Unsettling the Settler Within

Unsettling the Settler Within

Indian Residential Schools, Truth Telling, and Reconciliation in Canada

Paulette Regan

UBCPress · Vancouver · Toronto

20 19 18 17 16 15 14   10 9 8

Printed in Canada on FSC-certified ancient-forest-free paper
(100% post-consumer recycled) that is processed chlorine- and acid-free.

LIBRARY AND ARCHIVES CANADA CATALOGUING IN PUBLICATION

Regan, Paulette, 1949-
Unsettling the settler within : Indian residential schools, truth telling,
and reconciliation in Canada / Paulette Regan.

Includes bibliographical references and index.
ISBN 978-0-7748-1777-6 (cloth); ISBN 978-0-7748-1778-3 (pbk.)

1. Native peoples – Canada – Residential schools – History. 2. Reconciliation – Canada.
3. Truth commissions – Canada. 4. Canada – Race relations. I. Title.

E96.5.R44 2010   371.829'97071   C2010-904840-7

---

e-book ISBNs: 978-0-7748-1779-0 (pdf); 978-0-7748-5964-6 (epub)

Canadä

UBC Press gratefully acknowledges the financial support for our publishing program
of the Government of Canada (through the Canada Book Fund),
the Canada Council for the Arts, and the British Columbia Arts Council.

This book has been published with the help of a grant from
the Canadian Federation for the Humanities and Social Sciences,
through the Aid to Scholarly Publications Program, using funds provided by
the Social Sciences and Humanities Research Council of Canada.

UBC Press
The University of British Columbia
2029 West Mall
Vancouver, BC V6T 1Z2
www.ubcpress.ca

To the Hazelton Alternative Dispute Resolution Pilot Project
Indian Residential School survivors and the Gitxsan people,
and
to the memory of my mother, Lily Lee Regan,
who taught me that truth and justice always come from the heart;
may her grandchildren and great-grandchildren live her legacy

Contents

Foreword

Taiaiake Alfred

In a global era of apology and reconciliation, Canadians, like their counter-parts in other settler nations, face a moral and ethical dilemma that stems from an unsavoury colonial past. Canadians grow up believing that the history of their country is a story of the cooperative venture between people who came from elsewhere to make a better life and those who were already here, who welcomed and embraced them, aside from a few bad white men and some renegade Natives who had other, more *American,* ideas.

Canadians like to imagine that they have always acted with peaceful good intentions toward us by trying to fix "the Indian problem" even as they displaced, marginalized, and brutalized us as part of the colonial project. Canadians do not like to hear that their country was founded through frauds, abuses, and violence perpetuated against the original peoples of this land. Canadians are in denial, *in extremis.* For those who dispute this reality, Paulette Regan offers up the history and living legacy of colonial violence that characterizes the Indian residential school system as a case in point. She rejects a self-congratulatory version of Canadian history and challenges the benevolent peacemaker myth that forms the basis of settler identity.

We were always in the way. And we still are. It's just that now we do not present a physical obstacle so much as a psychological, or should I say spiritual, barrier to the peaceful development of the Canadian economy and society. Some may say, "Well, you know, things were different back then, two hundred years ago." But, really, how different?

The convenient way to deal with the founding injustice of Canada is to allow colonialism to continue by ignoring the truth, to erase it from our memory, ban it from the schools, and suppress it in public. Canadians can continue to glorify their country's criminality, from Cartier to Caledonia, and force those who suffered the fraud, abuses, and violence to accommodate the denial and artifice of justice that has been set up. But as the original people of this land, as the blood and spiritual descendents of the people who lived on the land and fought and died to preserve the loving relationship they had with this continent, we cannot forget what has been done to create the myth of the country now called Canada.

Writing from a settler perspective primarily for other settlers, the author avoids the trap that so many non-Native scholars fall into – telling Native people how we must live. Instead, she homes in on what settlers must do to fix "the settler problem." By this, she means that non-Natives must struggle to confront their own colonial mentality, moral indifference, and historical ignorance as part of a massive truth telling about Canada's past and present relationship with the original inhabitants of this land. The author argues that the settler version of national history denies a critical Indigenous counter-narrative. Populating the story of this country with Indigenous history and presence would mean that non-Natives will have to stop thinking of us as "obstacles" or "problems," which is counterintuitive in Canadian society.

Exposing the mindset that perpetuates "benevolent" colonialism, *Unsettling the Settler Within* urges settlers to take responsibility for decolonizing themselves and their country. The author argues that words of apology and reconciliation are not enough to make the significant social and political change that is so sorely needed. Words must be accompanied by concrete action at all levels of Canadian society. If such actions are to be transformative, they cannot be predicated on good intentions but must be rooted instead in a fundamental recognition of the human dignity and right to freedom of self-determining Indigenous peoples.

I am highly skeptical of the vision of reconciliation that is currently embraced by most Canadians. There is a growing sense, nationally, that, as we accept apologies and payments for the crimes of the residential schools, or jobs and contracts in exchange for stolen lands, forgiveness is implied. What is the message – that material compensation can address the crimes of colonialism? Yes. Most Canadians believe that, once money is paid to a Native or "Natives" in general, these questions are dead, and we will be able to move on. What is this notion of reconciliation doing for Canadian society, and what is it doing for Native people? More than anything else, it is obscuring. The author shares my skepticism and then proceeds to dig more deeply into what a process of ethical truth telling and genuine reconciliation entails. What she proposes is not an easy quick fix but gives Native and non-Native alike food for thought about how to break through the colonial impasse that continues to define our relationship.

Paulette Regan has offered us a necessary vision of being Canadian that reflects her hard-earned clarity and a fearless honesty. In writing my own book on the idea of decolonization, I had many conversations with Native people who are fighting to survive in all senses of the word and to restore dignity to their lives and nations.[1] Through these interactions, I came to understand what it is to be a true warrior and how crucial the warrior spirit is if we are going to challenge and defeat the falsehoods and violence at the core of our relationship today. Warriors put themselves forward to defend righteousness, even, or especially, when there are great risks attached to staking the claim to truth. In her own way, Paulette Regan embodies the warrior spirit too. And if taken seriously by its readers, the words and ideas she offers us in *Unsettling the Settler Within* have revolutionary and liberatory potential. They point the way toward something completely new in the five-hundred-year history of interactions between Indigenous people and settlers in this land: white people staking claim to justice and the generation of a relationship of honesty and mutual respect.

Acknowledgments

Writing this book would not have been possible without the support and encouragement of many scholars, professional colleagues, and friends who have inspired me to stay the course over the years: Taiaiake Alfred, Adam Barker, Leslie Brown, Sue Campbell, Jeff Corntassel, Scott Graham, Maggie Hodgson, Chief Robert Joseph, Michelle LeBaron, John Milloy, Catherine Morris, Leigh Ogston, Brock Pitawanakwat, Millie Poplar, Arthur J. Ray, Roger Simon, Deanna Sitter, Graham Hingangaroa Smith, Seetal Sunga, and Jim Tully, and Bob Watts. Thank you to Jean Wilson, former editor at UBC Press, who saw the potential in my work. My deep appreciation to UBC Press editors Darcy Cullen, Anna Friedlander, and Deborah Kerr, who helped bring this project to fruition. I am indebted to the anonymous readers whose suggestions for revisions improved the book immeasurably. Of course, I alone am responsible for its contents. I am Director of Research for the Truth and Reconciliation Commission of Canada, but the opinions expressed here do not represent the views of the Commission.

I especially thank Brenda Ireland for the energy, heart, and sense of humour that she brings to our work together and for her friendship, and to Ramona Rose for taking me home to Newfoundland. My deepest gratitude goes to my family, whose love sustains me: my husband, Les, my children, Paul and Denise, and my son-in-law, Thomas, for being there when I needed them most; my sister, Marion, and brother-in-law, Joe; my nephew, Rob, and his wife, Angela; my stepsons, Mike and Jeff; and my niece, Barb, her partner, John, and their children, Kristina, Brianna, and Matt. Finally, I want to acknowledge a very special little person, my granddaughter, Ella, who brings me such joy and reminds me that life is indeed a beautiful gift. I carry you always in my heart, little one.

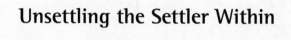

Unsettling the Settler Within

Introduction
A Settler's Call to Action

The government now recognizes that the consequences of the Indian Residential Schools policy were profoundly negative and that this policy has had a lasting and damaging impact on Aboriginal culture, heritage and language. While some former students have spoken positively about their experiences at residential schools, these stories are far overshadowed by tragic accounts of the emotional, physical and sexual abuse and neglect of helpless children, and their separation from powerless families and communities. The legacy of Indian Residential Schools has contributed to social problems that continue to exist in many communities today. It has taken extraordinary courage for the thousands of survivors that have come forward to speak publicly about the abuse they suffered ... The burden of this experience has been on your shoulders for too long. The burden is properly ours as a Government and as a country. There is no place in Canada for the attitudes that inspired the Indian Residential Schools system to ever prevail again. You have been working on recovering from this experience for a long time and in a very real sense, we are now joining you on this journey.

— FROM PRIME MINISTER STEPHEN HARPER'S
FORMAL APOLOGY FOR INDIAN RESIDENTIAL SCHOOLS,
AS DELIVERED IN PARLIAMENT, 11 JUNE 2008[1]

REFLECTIONS

On 11 June 2008, like many Canadians, I witnessed Canada's apology to Indian residential school (IRS) survivors. For me, as a non-Indigenous Canadian, a settler on these lands, the apology marked a watershed moment of national truth telling about Canada's past. It evoked powerful memories of the faces and voices of survivors I had encountered over the past six years. The apology was a public vindication of the many former IRS students who were not believed when they spoke out about what had happened to them in the schools. For those courageous survivors who first broke the silence and went to court to confront their abusers, it was an important symbolic recognition of the significant harms they suffered as children. For many survivors present in the House of Commons and those who watched from their communities across the country, the apology was bittersweet, as they remembered their grandmothers and grandfathers, mothers and fathers, husbands and wives, sons and daughters, aunties and uncles, sisters, brothers, and cousins who did not live to see this day. For some who rejected the apology, it was quite simply too little and too late.

As I listened to Harper's words of apology, I asked myself what it would mean in concrete terms for the settler majority to shoulder the collective burden of the history and legacy of the residential school system. History teaches us that, despite the cry of "never again," societies are quite capable of replicating in new forms the harmful societal attitudes and government policies of the past. In light of this reality, how will we actually make good on our promise to ensure that the attitudes that inspired the IRS system for over a hundred years never again prevail in this country?

If we are to join survivors on a journey to recover from the residential school experience, what is our particular role and responsibility? Is it to "help" Indigenous people recover from the devastating impacts of prescriptive policies and programs that we claimed were supposed to help them? Given our dismal track record, this seems a dubious goal. Or is it to determine what we who carry the identity of the colonizer and have reaped the benefits and privileges of colonialism must do to help ourselves recover from its detrimental legacy? How will we do so in ways that speak to truth, repair broken trust, and set us on a transformative decolonizing pathway toward more just and peaceful relations with Indigenous people?

My own journey into the visceral heart of Indigenous-settler relations began in the mid-1980s. It has taken me from the university classroom, where I studied fur trade history, to the safe haven of quiet archives, where I spent my days doing historical research on Aboriginal rights, land claims, and treaty issues, to the uncharted and highly contentious terrain of Aboriginal-government politics and policy. It eventually took me to small remote Native communities in northern British Columbia and southern Alberta, where I learned first-hand from residential school survivors not only about their experiences in the schools but about how the road to hell is indeed paved with good intentions.

Growing up in East Vancouver in the 1950s and '60s, I read about "Indians" in textbooks as part of a distant past. Occasionally, I would see the walking wounded, but I didn't distinguish Native people from the many other lost souls who wandered the streets of my neighbourhood. Unbeknownst to me, Indigenous children across the country who were the same age as myself were being sent to residential schools far from their homes and families. I knew nothing about the long history and presence of the Coast Salish on these lands that I call home. Today, when I walk through the city, I see it through new eyes. A history that was once invisible to me is now so apparent in the mountains, the outlying deltas and valleys, and the rivers and Pacific Ocean that were part of my childhood. I see Coast Salish presence and memory embedded everywhere in the city's landscape. When I look at the railway tracks that run through the city, what springs to mind is not so much the celebratory history of Canadian settlement but the lesser-known story of appropriating Indian reserve lands in the name of progress and the ensuing Native struggle for justice and restitution. When I see Indigenous people on the mean streets of the Downtown Eastside, or read about high incarceration rates or the low education success rates for children and youth, I now understand that much of the social dysfunction, violence, and poverty that exists in communities today is part of the intergenerational legacy of Indian residential schools.

But on this day of apology, I also know that these same communities have always resisted the attacks on their distinct cultural identities as they work to reclaim their histories and revitalize their languages, governance, and legal systems. I have been fortunate. I think about the many Indigenous teachers – scholars, friends, elders, community people, political leaders, and, most importantly, residential school survivors – who have been part of my journey thus far. Together, they have taught me hard lessons about the destructive impacts of colonialism. But they have also taught me something about the rich counter-narrative that exists across Turtle Island (North America). This long history and legacy of Indigenous diplomacy, law, and peacemaking reveals itself to those willing learners who have eyes to see, ears to listen, clear minds, and open, humble hearts. My teachers compelled me to question deeply the accepted wisdom that still prevails among majority Canadians, that we know what is best for Indigenous people. Why, despite all the evidence to the contrary, does this belief still persist? After all, it was this attitude of Euro-Canadian cultural superiority that justified the IRS system. Our government and various churches put into motion what is now described as a well-intentioned but ultimately devastating solution to what was known as the Indian problem.[2]

For me, Canada's apology was a call for settlers to take seriously our collective moral responsibility for the systematic removal and institutionalization of Native children, some of whom were abused and most of whom were deprived of their family life, languages, and cultures. Although the debilitating impacts of sexual, physical, and psychological abuse upon children are self-evident, and Canadians condemn such practices, the problematic assimilation policy that gave rise to such abuses is less understood by the Canadian public. To those who argue that they are not responsible, because they were not directly involved with the residential schools, I say that, as Canadian citizens, we are ultimately responsible for the past and present actions of our government. To those who say that we cannot change the past, I say that we can learn from it. We can better understand how a problematic mentality of benevolent paternalism became a rationale and justification for acquiring Indigenous lands and resources, and drove the creation of prescriptive education policies that ran counter to the treaty relationship. Equally importantly, we can explore how this mentality continues to influence Indigenous-settler relations today. Failing to do so will ensure that, despite our vow of never again, Canada will create equally destructive policies and practices into the future. To those who argue that former IRS students should just get over it and move on, I say that asking victims to bury a traumatic past for the "greater good" of achieving reconciliation does not address the root of the problem – colonialism. For all these reasons, I think of the apology not as the closing of what is commonly referred to as a dark, sad chapter in Canada's history but rather as an opening for all Canadians to fundamentally rethink our past and its implications for our present and future relations.

Setting the Context

Indian residential schools were jointly established and run by the federal government and various churches in most provinces and territories across the country.[3] This history is still very much alive – the last school closed in 1996, and approximately eighty thousand former students are still alive today. The history of Indian residential schools in Canada is complex and spans more than a century. One part of the story is about well-meaning paternalistic educators, government and church officials who sought to educate and assimilate Indigenous children into mainstream Canadian society "for their own good." To accomplish this task, children were removed from their families, in many cases forcibly, by Indian agents or police officers. They were forbidden to speak their own languages or practise their own cultural and spiritual traditions, and were punished for doing so. The other part of the story is about the devastating cultural, psychological, and emotional harms and traumatic abuses that were inflicted upon small children – an intergenerational history of dispossession, violence, abuse, and racism that is a fundamental denial of the human dignity and rights of Indigenous peoples. These aspects of the story have been revealed through the IRS litigation and claims process. But the whole story – the one that will provide new insights into how and why the system was able to flourish for so long, despite overwhelming evidence of its flaws – has yet to be told.

Telling the whole truth about the history and legacy of the IRS system means that settlers must consider the possibility that our relationship with Native people has never been predominantly peaceful or reconciliatory. Deconstructing our identity and history necessitates a rethinking of what constitutes violence as well as a closer investigation of its more nuanced forms. Why focus on violence? Some readers may think that I overstate the case and will resist this particular reading of Canadian history. They point to the many examples of cooperation, alliance, and intermarriage that also shape our past. Others rationalize, declaring that not all children had a bad experience in residential schools, not all teachers were abusers, and that some staff and officials spoke out courageously, criticizing conditions at the schools. I acknowledge these realities. In fact, if we are to fully understand the complexity and insidious nature of the attitudes, policies, and practices that gave rise to the residential school system, these aspects of the story must also be told. Important decolonizing lessons can be learned from the ways in which teachers, staff, and various officials chose to ignore, vigorously enforce, comply with, or resist residential school policies and practices in various times and places.

Despite the long history of Indian residential schools, characterized by the imposing presence of the school buildings that dotted the Canadian landscape and were embodied in the lives and memories of survivors, most ordinary citizens say that they know nothing about them. The schools, some of which are still standing, remain comfortably invisible to Canadians, as do the former inhabitants themselves. Perhaps we, as non-Indigenous people, can begin by asking ourselves some troubling questions. How is it that we know nothing about this history? What does the persistence of such invisibility in the face of the living presence of survivors tell us about our relationship with Indigenous peoples? What does our historical amnesia reveal about our continuing complicity in denying, erasing, and forgetting this part of our own history as colonizers while pathologizing the colonized? How will Canadians who have so selectively forgotten this "sad chapter in our history" now undertake to remember it?[4] Will such remembering be truly transformative or simply perpetuate colonial relations? Surely, without confronting such difficult questions as part of our own truth telling, there can be no genuine reconciliation.

Although the prime minister assured First Nations, Métis, and Inuit peoples that "there is no place in Canada for the attitudes that inspired the Indian residential school system to ever prevail again," my premise is that, unfortunately, such attitudes are still alive and well today, rooted in settler historical myths and colonial mindsets. To understand why this is so, it is instructive to explore how colonial violence is woven into the fabric of Canadian history in an unbroken thread from past to present, which we must now unravel, upsetting our comfortable assumptions about the past. At the same time, we must work as Indigenous allies to "restory" the dominant-culture version of history; that is, we must make decolonizing space for Indigenous history – counter-narratives of diplomacy, law, and peacemaking practices – as told by Indigenous peoples themselves.[5]

A Pedagogical Opening: Canada's Truth and Reconciliation Commission

Post-apology, Canada will embark on a national journey of remembering the history and legacy of Indian residential schools in the hope of repairing the damaged relationship between Indigenous peoples and settler Canadians. The Truth and Reconciliation Commission of Canada (TRC), which has been described as the cornerstone of the Indian Residential Schools Settlement Agreement (IRSSA), will guide this journey. The agreement was negotiated in response to over twelve thousand individual abuse claims and several class-action lawsuits filed on behalf of approximately seventy thousand former IRS students against the federal government and church entities who shared joint responsibility for the schools. Over the past several years, the Government of Canada and its various church co-defendants have paid monetary compensation to students whose sexual and physical abuse claims have been validated. In 2005, all of the involved parties – government, churches, the Assembly of First Nations, and legal counsel representing residential school survivors – began negotiations to resolve these claims. The IRSSA was finalized in 2006, approved by courts in every province and territory in 2007, and is now being implemented under court supervision. Although the settlement agreement is not without controversy, it is comprehensive in scope and multi-faceted, consisting of the following components: monetary reparation in the form of a common experience payment awarded to all former students based solely on verification of their school attendance; an independent assessment process that adjudicates physical and sexual abuse claims and awards financial compensation; a health support program for survivors that is administered by Health Canada; a commemoration program for memorial projects; and the creation of the TRC.[6]

The Truth and Reconciliation Commission was formally established on 1 June 2008 and got off to a rocky start with the resignations of the first chair and commissioners. The commission was reconstituted in the summer of 2009 with the appointment of a new chair, Justice Murray Sinclair, and two commissioners, Chief Wilton Littlechild and Marie Wilson.[7] Tumultuous beginnings aside, the creation of the commission marked a critical turning point in Indigenous-settler relations in Canada. During its five years, the commission is tasked with undertaking a truth-telling and reconciliation process, producing a report on the residential school system and its aftermath, and making recommendations to government based on its findings. It will do so in part by gathering the diverse stories of former students, staff and administrators, government and church officials, and all others who wish to make submissions.

For survivors and their families and communities, the consequences of the residential school system are profound. As the commission undertakes its task, it is vitally important that Canadians learn about and acknowledge what Indigenous people have suffered as a result of assimilation policy and actions. In doing so, we must also recognize the strength and resilience of those who, despite the harms perpetrated against them, continue to resist colonialism, reclaiming and reconstituting their own governance systems, laws, histories, languages, and ceremonies. Equally importantly, the TRC provides a rare opportunity for non-Native Canadians to undertake a deeply critical reflective re-examination of history and themselves.

Canada's TRC is also of interest to the international community as a potential model for addressing historical injustices affecting Indigenous peoples across the globe. The TRC is distinct from other commissions in several ways. It is the first commission in the world to be established as part of a judicially supervised negotiated agreement rather than by legislation or executive order. It is the only TRC to focus on Indigenous peoples, and more specifically on the historical experiences of children who were subjected to systemic abuse. The TRC must conduct its work in a manner that educates the Canadian public and enables participants to engage in truth telling about our past in a way that also facilitates long-term reconciliation.[8]

Within the international context, this TRC (unlike other commissions established in transitional democracies such as Chile, Peru, Guatemala, or South Africa) will conduct its work in a stable democracy. This may present certain advantages in that there are well-established democratic governance and legal institutions. Unlike many South Africans, for example, who viewed the long-standing institutions of apartheid as suspect, the majority of Canadians perceive their legal system to be fair. (Here I note that many Native people would disagree based on their negative experiences with the justice system.) Many South Africans thought that their country's commission (SATRC) was an inadequate substitute for the criminal prosecution of perpetrators who were instead granted amnesty for their crimes in exchange for their testimony. Equally problematic, the SATRC failed to provide financial compensation and symbolic reparations to the vast majority of victims who testified.[9]

In Canada, attempts to bring to justice the perpetrators of criminal acts and abuses related to the residential schools have taken a different trajectory, one that eventually led to the settlement agreement. In 1993, after a former school supervisor at the Alberni Indian Residential School was convicted and sentenced to eleven years in prison, the RCMP set up a Native Residential School Task Force to investigate allegations of criminal abuse. By 2000, it "had received 3,400 complaints against 170 suspects.

Only five people were charged."[10] In many instances, laying charges was no longer possible because alleged perpetrators had died. By far the vast majority of claims were filed in the civil courts, where the sheer volume of claims eventually threatened to overwhelm the system. But the early trials demonstrated that the civil litigation process itself often revictimizes plaintiffs, dehumanizing those who may seek not only financial compensation but a restoration of their human dignity. The procedural requirements of civil litigation make it difficult for plaintiffs to fully describe those experiences that are not directly associated with the abuse but nevertheless have had a significant impact upon them.[11] Moreover, civil litigation focuses on individuals and cannot address the collective and intergenerational harms, such as loss of language and culture, which many students experienced.

A substantive body of research indicates that symbolic and material reparations, psychological support for victims of trauma, and a public reckoning with past wrongs are all required to adequately address historical injustices inflicted upon minority groups. Canada's multi-pronged response to the IRS issue – the apology, financial compensation, a health support program, commemoration, and the creation of the TRC – hits close to the mark. Nevertheless, each component of the Indian Residential Schools Settlement Agreement has met with mixed responses from survivors. For example, the common experience payment process has been criticized by some students whose compensation claims were denied, whereas some recipients found the process itself retraumatizing. Yet others report that the payment was important to them as tangible recognition of the systemic harms they suffered at the schools.[12] Like its precursor, the Alternative Dispute Resolution Program (ADRP), which is the subject of Chapter 4, the independent assessment process has met with various criticisms and accolades. Finally, it should be noted that the settlement agreement has been disparaged because it deals only with students who attended Indian residential schools. People who attended day schools or were in foster care are excluded, and recently, new class-action lawsuits have been filed by representative plaintiffs of these groups.

Within this controversial milieu, the TRC will face the formidable task of sustaining survivor support and public interest in its proceedings over the course of its five-year mandate. Many Canadians may simply tune out, declining to observe or participate in the commission's activities, all of which are voluntary because the TRC is not a public inquiry and has no subpoena powers to compel witnesses to testify. Here, it is important to note that critics of the commission have already surfaced on all sides. Some say that genuine reconciliation is impossible until Indigenous people's right to self-determination is recognized, treaties are honoured, restitution is made for appropriated lands and resources, and socio-economic, health, and education outcomes improve substantively. Others view the TRC as a whitewash designed by government and churches to cover up genocide. Still others envision it as a massive public exercise in either inducing or alleviating settler guilt as survivors and former staff members tell their stories. Some fear that survivors' truth telling or public testimony about very personal experiences of abuse, trauma, and grief will simply be consumed by the public as spectacle and will have little real impact on changing Native lives or educating Canadians about the past in a way that achieves social justice or facilitates a just reconciliation.

The Canadian commission faces an additional challenge. In the public mind, there has been no epitomizing moment of genocidal crisis or mass human rights violations that would trigger a need for transitional justice mechanisms such as international criminal courts, tribunals, or truth and reconciliation commissions more commonly associated with so-called developing countries or despotic regimes. Most Canadians associate violence in this country with the kind of physical confrontation that occurred during the highly publicized conflicts at Oka, Gustafsen Lake, Burnt Church, and Ipperwash Park.[13] We are disturbed by these violent encounters as they call into question a core tenet of Canadian identity – that we are a nation of peacemakers in our relations with Indigenous people. We congratulate ourselves on the fact that armed confrontation is still a rare occurrence in Canada, taking this as proof of our own political and moral superiority. We tend not to attribute this absence of overt violence to Native people's methods of handling conflict and making peace. Nor do we see the more subtle forms of violence that permeate everyday Indigenous-settler relations – racism, poverty, cultural domination, power, and privilege.

We do not categorize the residential school system and other assimilationist strategies as acts of violence, yet their caustic effects are evident. In the seismic wake of destruction left by the public policy experiment that was the Indian residential schools, Indigenous communities struggle with poverty, poor health and education outcomes, economic disadvantage, domestic violence, abuse, addiction, and high rates of youth suicide. It is easy, from the safety of our relatively comfortable lives, to judge the apparent inability of Native people to rise above such conditions, thus pathologizing the victims of our well-intended actions. It is equally easy to think that we know what is best for them – hence our persistence in trying to solve the Indian problem. This singular focus on the Other blinds us from seeing how settler history, myth, and identity have shaped and continue to shape our attitudes in highly problematic ways. It prevents us from acknowledging our own need to decolonize.

On *Unsettling the Settler Within*

How can we, as non-Indigenous people, unsettle ourselves to name and then transform the settler – the colonizer who lurks within – not just in words but by our actions, as we confront the history of colonization, violence, racism, and injustice that remains part of the IRS legacy today?[14] To me, this is the crux of the matter. I unravel the Canadian historical narrative and deconstruct the foundational myth of the benevolent peacemaker – the bedrock of settler identity – to understand how colonial forms of denial, guilt, and empathy act as barriers to transformative socio-political change. To my mind, Canadians are still on a misguided, obsessive, and mythical quest to assuage colonizer guilt by solving the Indian problem. In this way, we avoid looking too closely at ourselves and the collective responsibility we bear for the colonial status quo. The significant challenge that lies before us is to turn the mirror back upon ourselves and to answer the provocative question posed by historian Roger Epp regarding reconciliation in Canada: How do we solve the settler problem?[15]

Unsettling the Settler Within is based on the premise that *how* people learn about historical injustices is as important as learning truths about *what* happened. Within this context, I explore the pedagogical potential of truth-telling and reconciliation processes. I agree with transitional justice experts who argue that history education in the wake of systemic violence and deeply rooted identity-based conflict must focus not only on curricula reform but on pedagogical reform as an effective means of transforming divisive histories and identities, and shifting negative perceptions of marginalized groups.[16] Although transitional justice theory and practice has focused primarily on "Third World" countries, "First World" states including settler nations such as Canada, Australia, New Zealand, and the United States can benefit from the lessons learned in less stable regimes. In a similar vein, what might the "Third World" learn from the Canadian TRC experience?

In dealing with historical and identity-based conflict in North America, a multidisciplinary group of scholars has raised critical questions regarding culture and power in neutrality-based alternative dispute resolution (ADR) negotiation models of the sort that have been used to resolve residential school claims.[17] At the same time, scholar-practitioners who focus on intercultural conflict resolution are now exploring the role of narrative, dialogue, ritual, performative practices, world view, and myth in developing transformative approaches to addressing socio-political conflict. But there has been little sustained interdisciplinary dialogue between conflict reso-lution scholar-practitioners who influence and participate in treaty nego-tiations and claims resolution processes, historians who study the complexities of Indigenous-settler relations and conflicts over time, and educators who focus on the pedagogical issues related to public history education and commemorative practices associated with remembering a difficult past. Rather, their works run on parallel tracks that rarely intersect, leaving a significant gap in theory, research, and practice.

Here, I bridge this gap, linking theory to my own practice – that is, research as praxis. In doing so, I emphasize the centrality of history and myth to settler truth telling about the past. Within this context, recon-necting reason and emotion – head and heart – is integral to an unsettling pedagogy. Although the strong emotions engendered by listening to resi-dential school survivors' stories are potentially decolonizing, they might also create a backlash of settler denial or, conversely, generate an empa-thetic response that, though well intentioned, is still colonial in nature. Reframing reconciliation as a decolonizing place of encounter between settlers and Indigenous people mitigates these possibilities by making space for collective critical dialogue – a public remembering embedded in eth-ical testimonial, ceremonial, and commemorative practices.

Themes and Structure of the Book

Unsettling the Settler Within is structured and written in a way that reflects my own ongoing decolonizing journey. More than a theoretical exposition, it is based on my lived experience. From 2002 to 2004, I worked directly with residential school survivors, church representatives, and lawyers in my capacity as an IRS claims resolution manager for the federal government. For me, this experience put a human face on the stark violence of colonialism. This book draws on my experience as a former claims manager and employs a conceptual framework for a decolonizing pedagogical strategy that is designed to teach Canadians about their history so as to initially unsettle and then transform how they view the past as it relates to contemporary Indigenous-settler relations. It also incorporates new material based on my university classroom teaching and an intercultural workshop titled "Unsettling Dialogues of History and Hope," which I co-developed and facilitated with my Anishinaabe Métis colleague Brenda Ireland.

I am currently the director of research for the Truth and Reconciliation Commission of Canada (the opinions I express in the book are solely my own and do not represent those of the commission[18]), so I continue to grapple with the question of how settlers might confront the Indian residential school narrative as part of a broader decolonization project without falling into the multiple traps that replicate colonizing attitudes and behaviours. Throughout the book, I situate and self-critique my decolonizing struggles through my own storytelling in a series of self-reflective critical personal narratives, or auto-ethnographic vignettes, that mirror an imperative to unsettle the settler within. *Webster's Dictionary* defines "unsettle" as "to loosen or move from a settled state or condition ... to perturb or agitate mentally or emotionally." I argue that we must risk interacting differently with Indigenous people – with vulnerability, humility, and a willingness to stay in the decolonizing struggle of our own discomfort. What if we were to embrace IRS stories as powerful teachings – disquieting moments in which we can change our beliefs, attitudes, and actions?

Chapters 1 to 4 guide the reader through a process of truth telling. I first explain the theoretical and methodological underpinnings of an unsettling pedagogy and explore various themes related to settler responsibility. I make the case for why disturbing emotions are a critical pedagogical tool that can provoke decolonizing, transformative learning. In Chapter 2, I contextualize apology and reconciliation initiatives in a comparative analysis of Australia and Canada to critique and rethink reconciliation discourse. This sets the stage for exploring how a restorying of

Canadian history through ethical testimonial encounters, public history dialogues, and commemoration of the IRS history and legacy can work as a decolonizing force.

In Chapter 3, I challenge the peacemaker myth that goes to the heart of settler identity. It reinforces the popular belief that the settling of Canada was relatively peaceful because our ancestors, unlike their more violently disposed American counterparts, made treaties rather than war with Native peoples, brought law and order to the frontier, and created well-intentioned (if ultimately misguided) policies designed to solve the Indian problem by civilizing and saving people seen as savages. I trace the persistence of this myth from its roots in nineteenth-century treaty making to a contemporary reconciliation discourse that purports to be transformative but actually replicates colonial relations, reinscribing a national narrative that celebrates settlers as peacemakers.

The peacemaker myth emerged full-blown in nineteenth-century public consciousness as the settlement process moved west. In highlighting the western numbered treaties on the prairies and Indian policy in British Columbia, my intention is not to discount the substantive history of earlier treaties but to emphasize that, during this time period, the peacemaker myth crystallizes, becoming fixed in the public mind. My purpose is not to cover old ground – the controversial history of treaty making and Indian policy in Canada is well documented. Rather, using historical-comparative analysis, I reveal the violent discursive and symbolic practices of historical treaty and policy making and demonstrate in Chapter 4 how these practices continue into the present in new forms.[19] Today, they are manifested in various claims settlement processes that, despite talk of healing and reconciliation, remain rooted in patterns of colonial violence. I illustrate this point in a case study of the Alternative Dispute Resolution Program, which was created by contemporary bureaucrats – policy makers, lawyers, and negotiators – to settle IRS claims as part of a broader government mandate of healing and reconciliation.

Chapters 5 through 8 then take the reader through a process of reconciliation. In Chapter 5, I explore a historical counter-narrative of Indigenous diplomacy, law, and peacemaking that stands as a corrective to settler history and the peacemaker myth. Settler and Indigenous visions of law and peacemaking are fundamentally at odds. I draw on various Canadian and American sources that set out this counter-narrative from Indigenous philosophical, cultural, and legal perspectives. Although the treaty literature in Canada and the United States is vast, the number of scholarly works that articulate Indigenous understandings of diplomacy, law, and peacemaking is much smaller, and I limit my focus to them. Conflicting Indigenous-settler historical narratives are most evident in Aboriginal title and rights cases where Indigenous people bring their oral histories and law into the courtroom.

Next, in Chapter 6, I probe the possibilities of apology and testimonial exchange that is experiential, subjective, and emotionally engaged, thus enabling settlers to bear ethical witness and learn to listen differently – with a decolonizing ear – to the accounts of IRS survivors, former teachers, and staff. The unsettling questions we then ask ourselves are ripe with potentially transformative possibilities. I compare Western and Indigenous criteria for making apology and restitution, emphasizing the importance of storytelling and ceremony as embodied testimonial and commemorative practice. Within this context, recognizing and respecting Indigenous criteria, protocols, and practices, without appropriating them, is essential.

In Chapter 7, I describe my own experience as a federal government representative who was honoured to be one of the non-Indigenous hosts of an apology feast held on 20 March 2004 at Hazelton, BC, in the Gitxsan Feast Hall for former Edmonton Indian Residential School students who participated in the Hazelton Alternative Dispute Resolution Pilot Project. In the feast hall, reconciliation is a place of intercultural encounter – a teaching/learning space wherein the Gitxsan use their diplomatic skills to adapt traditional law, protocols, and peacemaking practices within a contemporary context.

In the final chapter, I argue that incorporating an unsettling pedagogy into the design of truth-telling and reconciliation processes is essential if such processes are to be sites of decolonizing struggle and liberatory resistance that teach us to live in truth. Building on Rupert Ross' suggestion that, as residential school survivors bring their testimonies, their life stories, to the Truth and Reconciliation Commission, they are transformed into warriors, I return to the theme of Indigenous diplomacy. I consider the problematic way in which North American popular history and media juxtapose the "Indian warrior" as the diametric opposite of the "Indian peacemaker," when historically and paradoxically, "a true warrior ... is someone who carries the burden of peace."[20] I argue that, collectively, survivors have always been warriors of peace. By this, I mean that they have used various non-violent means to confront Canada with its own colonial history, speaking truth to power in the courtroom and in the IRS claims settlement process, at community gatherings, and in public forums. The very fact that a national Indian Residential Schools Settlement Agreement was negotiated and that Canada apologized to former students stands as a living testament to these peace warriors.

Settler identity can also be transformed from that of colonizer to ally. We can learn from peace warriors, whose moral imagination points us toward a decolonizing pathway – but as we travel on this long and arduous journey, we must also look to our own past, our own life stories, for guidance. What can we learn from historical Indigenous allies who, despite their own complicity in the colonial project, spoke up for justice and, in doing so, were often marginalized themselves? The work of the TRC will not lead us to the end of the path: rather, it gives us a place and space to begin. This entails a public truth telling in which settlers link critical reflection, enlightened vision, and positive action to confront the settler problem head-on. Truth as an act of hope nurtures peaceful yet radical socio-political change that is the necessary foundation of reconciliation.

Reconciliation as Regifting

In the final years of the twentieth century and into the first decade of the new millennium, settlers came bearing the promise of a new gift – reconciliation with former students, their families, and their communities. But as I argue in subsequent chapters, earlier attempts to address the residential school history and legacy were simply a regifting of the old package of settler promises, wrapped in pretty new paper – the language of reconciliation. For years, many residential school survivors have called for a national truth-telling and reconciliation process to heal the wounds left by the residential school experiment. But they are also understandably wary. To paraphrase an old adage, they have learned through hard experience to "beware of settlers bearing gifts," and their experience with the now defunct Alternative Dispute Resolution Program did little to alleviate this distrust. In a post-apology environment and as Canada's Truth and Reconciliation Commission undertakes its work, many former students and their families will choose not to participate. We must respect this choice. But others will offer the gift of their testimonies to Canada and Canadians.

How will we, as settlers, receive these gifts? What gifts will we ourselves bring to truth telling and reconciliation? Each of us must answer fundamental questions: Do we choose to remain colonial perpetrators – benign peacemakers – bearing the token gift of a false reconciliation? Or will we bear gifts offered with humility, respect, and a genuine willingness to experience our own unsettling so that we might learn from the profound teachings that this history holds for all of us? Will we view a truth-telling and reconciliation process simply as a way to put the past, and our guilt, behind us quickly? Or will we recognize the possibility of opening transformative pathways on a journey that starts within ourselves – a journey of critical reflection upon profoundly disturbing residential school stories? This book attempts to address these question honestly and constructively in ways designed to speak hard truths, while remaining mindful of the importance of nurturing critical hope if we are to plant the seeds of a more authentic, ethical, and just reconciliation.

A Settler Call to Action

Unsettling the Settler Within is a call to action for non-Indigenous Canadians who do not see a need to take part in a truth-telling and reconciliation process. It makes a compelling argument for why they should care about the history of the IRS system and actively participate in dismantling its ongoing legacy. For scholars, policy makers, and negotiators, it offers new insight into the influence of the peacemaker myth on historical and contemporary intercultural negotiation practices and the concomitant erasure of the history of Indigenous diplomacy, law, and peacemaking from the Canadian consciousness. For educators, conflict/peace studies scholar-practitioners, and historians, it links theory and practice to explore the pedagogical potential of truth-telling and reconciliation processes. For those who would be Indigenous allies in the fight for justice and peace, it demonstrates how examining myth and history enriches our thinking about, and participation in, the decolonization project.

At its heart, writing this book is an act of truth telling and witnessing whereby I continue to fulfill my responsibility as host at the Hazelton feast. In this way, I "remember my obligation" to polish the "chain of testimony-witnessing held together by the bonds of an ethics forged in a relationship of responsibility and respect."[21] Thus, my writing represents one way of honouring, not just in words, but through my actions, those IRS survivors who offered me the gift of their testimonies. Somehow, these testimonies cut to the heart of the matter. The people and their stories teach us. Indigenous people have broken the silence in order to name the violence that has been directed at them, and in doing so they call us, as settlers, to account. For two years, in both private and public settings, I listened to former students describe their experiences in the residential schools. During this time, I began the difficult process of learning how to listen differently to these stories – to engage in the act of bearing witness as an ethical undertaking.

In 2005, when I left my job to return to the Indigenous Governance Program at the University of Victoria to begin the research on which this book is based, I was unsure where the journey would take me. As I began to write, I realized that, as a non-Native woman who had worked both for and with Indigenous people for over twenty-five years, mostly in non-government contexts, my own deepest learning has always come when I was in unfamiliar territory culturally, intellectually, and emotionally. It seems to me that this space of not knowing has power that may hold a key to decolonization for settlers. Back then, I was just beginning to appreciate the richness of the gift I had received from residential school survivors. Sometimes, we are offered a gift that we are reluctant to accept. Perhaps we do not recognize it as a gift because it feels like a burden, like a heavy responsibility that we don't quite know how to carry, and we are afraid that we will do so poorly. I now realize that their gift is a life teaching that I will always carry with me and continue to learn from in new, unsettling ways.

Part of the struggle of writing as truth telling has been to make sense of my own decolonizing journey in a way that honours the gift. I write as honestly as I can about what I have learned in the critical hope that it might serve as some small catalyst in thinking about how we, as settlers, might breathe life into Canada's apology. This is my truth. So I write not about survivors' stories, for they are not mine to tell, but of my own unsettling. This is my reciprocal gift to Indian residential school survivors – offered with humility, in the spirit of acknowledging, honouring, and remembering their teachings.

1

An Unsettling Pedagogy of History and Hope

REFLECTIONS

"The title of your workshop, 'Unsettling Dialogues of History and Hope,' may be threatening and turn people off. Is there another one?" This question jumps out at Brenda and me as we review the evaluation sheets that we have collected from our workshop participants. It reminds us that, for some, the very notion of "unsettling" or decolonizing struggle seems frightening and counterintuitive. Yet over the years, our own experiences as an intercultural team – one of us Anishinaabe Métis and the other Euro-Canadian – tell us that, without this unsettling, little will change. We had both been in situations where people's attempts to work together became bogged down in recriminations, denial, distrust, and guilt. We wanted to explore whether using dialogue circles as a way to learn about Indigenous-settler history could be a catalyst for changing this destructive dynamic.

Our work together is grounded in a conceptual and pedagogical framework that emphasizes the importance of circle work and ceremony when sharing our stories. Circles are universal places of connection that invite paradigm shifts. Although circles have a certain structure and format, what happens within each circle is unique and unpredictable.[1] Brenda and I create opportunities for people to experience decolonization so that history is understood both intellectually and emotionally as an embodied place of connectivity that is essential to reconciliation. We aim to move people outside their comfort zones by putting a human face on the impacts of colonization as we share our own stories. As an intercultural team, we work with shared principles and ethics of mutual respect, recognition, and responsibility, coupled with trust and good humour. Several workshop participants have commented that how we interact with each other models what we teach. At the same time, we are mindful that, despite the many years we have known each other, there are sometimes still moments of tension between us that reveal the colonizer/colonized dynamic in our own relationship.

Using circle protocol, Brenda and I begin the workshop by creating a safe space for participants to challenge their understanding of our shared history, examine their differing world views, values, and cultural systems, and explore how these affect Indigenous-settler relations today. Basing her approach on her elders' teachings, Brenda invites participants to join us in ceremony – those that she conducts or ones of their own choosing. Ceremony prepares everyone to work together in a good way with clear heads and open hearts.

In the first part of the workshop, we explain why decolonization is necessary to authentic reconciliation. We talk about how we have seen first-hand that, in the headlong rush toward reconciliation, there are very few opportunities for people to engage in honest, reflective dialogue about our shared but conflicting stories – our histories. For Indigenous people, the past is a painful chronicle of broken treaties, stolen lands, Indian residential schools, and the Indian Act. For non-Indigenous people, the past is a celebratory story of settling new lands, nation building, and helping unfortunate "Indians" to adjust to a new way of life. Yet this problematic history is not in the past: it sits with us in many places – government offices, boardrooms, negotiating tables, churches, hospitals, classrooms, and community halls. Whether or not we acknowledge its presence, we know intuitively that this history is still alive. But because we cannot change the past, we try to ignore it. Talking about the burden of history makes us feel frustrated and overwhelmed. We don't know how to put the past behind us, so rather than engaging in meaningful dialogue, we get stuck in destructive monologues. We talk past each other, not hearing the deeper truths residing in stories that are troubling for both teller and listener, albeit for different reasons.

Brenda and I then restory Canadian history, describing the past and present impacts of colonial policies such as Indian residential schools, the Indian Act, and involuntary enfranchisement. Although most Indigenous participants are very familiar with this history, many settler participants know only rudimentary facts and have little understanding of Indigenous-settler relations. In correcting the record, we intertwine historical facts with life stories that make the history come alive. In this way, abstract facts become connected to human experience. People find this to be a powerful and compelling way of presenting history. As one participant said, "This is the real history." We then encourage participants to explore the coping strategies that both Indigenous and non-Indigenous people have developed – distrust, anger, denial, distancing, shame, fear, and guilt – that keep us mired in a colonial relationship. We have found this to be a critical part of the workshop as participants experience an "aha" moment in which they see how their own coping strategies are self-limiting.

We encourage participants to explore how their conceptions and misconceptions about the past limit their ability to work together in the present at the individual and community level. This process evokes strong emotions. Facing our feelings and being willing to risk taking action can seem futile, given what seem to be insurmountable challenges. Debriefing this part of the workshop can be intense, so an eagle feather is passed around the circle, reminding everyone of the sacredness of the work that we are doing and honouring the courage and honesty of all those present.

At mid-day, the sharing of food and laughter lightens the energy in the room and creates a sense of camaraderie that carries over into the second part of the workshop. We work with people to identify personal strategies and practices – those concrete steps that help move them beyond overwhelming feelings of in-adequacy and instill a sense of critical hope – to progress, as one participant said, "beyond 'where do we start?' to 'this I can do!'" People have a better understanding and greater respect for the role that history plays in everyday Indigenous-settler relations. They begin to get excited about applying what they have learned to their own circumstances. The workshop ends with a sharing circle. It is not unusual for everyone, including ourselves, to feel exhausted yet exhila-rated at the end of a long, emotionally draining yet curiously uplifting day.[2]

Linking Theory, Critical Reflection, and Action

Our workshop experiences showed me that most non-Native people resist the notion that violence lies at the core of Indigenous-settler relations. This is understandable, as it raises disturbing questions about settler identity and history. Thus, following Henry Giroux, my pedagogical strat-egy links historical consciousness and collective struggle to elements of critique and hope in ways that are potentially uncomfortable.[3] I aim to "uncover myths, reveal hidden truths ... accurately describing reality ... to suggest or undertake action ... [thus] challeng[ing] the claim that research can or should be neutral."[4] In my experience, once most non-Natives understand the ways in which colonial violence is embedded in the institutional structures of Canadian society that gave rise to the residential school system, they genuinely want to do something to remedy the situation. This is a critical juncture, as they have a strong tendency to focus on how to fix things for Native people. This stance is familiar to us, and it seems like the right thing to do. At the same time, few people are enthusiastic about exploring difficult emotions that may leave them feeling hopeless and stuck in a quagmire. Stirring up unacknowledged denial, guilt, shame, and anger seems counterproductive to the task at hand. I was perplexed as to how to inspire learners to risk taking this approach. Ironically, this dilemma led me to consider more carefully what role hope might play in decolonization.

On Critical Hope

In *Pedagogy of Hope,* educator and activist Paulo Freire identifies the importance of linking struggle with hope in spite of the apparent hopelessness of our situation. He does not mean that we should cling to an idealistic, naive kind of hope that is in actuality "an excellent route to hopelessness, pessimism, and fatalism" but rather that we should strive to maintain a critical hope that is rooted in struggles for freedom. Freire argues that, "to attempt to do without hope, which is based on the need for truth as an ethical quality of the struggle, is tantamount to denying that struggle one of its mainstays." He says simply that, "without a minimum of hope, we cannot so much as start the struggle. But without the struggle, hope ... dissipates, loses its bearings, and turns into hopelessness ... Hence the need for a kind of education in hope."[5] Yet simply acquiring knowledge and reflecting upon historical wrongs is insufficient to generate critical hope. Transformative educator Daniel Schugurensky points out that individual critical reflection is "not only unlikely to lead to transformative social action, but in some cases it may even lead to the opposite situation, which is cynicism, paralysis, and a general feeling of helplessness." As people become "more aware of the structures of domination and the role of ... institutions in reinforcing them ... in the absence of a coherent social movement to promote an alternative ... we fall into a state of paralysis, pessimism, and cynicism," and therefore transformative learning can occur only when "critical reflection and social action are part of the same process."[6] Maintaining critical hope reinforces our capacity to understand that, though we cannot change the past, neither are we held prisoner by it.

In *Teaching Community,* black American feminist scholar and educator bell hooks builds on Freire's work to write with passion and warmth about the importance of generating critical hope from an anti-racist standpoint. As an educator, she strives to create a community of learning that goes beyond the classroom and encourages learners to embrace the challenges that lead to systemic social change: "In the last twenty years, educators who have dared to study and learn new ways of thinking and teaching so that the work we do does not reinforce systems of domination, of imperialism, racism, sexism, or class elitism have created a pedagogy of hope ... Hopefulness empowers us to continue to work for justice even as the forces of injustice may gain greater power for a time ... My hope emerges from those places of struggle where I witness individuals positively transforming their lives and the world around them."[7] In her teaching practice, she sees transformative educative possibilities for white people who choose to resist their privilege and racism through critical reflection and social action. She argues that to be anti-racist is a moral choice and reminds us that we will always be engaged in the struggle to unlearn racism in our homes, schools, workplaces, and communities, and that we will inevitably make mistakes along the way. What makes the difference in terms of a life-long commitment to anti-racism is the willingness to continuously face our mistakes and take the actions necessary to make amends on personal and political levels.[8]

Like Freire and others, I believe that education is not simply about the transfer of knowledge but is a transformative experiential learning that empowers people to make change in the world. Failure to link knowledge and critical reflection to action explains why many settlers never move beyond denial and guilt, and why many public education efforts are ineffective in bringing about deep social and political change. At the same time, I am mindful that, because radical change is not ultimately in its best interest, the dominant majority is apt to reinforce benevolent imperialism and colonial attitudes, often unconsciously, in ways that are antithetical to decolonization.[9] An unsettling pedagogy is therefore based on the premise that settlers cannot just theorize about decolonizing and liberatory struggle: we must experience it, beginning with ourselves as individuals, and then as morally and ethically responsible socio-political actors in Canadian society.

Situating Myself

> It is the strangeness of difference – the unfamiliar space of not know-ing – that is so hard to tolerate for the colonizer whose benevolent imperialism assumes both herself or himself as the center of knowing and that everything can be known. For the colonizer-settler engaged in critical inquiry there is an inevitable and disturbing moment when the indigenous teacher or informant speaks. It is a moment of recognition – perhaps unconscious – that some things may be out of one's grasp. It is a fleeting, slippery glimpse of (the possibility of) something inaccessible and unknowable.
>
> – ALISON JONES, WITH KUNI JENKINS, "RETHINKING
> COLLABORATION: WORKING THE INDIGENE-COLONIZER HYPHEN"

Epistemologically, I am a willing learner in this "unfamiliar space of not knowing," who writes from multiple overlapping standpoints. I am at once a non-Indigenous woman, colonizer-perpetrator, colonizer-ally, and a scholar-practitioner. In drawing on feminist theory in this study, I note that Mayan American scholar Sandy Grande rightly criticizes white feminist theorists who are "unwilling to examine their own complicity in the ongoing project of colonization," thereby ignoring the implications of power and privilege.[10] Although she acknowledges that anti-racist critical feminists provide insightful analyses with regard to the intersections of gender, race, and class in colonial contexts, she remains skeptical of feminist theory's usefulness to the Indigenous struggle for self-determination. Métis feminist scholar Emma LaRocque also addresses the problems associated with "white-constructed feminism" and challenges non-Indigenous scholars to "do some consciousness-raising about the quality of life and the nature of political and intellectual colonialism in our country." But she cautions that rejecting feminist theory out of hand as "irrelevant because white women have conceptualized it" is counterproductive.[11] She points out that feminist theoretical and critical insights regarding racism and sexism are vitally important to Indigenous women as they confront these challenges in their own lives and communities.

Cherokee scholar Andrea Smith resists creating a feminist/non-feminist dichotomy and argues that feminism is not antithetical to self-determination. Rather, what is needed are "political projects that both address sexism *and* promote Indigenous sovereignty simultaneously." Within this context, "Native women activists' theories about feminism ... and about the importance of working in coalition with non-Native women are complex and varied."[12] Maori scholar Makere Stewart-Harawira goes a step further to call for a more inclusive non-essentialist feminism that "recognizes difference but seeks to disrupt the privileging impact of the unequal structures of power."[13] For her, the most critical decolonization agenda involves not only achieving Indigenous self-determination but resisting new forms of imperialism that now threaten the globe.[14] She declares that, as a Maori Celtic academic, activist, and grandmother, she herself writes from a position of privilege that carries with it a responsibility "to bear witness against the wanton violence that marks humanity's headlong slide into the abyss of self-destruction in the twenty-first century, and to call for a new model of being in the world, a political ontology grounded in spirit." Thus, Stewart-Harawira argues that many post-modern, post-colonial white feminist theorists miss the mark when they insist that the representational linking of women and nature further op-presses women. She rejects this position as antithetical to an Indigenous world view that recognizes and values the interconnectedness between human beings, nature, and spirit.[15]

Despite their conflicting views on feminist theory's efficacy for Indigenous women, all these scholars explore the complexity of their own positionality and responsibility as researchers to make a compelling argument for why non-Indigenous scholars and activists must do the same as part of their own decolonizing struggle. Their critique serves as a cautionary tale for settler scholar-practitioners about the importance of truth telling in our own work and in collaborative Indigenous-settler coalitions and partnerships more generally. It is therefore important that I acknowledge my own complicity in the colonial practices related to the IRS claims process that I critique even as I aspire to work in solidarity with Indigenous people as an ally. I have worked "in the belly of the beast," yet I have also fought to resist the hegemonic structures, institutions, and bureaucracies that reproduce colonialism.

Writing from an anti-racist feminist perspective, critical theorist-activist Mehmoona Moosa-Mitha describes the importance of situating oneself not as an expert but as a learner in anti-oppressive experientially based research. Thus, in seeking to know the Other, the researcher comes to know herself and to understand her own complicity: "The researcher holds the attitude of a learner, of one who is a 'not-knower,' but through the act of empathetic imagination and by possessing critical self-consciousness, comes to gain a sense of what the Other knows. The researcher is reflexive in her practice, whereby the knowledge of the subaltern or subjugated is used to reflect dominant practices and assumptions in which the researcher herself is complicit ... Anti-oppressive theorists ... make a connection between knowing and doing, and research as 'praxis' ... Knowledge, therefore, is not conceived of as neutral, nor is it abstract in nature."[16] This led me to question whether objectivity and neutrality – qualities that are highly valued in Western research and conflict resolution practices – are either morally possible or ethically responsible when it comes to addressing the injustices of the IRS system.

More recently, some scholars have pointed out that even those researchers who attempt to know the Other empathically run the risk of simply perpetuating an imperial belief that their status as researchers entitles them to acquire such knowledge. A more preferable approach, they say, is one in which non-Indigenous researchers fully embrace the uncomfortable epistemological tension that comes with the realization that they can never fully know the Other; nor should they aspire to do so. From this stance, a more nuanced reworking of non-Indigenous positioning is evident in the literature.

For example, Alison Jones (Pakeha) and Kuni Jenkins (Maori) describe their intercultural collaboration as educators "working the Indigene-Colonizer hyphen," in which they "attempt to create a research and writing relationship based on the tension of difference, not on its erasure."[17] Wanda D. McCaslin (Métis) and Denise C. Breton (Euro-American) collaborate in ways that acknowledge this tension as they critique restorative justice models that they assert have failed to live up to their decolonizing potential within Indigenous communities and in the field of restorative justice itself. These shortcomings reveal the need to get to the root of the problem, which is colonialism, and illustrate why "decolonization is critical for both Indigenous and non-Indigenous people."[18] Both Jones and Breton, as non-Native scholars, emphasize the importance of continually interrogating their own colonial position within their work. Jones describes her effort to engage in collaborative dialogue while being ever mindful of the need to examine her own attitudes and actions: "To rethink collaboration between indigene and colonizer is both to desire it and to ask troubling questions about it ... Interrogating the logic of (my own) White/settler enthusiasm for dialogic collaboration, I consider how this desire might be an unwitting imperialist demand – and thereby in danger of strengthening the very impulses it seeks to combat. I do not argue for a rejection of collaboration. Rather I unpack its difficulties to suggest a less dialogical and more uneasy, unsettled relationship, based on learning (about difference) from the Other, rather than learning about the Other."[19]

In a similar vein, Breton notes that her very sense of identity is rooted in "all the mental, emotional, and material habits" associated with taken-for-granted white privilege, which support ongoing oppression and are often invisible to her. Thus, "the decolonizing work begins here with naming these dynamics, so that I can engage in the lifelong work of breaking their hold."[20] Acknowledging that decolonization threatens their own privileged position, Jones and Breton seek to make visible to themselves and others the ease with which the colonizer unconsciously reasserts herself.

Viewed from a colonizer-ally's perspective, the challenge of learning from rather than about the Other, from "an unfamiliar space of not knowing," seems a particularly appropriate standpoint for a study that focuses on the personal and socio-political unsettling of settlers. It is also congruent with a broader Indigenous research agenda that supports decolonization and self-determination in ways that confront the historical and theoretical foundations of Western research paradigms and practices that privilege objectivity and neutrality over subjectivity and engagement. Like Jones and Breton, I aim to interrogate my own positionality as both colonizer-perpetrator and colonizer-ally as I work through the complexities of settler participation in truth-telling and reconciliation efforts. Therefore, I make settlers (myself and others) the subject of this study, linking it to my own practice as a former claims resolution manager through critical self-reflective storytelling.

On Settler Storytelling

> In her auto/ethnography, Pieces of White Shell: A Journey to *Navajo-*
> *land*, [Terry Williams] praises the wisdom of Navajo storytellers and
> the stories they tell. But she warns the reader we cannot emulate
> Native peoples: "We are not Navajo ... Their traditional stories don't
> work for us. Their stories hold meaning for us only as examples. They
> can teach us what is possible. We must create our own stories." As
> nonindigenous scholars seeking a dialogue with indigenous scholars,
> we ... must construct stories that are embedded in the landscapes
> through which we travel. These will be dialogical counternarratives,
> stories of resistance, of struggle, of hope, stories that create spaces.
>
> – NORMAN K. DENZIN AND YVONNA S. LINCOLN, "INTRODUCTION:
> CRITICAL METHODOLOGIES AND INDIGENOUS INQUIRY"

Settler stories as counter-narratives that create decolonizing space are both
interior and relational. As such, they require us to risk revealing ourselves
as vulnerable "not-knowers" who are willing to examine our dual positions
as colonizer-perpetrators and colonizer-allies. Canadian historian Robin
Jarvis Brownlie writes that, "in the field of Aboriginal history, the belief
that oral history is important has come to be almost universally accepted
... It is becoming almost a platitude to state that oral history is essential,
but oral history is difficult to do." She cites various reasons for this, including an understandable reluctance on the part of Native communities to
share their knowledge with outsiders, the difficulty of establishing long-
term collaborative research relationships with communities, and the
academic institutional and timeline pressures scholars face with regard to
publication, which is linked to achieving tenure.[21] Brownlie does not suggest that such difficulties are reasons to avoid conducting oral history but
rather aims to alert the reader to the ethical and practical complexities of
undertaking such projects. I will add that one should also consider whether interviews or other oral history methodologies are best suited to the
research task at hand. Within emergent qualitative research design, oral
history methodology and data collection are not restricted to interviews
but can take many other forms, including auto-ethnography, or critical
personal narrative.

Despite the fact that it has become almost standard for non-Native researchers to conduct oral history interviews with Native people in studies dealing with Indigenous-settler relations, I did not follow suit for this book. The reasons are threefold. First, applying a research ethic of "do no harm," I consider it ethically questionable to ask survivors to relive events associated with their residential school experiences for a book that is focused on examining settler attitudes, perspectives, and responsibility. Through the work of the Aboriginal Healing Foundation and other organizations that work directly with survivors, we now know that the constant retelling of traumatic personal histories may trigger unintended but potentially harmful consequences.

Second, I believe strongly that Gitxsan stories about the Hazelton feast (which is the subject of Chapter 7) are not mine to tell: instead, they belong with the survivors and with the Gitxsan, who are documenting their history of Indian residential schools in their own voices. But neither was this study written in isolation. I consulted with and received invaluable feedback from various feast participants and witnesses, as well as several Indigenous scholars and professional colleagues as I presented earlier versions of this study at symposia and conferences. Without exception, they all encouraged me to tell my own story, not theirs. This entailed adopting an oral history methodology that was congruent with my research focus on unsettling the settler within. By incorporating my own ongoing decolonizing journey into the book, I intend to demonstrate the transformative personal and socio-political pedagogy I am advocating. However, in doing so, I am also aware that injecting a critical personal voice into an academic work is fraught with its own difficulties precisely because it is not neutral, objective, or abstract.

My methodology thus involves using oral history evidence in the form of auto-ethnography – my own storytelling – to document and analyze my own lived experience. This approach is common in Indigenous scholarship but still not as widely used in the social sciences and history disciplines. Yet it is particularly well suited to the parameters of this study. The authors of *Telling Stories* note that

there has been an increasing interest among a number of scholars in writing ... "auto/ethnography" ... These scholars are interested in narratives of self-inscription, but rather than studying the "other" they write critical ethnographies of themselves, or themselves in relation to others. Informed by developments in postmodern, feminist, and postcolonial theory and methods, auto/ethnographers build on recent reconsiderations of the uses and meanings of personal narratives to examine the ways in which selves and social forms are culturally constituted through biographical genres ... [They] reject the search for universal and objective "truths" in favor of the personal and the subjective ... [They] address, for example, the emotional and personal experiences that characterize and shape fieldwork. What makes these works distinct from an autobiography or a life history is the narrator's attempt to turn the ethnographic gaze on his or her own life and work. In this respect ... auto/ethnographers are at once narrator and analyst.[22]

Auto-ethnographic methodologies incorporate textual and performative components as embodied research in which "researchers use their own thoughts, feelings and experiences as a means of understanding the social world."[23]

Very few non-Indigenous negotiators or policy makers who have been involved in attempts to resolve Indigenous-settler conflicts or in treaty or claims resolution processes have written about the personal and sociopolitical insights they have gained from their experience. Yet their stories, forged within the harsh realities of their everyday work, have much to teach us about the importance of building trust, attending to history, and repairing relationships. These stories can also reveal the emotional toll exacted upon non-Native people who work in Indigenous contexts, grappling with the moral and ethical issues that confront them. Writing from two very different perspectives, BC treaty negotiator Tony Penikett and John Ciaccia, minister of Native affairs for Quebec during the Oka crisis, both describe themselves as "peacemakers" who became increasingly frustrated by the actions of recalcitrant politicians and resistant bureaucrats. They argue that a fundamental lack of leadership, political will, and creativity bogs down negotiations. Both emphasize how important it is for the Canadian public to understand the destructive impacts of colonial history on contemporary Indigenous-settler conflicts.[24] Ciaccia also reveals the deeply transformative journey he embarked upon and the emotional, physical, and spiritual consequences of his own ethical and moral crisis. In *The Oka Crisis*, published in 2000, he writes, "My plans, and my life, were changed by the Mohawks of Kanehsatake and Kahnawake. For years, I wasn't able to talk about the events that occurred that summer of 1990. Now, some healing has taken place ... The Oka Crisis, as it came to be known, was not only about Native people. It was about government, idealism and the realities of power. It was about history, about human nature, about the clash of cultures, survival and soul."[25]

In a similar vein, and writing within the IRS context, I think it important that I reveal something of my own emotional turmoil and the moral and ethical dilemmas that confronted me in my work with survivors. My intended primary audience is not survivors but other settlers. The former should not be asked to carry the additional burden of my decolonizing struggle. Moreover, it would seem unconscionable that, having listened to survivors who had the courage and strength to tell me about their intimate experiences of abuse, neglect, and suffering, I would not have the fortitude to openly and critically reflect on how their stories affected me. Thus, telling my own story "is a particular kind of critical method that is able to give expression to metaphor, paradox, identity and emotion" in ways that reflect my lived experience.[26]

Third, and finally, many survivors and Indigenous scholars and colleagues told me that my approach is long overdue. More importantly, they indicated that I had a moral and ethical responsibility to share my story with other settlers.[27] This is consistent with Indigenous pedagogy in which stories are teachings, and the storyteller has a responsibility to "give away" – to share with others what he or she has learned. Sto:lo educator Jo-ann Archibald (Q'um Q'um Xiiem) explains that Indigenous storywork involves sharing as a foundational ethical principle: "Sharing what one has learned is an important Indigenous tradition. This type of sharing can take the form of a story of personal life experience and is done with a compassionate mind ... [that] combines physical, spiritual, emotional and intellectual learning with humility, truth, and love ... Some teachings ... are about cultural respect, responsibility and reciprocity ... If one comes to understand and appreciate the power of a particular knowledge, then one must be ready to share and teach it respectfully and responsibly to others in order for this knowledge, and its power, to continue."[28]

Such storywork is not undertaken from the position of experts who impart knowledge to passive listeners. Rather, storytellers share their own life experiences with humility as a way of provoking critical reflection in others, while continuing to learn themselves. Decolonizing stories told in this manner are an interactive exchange between teller and listener in which both learn and teach.

Writing about the obstacles facing non-Native critical theorists working in Indigenous contexts, Norman K. Denzin argues that "all inquiry is moral and political" and that "narrative, performative methodologies and research practices ... are reflexively consequential, ethical, critical, respectful and humble."[29] Stacy Holman Jones suggests that auto-ethnography can facilitate "radical democratic politics ... committed to creating space for dialogue ... that instigates ... social change."[30] Ultimately, decolonizing counter-narratives have the potential to "disrupt and disturb discourse by exposing the complexities and contradictions that exist under official history."[31] How the story is told is integral to its critical credibility and ethical integrity. Thus, my settler account "includes the obligation to bear witness – to re-testify, to somehow convey what one has heard and thinks important to remember."[32] This book constitutes my retestifying, in which, through a series of personal reflections, I try to convey the teachings and responsibilities that have been gifted to me by IRS survivors.

From the Personal to the Political: A Decolonizing Pedagogical Strategy

Although various scholars make a compelling argument as to why settlers should acknowledge and accept responsibility for past wrongs and enrich our thinking about the politics of knowing/not knowing, what remains unclear is *how* we might actually undertake such a task. This requires adopting a pedagogical approach to truth telling and reconciliation that not only challenges mainstream society's deeply held myths about history but also fosters a genuine willingness and ability among settlers to accept responsibility for the residential schools. Thus, it is necessary to link the individual's sense of personal responsibility to the collective socio-political, moral, and ethical responsibility that we carry. This involves learning to bear deep witness to survivors' testimonial stories, paying careful attention to our responses as indicators of our empathy for, or resistance to, the hard historical truths we are hearing. These personal responses, if reflected upon self-critically, are a springboard for socio-political action. Here, the works of Indigenous, critical, and feminist theorists provide valuable insights as to why this is best done from within a decolonizing framework.

Maori scholar Linda Tuhiwai Smith sets out the parameters of decolonizing methodologies for Maori researchers, and in doing so she also challenges their non-Indigenous counterparts to question the cultural, theoretical, and methodological traditions that define our work.[33] Like other Indigenous scholars, she points out that many Western academics continue to oppress and colonize Native people, excluding or marginalizing their knowledge systems, world views, and pedagogy. Western research often exploits or revictimizes and further harms individuals and whole communities. Most importantly, Indigenous people must speak with their own voices about their histories, cultures, and experiences as people who continue to resist the onslaught of colonial structures, policies, and practices.[34] They rightly criticize non-Native scholars who research and write in ways that either appropriate or ignore Indigenous knowledge systems.

This does not absolve settlers from the responsibility of addressing our shared colonial history. Rather, as Mohawk scholar Patricia Monture-Angus suggests, we should do so from our own perspectives, using approaches that acknowledge complicity and move us away from the objectifying thinking that situates Indigenous people as the Other and problematizes them accordingly.[35] In 2005, as I began my research, I thought about these thorny issues of voice, legitimacy, power, and representation in writings produced by non-Native scholars about Native peoples and issues. It became obvious to me that we are still overly focused on researching, analyzing, and interpreting Indigenous experience. What is missing is a corresponding research emphasis on understanding our own experiences as the descendants of colonizers and the primary beneficiaries of colonialism.[36] As I pondered the possibility of focusing my research on settlers, I began to see its potential as a decolonizing strategy, though I was also aware that, in making settlers the subject of study, I might simply replicate colonizer epistemic privilege by making the issues all about us.

However, Cree Saulteaux Dunne Zah legal scholar Val Napoleon observes that a settler lack of critical self-reflexivity is highly problematic. She notes, for example, that many cross-cultural sensitivity training programs are designed solely to educate settlers about Indigenous people without any reciprocal sharing by the former about their own history, cultural practices, world views, and values. Consequently, she argues, settlers "have their awareness increased, but not about themselves. Instead, it is a one-way street, another example of the 'Aboriginal people under glass' phenomenon."[37] Thus, for settlers, as Roger Epp argues, "making [ourselves] the subject under closest scrutiny" becomes essential as part of the decolonization project.[38]

On Settler Denial and Identity Crisis

> If a community has to recognize that its members, instead of being heroes, have been perpetrators who violated the cultural premises of their own identity, the reference to the past is indeed traumatic. The community can cope with the fundamental contradiction between identity claims and recognition only by a collective schizophrenia, by denial, by decoupling or withdrawal.
>
> – Bernhard Giesen, "The Trauma of Perpetrators: The Holocaust as the Traumatic Reference of German National Identity"

As a settler nation, Canada has consistently sought bureaucratic solutions to a long list of "Indian problems" such as poverty, low education levels, poor health, and social dysfunction. At the same time, Canadian society subscribes to the peacemaker myth as we cast ourselves as heroes on a mythical quest to save Indians. In this way, we deflect attention from the settler problem. To do otherwise would engender our own collective identity crisis and expose us to the trauma of admitting uncomfortable truths.

The peacemaker myth is an epitomizing characteristic of Canadian national identity and history. As settlers, we much prefer this identity, and understandably so. Being cast as a perpetrator is far less appealing. In his study of restitution as a "mechanism for moral action," American historian Elazar Barkan notes that, when victims of injustice speak out, their histories "dramatically contradict the public's self-perception and necessitate the rewriting of a heroic national history as one that inflicted pain and suffering and even perpetrated crimes."[39] Philosopher Trudy Govier writes about the Canadian propensity to deny by ignoring or minimizing already known truths because they "are incompatible with the favoured picture we have of ourselves," but she reminds us that, "through patterns of colonization, land use, racism, disregard for treaties, and the residential school system, we are linked significantly to the institutions that are responsible ... As members of the society and as citizens of the state, we share responsibility for these things ... We ... are beneficiaries of the injustices."[40] Viewed in this way, our willingness to negotiate outstanding historical claims with Indigenous people is mediated by our wilful ignorance and our selective denial of those aspects of our relationship that threaten our privilege and power – the colonial status quo.

Settler denial and moral indifference are closely linked to expressions of "violent innocence" in which individuals, organizations, or whole societies take on an "innocent gaze ... a collective mindset that protects illusions from uncomfortable truths ... Strategic myths are crafted about the organization's high morality."[41] Sociologist Stanley Cohen observes that "most countries with a democratic image to maintain ... cannot indefinitely sustain strategies of ignoring allegations completely, crude denial, ideological justification or aggressive counter-attack." Rather, they tell victims, "we welcome constructive criticism ... but the situation is difficult; things can't be changed overnight; you must be patient."[42] Governments claim that past wrongs were exceptional and that remedial steps are being taken. But the proposed legal and bureaucratic solutions deflect the more substantive political recognition necessary to make radical changes within more conservative systems, structures, and institutions.[43] At the same time, public denial of political violence (defined as the "repression and persecution of social groups by a state in order to establish and retain political control") against targeted groups works to silence the voices of victims, minimizing or discounting the extent of the harms inflicted upon them.[44] In stable democracies such as Canada, where the rhetoric of reconciliation now dominates Indigenous-settler public discourse, violence is most often although not exclusively expressed symbolically in a range of negotiation and claims settlement processes that replicate hegemony.

Historian Bernhard Giesen studies how ordinary German citizens denied their own role as perpetrators of the Holocaust by creating a national post-war narrative that rationalized genocide as the act of a few exceptionally evil individuals and cast the majority population as their innocent and unwitting victims. Thus, perpetrators become victims, the innocent bystanders who disavow responsibility for harmful government policies enacted on their behalf. The nation denies its guilt by focusing on the acts of individuals. He explains that, by "denying any collective responsibility, the rituals of trials confined the question of guilt strictly to individual acts, in particular as evidenced by formal decisions within organizations."[45] Stanley Cohen describes such tactics as "legalistic games of truth ... Harm may be acknowledged, but its legal or common sense meanings are denied, contested, or minimized."[46] If we apply a similar analysis to the Canadian context, we see striking similarities in the IRS claims settlement process. Initially, in the late 1990s, residential school trials focused public attention on the acts of individual perpetrators, as the state engaged in protracted legal battles with churches over the apportionment of liability and challenged class-action lawsuits whose claims included harms such as cultural loss and intergenerational trauma. During this period, the government refused to consider financially compensating survivors for systemic harms or to establish a public inquiry. The Alternative Dispute Resolution Program (ADRP) that was subsequently created in 2004 resolved individual claims and provided compensation based on validating and settling claims on a balance of probability that the acts of individual perpetrators constituted tort wrongs.

These kinds of legal and policy negotiations take place within a global environment of what sociologist John Torpey calls "reparations politics," which he defines as a broad field of activities, including material compensation, apologies, the rewriting of historical narratives, and commemoration, designed to address historical injustices.[47] He observes that Indigenous people whose individual and collective rights have been circumscribed challenge the very legitimacy of liberal democracies, which are built on the promise to protect rights and ensure equal justice for all. He makes a point that is central to my argument. When the focus is on colonizers as individual perpetrators, the number of victims is smaller; when colonizers are understood as collective beneficiaries of a system that created and perpetuates inequities and breaches the human rights of oppressed groups, the number of victims increases exponentially. Dealing with legal claims based on the actions of individuals is a matter of criminal or civil justice. But when the benefits, privileges, and wealth that colonizers have reaped from Indigenous lands and resources are factored in, the stakes become significantly higher. It is this "link between conquest and dispossession, between racialized power and racialized privilege, *between perpetrator and beneficiary,*" that must be made more visible and taken into account.[48]

Canada's response to IRS claims, which began with a focus on individual acts of wrongdoing, eventually widened to include a national apology and a mechanism for providing a collective response to the IRS history and legacy through the Truth and Reconciliation Commission. But though Canada's political and legal response is now fairly comprehensive in scope, much remains to be done to address settler denial, particularly through educating not only the Canadian public but negotiators, policy makers, and bureaucrats who work in Indigenous contexts. Peter Harrison, former deputy head of Indian Residential Schools Resolution Canada (IRSRC), points out that widespread ignorance about Canada's colonial history as it relates to the residential school system is common not only in the Canadian public but also among civil servants who work on Aboriginal negotiations, policy, and programs.[49] This ignorance, coupled with various degrees of denial and resistance to the stories of survivors, presents a significant pedagogical challenge related to truth-telling and reconciliation processes. It also has implications for the development and implementation of various policies and programs related to the reconciliation agenda that is now a strong focus in all federal government departments.

Confronting Violence

My experiences working with survivors compelled me to face my own denial and to rethink my understanding of violence. Demythologizing the long history of the residential schools has already begun, captured in numerous academic studies and in the *Report of the Royal Commission on Aboriginal Peoples,* which, along with histories written by former students, stands as a counter-narrative to those of Canada's celebratory past. These stark testimonials reveal the systemic long-term violence that characterized IRS policy and practice.[50] They call upon us to rethink our ideas about what constitutes violence and to recognize the more subtle forms of violence embedded in Indigenous-settler relations. This enables us to consider how we might disrupt these destructive and deeply ingrained colonial attitudes and patterns of behaviour.

In *Accounting for Genocide,* Dean Neu and Richard Therrien draw insightful connections between cultural genocide and the administrative solutions to the Indian problem that are designed using seemingly innocuous bureaucratic practices.[51] They argue that soft technologies such as strategic planning, law, and accounting, which combine legal frameworks, accounting techniques, and economic rationalizations with program and funding mechanisms, actually constitute violence – a slow form of genocide enacted over time:

> When faced with the evidence of the Holocaust, we are almost always overwhelmed by its naked brutality; the degree of inhumanity expressed through such an undertaking seems incomprehensible. And yet the same undertaking applied to Indigenous peoples – stretched over a century or two, dressed in a rationale of progress, economics and civilization – seems somehow to lose this quality of brutality and becomes not only comprehensible but defensible ... If genocide is gruesome in its lack of subtlety, then forced assimilation as a means of cultural annihilation is sly in its false generosity – the Indians were treated as children "for their own good," the King "watchful over their interests and ever compassionate."[52]

From this view, historian John Milloy's careful documentation of the destructive history of Indian residential schools from 1879 to 1986 takes on new meaning. In an analysis of government documents, he presents a damning indictment of the false generosity that guided the administration and operation of these schools of forced assimilation – a record of cultural annihilation, chronic underfunding, poor management, systemic abuse, neglect, and poor living conditions that had catastrophic impacts on the students who attended them. Using various reports and letters that were sent to government and various church officials over the years from teachers, staff, health officials, and others criticizing the residential school system, Milloy demonstrates convincingly that these officials knew about the problems but failed to take effective remedial measures.[53]

In a study of contemporary treaty negotiations in British Columbia, sociologist Andrew Woolford argues that colonial violence is entrenched in Canadian Aboriginal policy and bureaucratic practices, and manifested in treaty and claims negotiation processes and mandates. He builds on Pierre Bourdieu's concept of symbolic violence as a "gentle, invisible violence" in which the oppressor's subtle exercise of power reinforces hegemony and the colonial status quo. He reveals, for example, how discussion of Native peoples' historical grievances is excluded from negotiation tables:

"At treaty tables, following a First Nation's presentation on the hardships it experienced due to the policies of the federal and provincial governments, it is not uncommon to hear one of the non-Aboriginal government representatives remark: 'We are here to talk about the future, not the past.' With this statement, the non-Aboriginal representative performs, however unwittingly, an act of symbolic violence, using a position of power and discursive competence to attempt to 'name' or define the negotiation context in terms suitable to government interests."[54]

Not surprisingly, Woolford concludes that these negotiating strategies, based on dominant-culture beliefs about what constitutes the appropriate parameters of negotiation, deliver only minor reforms. As a result, they are not transformative but rather ultimately serve as a tool of assimilation.[55] This dynamic plays itself out in a particular manner during negotiations and public forums where Indigenous participants convey their points in highly emotional ways, whereas government officials listen from a neutral stance that may not be explicit in their responses but is nevertheless conveyed through body language and tone of voice. The theme of settler neutrality versus Native emotionality constitutes a critical subplot in the Indigenous-settler mythos, or storyline, one in which neutrality is actually an expression of settler symbolic violence, or power over, Indigenous people. At the same time, oppressed groups may choose to ignore dominant-culture assumptions about emotion, employing it as a political strategy.[56] Together, these studies expand our thinking about the nature of denial, what constitutes violence, and how these patterns remain entrenched in Indigenous-settler relations.

Scholars who look at the role of perpetrators in societies that are marred by violence identify various ways in which perpetrators deny their complicity by minimizing or neutralizing their role in illegal and/or immoral acts. Here, Cohen's analysis of denial is particularly instructive. He argues that, in the face of the accusatory testimonies of victims, perpetrators must give an account of their actions in which they are "not just telling a story ... but being morally accountable." In doing so, they may attempt to justify or excuse their actions, accepting partial responsibility in "accounts that are passive, apologetic and defensive."[57] Cohen notes that they may also disavow wrongdoing by separating their "personal selves from their work selves."[58] Writing in the Canadian context, Woolford identifies this same phenomenon in what he calls "the bifurcated consciousness" of government treaty negotiators who support mandates that may be at odds with their personal ethics and visions of moral justice. They are not unsympathetic and may in fact express sincere empathy for the victims of historical injustices. Nevertheless, they "are able to separate these personal and embodied feelings from their public role as negotiator ... from a space outside of the body ... that corresponds to the rational interests of non-Aboriginal governments."[59] As I discuss in more detail below, this form of disembodied empathy is ultimately colonial in nature.

Here, it is important to point out that this ability to separate feelings from thoughts in order to be a "neutral" participant in negotiation and adjudication processes is a core principle in North American ADR training provided for government lawyers, negotiators, policy makers, and program managers. The Western cultural preference for mediators who are neutral practitioners rather than, for example, respected community elders, and for separating rational thought from somatic, emotional, and spiritual responses to conflict is highly problematic for oppressed people.[60] It is also at odds with Indigenous diplomacy and peacemaking. Conflict studies scholar-practitioner Michelle LeBaron observes that dominant-culture ADR processes reflect this mind/body split by privileging fact finding, cost savings, and efficiency over emotional expression and relational issues, which, from a Western perspective, may seem superfluous. She suggests that, in disagreements between Indigenous and non-Indigenous, "it is not surprising that dominant culture legal processes and systems have been experienced by First Nations people as exclusionary, disempowering, and unfair. Bringing different cultural assumptions, values and behaviours, they have not accepted procedures and structures that reflected dominant culture 'common sense.'"[61]

Philosopher David Kahane also challenges the myth of neutrality that forms the basis of liberal philosophical ideas about what constitutes the just resolution of conflicts. Like others, he argues that ADR that claims to be neutral, fair, and rational is in fact a culturally bound, highly political process that reinforces dominant-culture values and replicates colonial power relations: "The common sense story of just adjudication has deep roots in Western cultural, legal and philosophical traditions and is closely tied to accounts of political legitimacy ... In its common sense version, this story of neutrality and justice has tremendous currency in North America:

it is seen as describing not only the aspirations of our legal and political systems but even their typical operation. Seen from the standpoint of Aboriginal struggles for survival, equality and self-determination, however, this dominant Western account of justice looks deeply corrupt."[62] Increasingly, ADR neutrality-based models that fail to take culture, power, and political relations into account are criticized by those who argue that they reinforce the status quo and fail to address the identity concerns and the political or socio-economic realities of oppressed, marginalized peoples. Within this context, the ability to act as a neutral observer of painful Indigenous historical experience constitutes a colonial form of empathy.

Settler Responsibility: Knowing versus Not Knowing Indigenous People

I take as my starting point that the creation of decolonizing, potentially transformative space in truth-telling and reconciliation dialogues must encompass both survivor and perpetrator stories in ways that enable Indigenous people to draw upon their own history, law, and peacemaking as they see fit. At the same time, settlers who have hitherto relied upon colonial ways of knowing Indians empathetically in order to solve the Indian problem must instead enter willingly into a more vulnerable, unsettling space of not knowing as we listen to Indigenous testimonies and share our own. Reconciliation conceptualized as an intercultural encounter involves creating a space for critical dialogue – rooted in testimonial, ceremonial, and commemorative practices – between Indian residential school survivors and settlers who are either directly or indirectly implicated in the school system itself as well as other assimilationist policies. Yet designing appropriate truth-telling and reconciliation processes will be especially challenging given the relatively high level of settler ignorance about Native issues in general, and more specifically, those related to Indian residential schools. Here, I want to distinguish between ignorance as a form of collective settler denial, and the concept of "not knowing" that I advocate as a decolonizing stance.

Claiming ignorance is a colonial strategy – a way of proclaiming our ignorance because "we did not know." The results of a national benchmark survey conducted in May 2008 confirm that, though Canadians are somewhat familiar with the sexual and physical abuse that occurred in the schools, very few have any substantive knowledge concerning the policy goal of assimilation that lay behind the IRS system. Clearly, an enormous public education task lies ahead. According to the survey, fully "one-third of Canadians (32%) feel they are not very familiar with Aboriginal issues, while just under two in ten (17%) are not at all familiar."[63] The survey also found that "just over one-third of Canadians are familiar with the issue of native people and residential schools, although only one in twenty are very familiar. Familiarity with this issue is much higher among Aboriginal people, especially those living on reserve."[64] Among the general population who were aware of residential schools, 37 percent knew that students had been abused and molested, 20 percent knew that they had been separated from their families, 14 percent identified the mistreatment of Aboriginal people and discrimination, 10 percent knew that Aboriginal children were forbidden to speak their own languages in the schools, 9 percent knew about the settlement agreement and financial compensation, 3 percent were aware that lawsuits and claims had been filed, 7 percent knew that the goal of the schools was assimilation into mainstream society, 4 percent knew that the schools were run by government and churches, 3 percent thought that they provided students with an education and taught their culture, and 2 percent thought that the schools had been closed because of poor living conditions.[65]

These results are consistent with my hypothesis that, regardless of whether settlers participate in truth-telling and reconciliation processes in the well-meaning belief that they can help solve the Indian problem or as those who rationalize perpetrator actions, neither group, in their rush to put the past behind them, will closely examine the cultural attitudes that influence understanding of the responsibility that Canadian society bears for the residential schools. Without understanding the subject as symptomatic of a colonial relationship that must be dismantled, we are unlikely to live up to our promise that Canada will never again formulate public policies of oppression that target Indigenous people or other minorities while the silent majority does nothing. That settlers fail to see the importance of accepting responsibility for the IRS system is hardly surprising. Maintaining a comfortable intellectual, psychological, and emotional distance from the harsh realities that the system engendered enables us to retain an identity as well-intentioned, humane citizens – benevolent peacemakers – who have always sought only to observe or know Indians in order to help them.

Yet such a response is inadequate if we are to take real responsibility for the IRS story. Canadian author Susan Crean argues that, to provide the necessary corrective to Canada's history, we must publicly acknowledge our complicity in producing and maintaining the residential school system as a colonial project that was entirely consistent with the cultural values and attitudes of imperialism:

> To my mind, ownership means understanding the how, who, and why of something like the residential school solution – how it was set up, who helped it function, and why the abuse was tolerated. Like other chapters in the saga of white/Aboriginal relations, we need to go deeper than just recognizing that Aboriginal peoples were betrayed and victimized ... We need a public reckoning with the fact that whole cultures were broken, children brutalized, and poverty and racism institutionalized by design. We need to acknowledge that all of this was sanctioned by the prevailing value system, which is to say the race-based conventions of British imperialism, and that it required institutions and individuals to pull it off ... Even with the *Charter of Rights,* equity laws could come and go, and no apology in the House of Commons, made to the sound of land claims stalling in the background, can atone for, much less change, the culture that produced residential schools. That culture must take it upon itself to alter the stereotypes, correct the history, fill in the gaps, or re-educate the public. What is the public to make of it anyway, given the government's continuing refusal to sign the United Nations' *Declaration on the Rights of Indigenous Peoples?* This confusion is symptomatic. The mixed signals are a product of a lack of leadership by non-Native elites and intellectuals and an absence of any real discourse in mainstream society.[66]

Thus, Crean identifies what settler society must do: we must own the residential school history and legacy in order to effect change in Indigenous-settler relations.[67] This is a moral and ethical obligation that settlers have yet to undertake.

Other scholars provide further insight into why the concept of responsibility vis-à-vis rights is so central to framing historical injustices as moral and ethical issues. Communications theorists W. Barnett Pearce and Stephen W. Littlejohn argue that public policy conflicts are in fact moral issues in which various parties cannot agree, because they have incommensurate social or moral values.[68] Conflict studies scholar E. Franklin Dukes declares that North Americans are facing a governance and public policy crisis because society is overly focused on rights rather than responsibilities, to the detriment of the public good. He points out that public policy disagreements are not just disputes over competing interests but that they "involve struggles for recognition, identity, status and other resources."[69] Moreover, whereas rights are socially constructed and legally granted (usually to individuals), responsibilities are more informal, carry more of a collective obligation, and can vary according to cultural teachings.[70] Thus, it is not enough to treat Indigenous demands for justice for historical wrongs and harms as strictly legal obligations that need be met only by the state and those institutions directly responsible. Rather, these wrongs also require a moral response from society that goes beyond resolving individual claims, which might satisfy black letter law but would fail to provide justice. The impetus behind the creation of the Truth and Reconciliation Commission as part of the national Indian Residential Schools Settlement Agreement is a case in point and stands as a testament to this hard reality.

In *Taking Responsibility for the Past,* philosopher Janna Thompson argues convincingly that societies and nations have intergenerational moral responsibilities that encompass past, present, and future relationships. She suggests that focusing solely on legal rights and obligations is insufficient to address grievances that are rooted in history but continue in the present. She says that citizens must understand that the moral and political integrity of nations as "intergenerational communities" rests upon fulfilling their collective moral obligations. Just as we bind our successors to treaties and agreements that we make today, so too are we bound by those made, and sometimes broken, by our ancestors. We inherit moral as well as legal obligations, and thus historical claims "require a response from us as moral agents."[71] Finally, she argues that negotiating reparations must necessarily involve addressing the "injustices done to family lines." It follows that, even if individuals were not harmed, the damage done to the cultural identity of a people demands public moral reparation.[72] Given this, it becomes more difficult for settler societies to deny history and their own responsibility.

Canadian philosopher Trudy Govier makes an important distinction between knowledge and acknowledgment as they relate to the politics of knowing or not knowing about the harms inflicted on oppressed groups, including Indigenous people in Canada. She argues that knowing about something does not necessarily lead to acknowledgment but instead can result in denial, which has implications for both personal and political relationships:

> Many South Africans denied the humanity of the black people who were their workers and servants. Many Canadians have similarly denied the humanity of Aboriginal peoples in Canada. We have chosen to ignore many facts, problems, and cries of pain. As a result of our ignoring we know little. Then, if we are charged with responsibility, we are apt to protest that we did not know. But we did know something – enough to ignore the situation in the first place, to avoid paying attention to it. We knew enough to know we did not want to know more. We did not know because we did not want to know. We did not want to know because the truths we would face would be unpleasant and incompatible with our favoured picture of ourselves, and they imply a need for restitution and redress, threatening our rather comfortable way of life.[73]

Govier's indictment of settlers' wilful ignorance and studied innocence is a powerful reminder that, without both knowledge and acknowledgment, there can be no authentic coming to terms with the past or, indeed, any fundamental change in Indigenous-settler relations. Yet this call to know – to accept responsibility – must be answered cautiously, given that seemingly benign ways of "knowing the Other," which are meant to provoke an empathetic response to historical injustices, are highly problematic in their own right.

On Confronting Colonial Empathy

Viewed from a critical standpoint, "the sympathetic humanitarian eye is no less a product of deeply held colonialist values, and no less authoritative in the mastery of its object than the surveying and policing eye."[74] With this caution in mind, it becomes clear how well-intentioned attempts to listen with empathy to IRS survivor testimonies can easily become mere observation or, worse, degenerate into public spectacle. Drawing on Indigenous and Western critical transformative pedagogies that emphasize the experiential and embodied nature of learning, one can consider how empathy might play out problematically in the testimonial practices associated with truth-telling and reconciliation processes. Critical theorists informed my thinking about why colonial empathy is an inadequate response here. It is integral to the misguided settler belief that our primary responsibility is to channel our caring impulses into solving the Indian problem. It enables us to observe the plight of Indigenous people from a safe distance that requires no substantive change on our part.

Writing about the "problematics of listening" to survivor testimonies as it relates to the TRC's public education mandate, cultural theorist Roger Simon cautions that the commission should not simply assume that the strong emotional responses evoked by survivor narratives will necessarily motivate non-Indigenous Canadians to "undertake an active, ethical engagement with this past, one that might forge new relations of solidarity with Indigenous communities in a collective struggle for a more just future."[75] He points out the danger that such testimonies will simply reinforce negative stereotypes of victimhood rather than "elicit a form of natural empathy and critical historical judgement" that could lead to a just reconciliation.[76] Although settlers may be sympathetic listeners, their empathy could be short-lived, serving only to confirm their own humanitarianism and failing to generate a sense of moral responsibility for the IRS legacy that would lead to material change.

In a similar vein, Ravi de Costa examines the reconciliation movement in Australia in order to "highlight the dangers of national efforts to shift [the] hearts and minds" of non-Indigenous citizens in stable democracies where, unlike in post-war Germany or post-apartheid South Africa, there has been no definitive "rupture in the ideological conditions that make settler or national identity possible. That is, a widespread acceptance amongst both victims and perpetrators that the fundamental ideas underpinning social and political arrangements are untenable."[77] In the case of Australia, he observes that reconciliation discourse, which originally focused on Indigenous rights, subsequently transformed into a justification for instituting new prescriptive government policies to address a "national emergency" – the dysfunctional social conditions and high addiction rates of children in Native communities.[78] Taking action in this instance reinscribed colonial relations in ways that ultimately reinforced rather than deconstructed the legitimacy of the benevolent colonizer. De Costa remarks that "benevolent urges recur throughout the histories of imperialism and colonialism, including forms of humanitarianism and 'benign imperialism,' providing ground[s] for policies of modernization and development, assimilation and integration, charity and aid. Indeed, these motivations are foundational to the colonial enterprise in legitimating Europeans' presence and presumed superiority. Reconciliation is in danger of reproducing these impulses."[79] Simon's and de Costa's prudent cautions make it all the more urgent to consider how truth and reconciliation endeavours can avoid appropriating survivors' pain in voyeuristic ways that enable non-Indigenous people to feel good about feeling bad but engender no critical awareness of themselves as colonial beneficiaries who bear a responsibility to address the inequities and injustices from which they have profited.

Canadian philosopher Sue Campbell argues that, in the TRC context, it will be important for Canadians to understand the difference between forensic and narrative forms of truth telling as it relates to legal versus political testimony. She points out that, although the commission is not a courtroom or a public inquiry, many Canadians may not distinguish "the political testimony of grave harm ... and the kinds of respect and deference appropriate to witnessing such testimony, from Western norms of legal testimony ... [in which] the adversarial setting of the courtroom encourages a skeptical response to testimonial speech."[80] She cautions that the commission's work "will be a challenge to the myths that have rationalized Canada's colonization of Aboriginal peoples ... Challenges to memory, which may be especially intense in political contexts, are sometimes expressions of disrespect meant to undermine the credibility of groups that have suffered harm. Learning to share memory in ways that are respectful, reflective, and appropriately challenging, as well as learning to recognize and avoid disrespectful challenge, are important ethical responsibilities in the context of the IRS TRC."[81] In identifying the need to share memories respectfully during truth-telling and reconciliation processes, Campbell reinforces the concerns raised by Simon and de Costa. As the TRC undertakes its work, it is possible that some non-Native Canadians may listen to residential school survivors' stories with little more than colonial empathy. Others may feel hostile or defensive and be active deniers, questioning the very credibility of the testifiers.

Unsettling Emotions as Decolonizing and Liberatory Struggle

The concerns regarding the politics of emotion raise important questions about the function of emotion in truth and reconciliation processes. Roger Simon provides insight into why, in and of themselves, emotional responses will do little to transform Indigenous-settler relations. We must reconsider "the tendency to give stories of heartfelt pain and suffering an almost magical power, as if ... listening to the story is itself enough, as if it does not take hard work – political work as well as emotional – to create a world in which we can truly say 'Never Again' will such violence and violation be tolerated."[82] This is consistent with an unsettling pedagogical approach in which strong emotions are linked to a broader decolonizing and liberatory struggle – the political work necessary for transformative sociopolitical change.

In *Feeling Power,* Megan Boler argues that, though multicultural democratic societies cultivate the sort of passive empathy that individuals may feel in reaction to testimonies of social and political injustice, ultimately "emotions are inseparable from actions and relations, from lived experience."[83] She writes that, though the theoretical study of emotion has focused primarily on emotions as an individual response to an event – as part of the private sphere – feminist theorists are engaged in "rethinking emotions as collaboratively constructed and historically situated, rather than simply as individualized phenomenon located in the interior self."[84] Emotions are therefore "structures of feeling" that constitute "a medium, a space in which differences and ethics are communicated, negotiated and shaped."[85] Within this greater context, Boler examines the ethical relationship between readers and published testimonies that describe traumatic personal experiences related to war, genocide, and other atrocities that mark the systematic dehumanization of a targeted group.

Boler distinguishes between individualized passive empathy and a testimonial reading of such accounts in which readers assume responsibility for challenging their own world views, engaging in truth telling about the past, and taking action to address historical wrongs. In contrast, when readers engage the text with passive empathy, they do so from a safe distance that, though genuinely sympathetic, requires no further self-reflection or action:

> The primary difference between passive empathy and testimonial read-ing is the responsibility borne by the reader ... Rather than seeing reading as isolated acts of individual response to distant others, testimonial read-ing emphasizes a collective educational responsibility ... What is at stake is not only the ability to empathize with the very distant other, but to recognize oneself as implicated in the social forces that create the climate of obstacles the other must confront ... What might it mean for the reader to "take action"? ... This task ... involves challenging my own as-sumptions and world views ... In response to crisis the reader accepts responsibility as a co-producer of "truth." This responsibility requires a committed interrogation of the reader's response as she faces the other's experience. To turn away, to refuse to engage, to deny complicity – each of these responses correlates with a passive empathy and risks annihilat-ing the other.[86]

Boler's observations suggest that, if it is structured appropriately, the col-lective testimonial exchange that will occur as part of the TRC's work could also open up new possibilities for shifting Canadian historical conscious-ness in decolonizing, liberating ways. The need to question one's assump-tions, attitudes, and world view in the face of overwhelming evidence regarding the destructive impact of the residential school system points to the importance of balancing the inevitable tensions that arise between truth telling and reconciliation. It further points to the necessity of fram-ing the IRS legacy within the comparative colonial experience in settler nations including Canada, Australia, New Zealand, and the United States.

Such an undertaking would enable us, as Simon states, not only to "correct memory" by "engag[ing] in an active re/membering of the actu-alities of the violence of past injustices" but also to "initiate remembrance of the discursive practices that underwrote the European domination, subjection, and exploitation of indigenous peoples."[87] Engaging in these acts of "insurgent remembrance" makes visible to non-Indigenous people the colonial roots of historical patterns and structures that shape our contemporary thinking, attitudes, and actions toward Indigenous people:

> At stake is a pedagogy that moves away from the exclusive concern of historically isolated discussion of who did what to whom ... What moves more centrally into focus are the forms through which relationships with those who are other to ourselves are established and negotiated ... Such remembrance would ask us to grasp the ways the encounter between indigenous and nonindigenous peoples were structured and continue to be structured ... For this recognition to be possible, it is necessary to find a way to enable non-natives – as individuals who draw meaning from their own cultural identities – to directly engage in the record of European-initiated genocide and colonialism without distancing themselves from this history.[88]

Building on Simon's work, my own act of insurgent remembering involves deconstructing the peacemaker myth, linking the discursive practices of nineteenth-century treaty making and Indian policy to a flawed contemporary discourse of reconciliation, and thus tracing the continuity of the violent structures and patterns of Indigenous-settler relations over time. In doing so, I conceptualize history not simply as the intellectual study of the past – the facts and interpretations through which we gain knowledge about our social world – but as a critical learning practice, an experiential strategy that invites us to learn how to listen differently to the testimonies of Indigenous people. Yet my experiences in classroom teaching and the workshop described at the beginning of this chapter have taught me that undertaking such a task can be emotionally disturbing for settlers.

For many non-Native Canadians, residential school survivors' stories will provoke powerful feelings of denial, guilt, and shame. We find these narratives of violence, trauma, and loss deeply disconcerting. We may resist hearing such stories, partly because they challenge our own identity as a nation of benevolent peacemakers. Moreover, we may resist framing the survivors' stories using a lexicon of trauma that we associate primarily with genocide and other acts of collective violence in Third World countries.[89] Or we may dismiss Indigenous talk of violence and trauma as the hyperbole that has become part of the political lexicon of Indigenous-settler relations. We see this most clearly when survivor testimonies are rejected outright, as Campbell indicates. But this is also the case when settlers listen with a more empathic ear as consumers of, not witnesses to, historical accounts of injustice and trauma.

Although reflexivity is essential to the task of confronting unsettling stories, historian Dominick LaCapra, like Boler and Simon, argues that individual self-reflection merely encourages passive empathy or a neutral distancing from the Other that is insufficient to effect social and political change. Rather, he says that one must engage with the Other through what he describes as an "empathic unsettlement," or a working through of "one's own unsettled response to another's unsettlement."[90] This is a necessary precondition to a more ethical response to stories of historical oppression. Boler cautions that "self-reflection, like passive empathy, runs the risk of reducing historical complexities to an overly tidy package that ignores our mutual responsibility to one another. Empathy ... often works through reducing the other to a mirror-identification of oneself, a means of rendering the discomforting other familiar and non-threatening ... The simple identifications and passive empathy produced through this 'confessional reading' assures no actual change. [In contrast,] 'testimonial reading' ... carries with it a responsibility for the 'forces raging within us' – we are asked to turn the gaze equally upon our own historical moment and upon ourselves."[91]

Relating these scholarly observations to the work of Canada's Truth and Reconciliation Commission reinforces the potential risk that settlers – the general public and former IRS staff, government, and church officials – could react to survivor stories as confessional readings. Such responses, although empathetic and perhaps even self-reflective, would fail to engender widespread accountability for the schools. From a decolonizing stance, settlers as ethical witnesses must assume a "posture of alert vulnerability to or recognition of difference, rather than a pose of empathetic understanding that tends to reduce difference to the same."[92] In this way, the dynamics of testimonial exchange create space for the sharing of difficult stories that potentially decolonize and transform both teller and listener. A testimonial reading or witnessing necessitates the kind of owning or taking responsibility for the history of colonialism that Crean and others advocate. This involves a disquieting working through of historical and cultural trauma in the relationally engaged and ceremonial ways that are integral to Indigenous pedagogy and peacemaking practices. In thinking about what kind of pedagogical approach would be best suited to this task, I turned to Indigenous and Western critical theorists and transformative pedagogy scholars.

Various Indigenous scholars describe the holistic, experiential methods of Indigenous pedagogy. Yuchi Muscogee scholar Daniel Wildcat compares Western scientific knowledge, with its emphasis on "universal, objective truth," to Indigenous knowledge systems that "literally emerge from a place – an experience of the world ... You experience places and you learn, if attentive, about the processes and relationships in those places."[93] Métis elder Elmer Ghostkeeper explains that "we observe and analyze everything holistically using our mind, spirit, emotion, and body. Our wisdom views experiential interactions as the primary learning process."[94] Kanien'kehaka (Mohawk) scholar-activist Taiaiake Alfred says that the Indigenous "method of learning is really one of transformation, and it is experiential, observational and practical."[95] Similarly, some Western scholars suggest that we do not learn solely or even primarily through reason but through our emotions, body, spiritual presence, and imagination. Thus, transformative learning "involves experiencing a deep structural shift in the basic premises of thoughts, feelings, and actions. It is a shift of consciousness that dramatically alters our way of being in the world."[96] Megan Boler and Michalinos Zembylas' "pedagogy of discomfort" influenced my thinking about the role emotion can play in practising a decolonizing, transformative, unsettling pedagogy: "To engage in critical inquiry often means asking students to radically alter their worldviews. This process can incur feelings of anger, grief, disappointment and resistance, but the process also offers students new windows on the world ... In short, this pedagogy of discomfort requires not only cognitive but emotional labor ... [It] emphasizes the need for both educator and student to move outside their comfort zones. By comfort zone we mean the inscribed cultural and emotional terrains that we occupy less by choice and more by virtue of hegemony."[97] This process of stepping outside comfort zones resonated strongly with me in relation to my own work in the IRS context and in my subsequent teaching and workshop activities. Within these different contexts, the challenge is to design ethical teaching/learning environments in which testimonial exchange functions as a catalyst for engaging in constructive critical dialogue.

In a study of public deliberative planning processes, American urban planning theorist John Forester suggests that designing public dialogue processes to include storytelling and ceremonial ritual helps us to address power imbalances, cultural differences, and traumatic histories, thus providing safe space for emotional expression. Doing so ensures that participants who have been historically oppressed and have suffered serious harms are not required to "leave their pain at the door."[98] At the same time, dominant-culture participants must be mindful that "deliberation in the shadow of trauma may require much more than a neutral political space in which to debate claims."[99] The dialogue circle methodology I describe at the beginning of this chapter attempts to provide such a space. I began with a story about how the name of the workshop, Unsettling Dialogues of History and Hope, prompted someone to suggest that Brenda and I consider renaming it. After serious consideration, we have not done so. For my part, the question caused me to reflect more deeply on why I am drawn to unsettling pedagogical approaches and to write more explicitly about my theoretical roots; that is, the theory that informs my practice.

2

Rethinking Reconciliation
Truth Telling, Restorying History, Commemoration

REFLECTIONS

My class has been studying the history of Indian residential schools in Canada. With a few exceptions, the students did not previously know anything about the subject. On this particular day, I have invited Kwakwaka'wakw chief Robert Joseph, a residential school survivor who often speaks publicly about his experience, to talk to them. Chief Joseph, former executive director of the Indian Residential School Survivors Society, has been working on IRS issues for many years at community, national, and international levels. Prior to this class, the students had done various readings, and I had spoken briefly about my own experience in the claims settlement process. But it is Chief Joseph's powerful talk about his own truth-telling, healing, and reconciliation journey that really makes this history come alive. My students are inspired by his honesty, his genuine warmth, and the sense of hope he brings to his work, despite all that he has been through. He answers their many questions afterward with a frankness that they appreciate and encourages them to find their own ways to get involved in the work of reconciliation.[1]

Students have also been learning about other aspects of Indigenous-settler relations, including treaties, the Indian Act, Aboriginal policy issues, and litigation and land claims processes. Most have minimal knowledge, with the exception of three Native students and a couple of others. In our dialogue circle, some students are dismayed by the fact that they learned so little about this history in elementary or high school. As one student said, "I'm twenty-four years old, and I don't want a sugar-coated version of Canadian history. People need to know that this stuff happened." Several new Canadian students share their own family histories - of fleeing from oppression, poverty, and violence, and of new opportunities in their adopted homeland. They are learning about an aspect of Canadian history that wasn't covered in their citizenship classes. Other students talk to me during my office hours, struggling with their feelings as they discover that the version of Canadian history they grew up with is only half the story. One student whose family settled in Canada during the early twentieth century asks, "Does this mean that I can't feel proud of my own family's history? They worked hard to build a good life in Canada. But, as I'm finding out about all the bad things that happened to Indigenous people, I feel confused, guilty, and ashamed." We talk about the possibility that her negative feelings are not necessarily bad. I gently remind her that, as she learns about this difficult history, it is important not to become paralyzed by troubling emotions but to work through them. In my experience, this often sparks new insights. The student eventually wrote a term paper on what role the community museum in her hometown has played in silencing the history of local Native people and how this might be rectified.

Throughout the course, I emphasized that, with newfound knowledge, comes an obligation to act – that is, for each of us to find our own ways to share this knowledge with others and to integrate it into our everyday work and civic life. These seemingly small but empowering acts have a ripple effect as settlers speak up, challenging other settlers to rethink their views. I have encountered ample opportunities for such informal teaching moments. Often, a media story ignites interest. Thus, Caledonia becomes a lesson in the land claims process; an article about monies paid to survivors to resolve their claims becomes a lesson about the residential school system; a story about an Aboriginal title and rights case in the courtroom becomes a lesson in the controversies surrounding treaty negotiations and conflicts over lands and resources. Armed with knowledge about these various issues, students are better equipped to understand the complex genesis of contemporary Indigenous-settler conflicts and to share this information with others in ways that challenge ingrained attitudes and deepen understanding. Speaking up is an act of truth telling.

Apology and Reconciliation: The International Context

There is a huge chasm in public perception and belief that ranges on the one hand from those who whitewash history and deny the impact of colonialism on Aboriginal peoples to those who admit to past wrongdoings and move forward to begin the politics of reconciliation. The neo-conservative right in ... Canada ... fears a truthful telling of the history of European-Aboriginal relationships ... This fear is, perhaps, easily understood; to admit the history is to admit both to a record of racism in the past and to the possibility of continued racism ... against Aboriginal peoples in the present. It is time to end this denial, to acknowledge the truth about our recent past, and to accept that the mistreatment of Aboriginal peoples should never be forgotten. Only then will an era of true reconciliation between Aboriginal and non-Aboriginal peoples begin.

> – WAYNE WARRY, *ENDING DENIAL:*
> *UNDERSTANDING ABORIGINAL ISSUES*

Wayne Warry touches on key conceptual themes – truth telling, reconciliation, restorying history, and commemoration – that involve making choices about how we, as Canadians, will come to terms with, and remember, a problematic past in relation to the future. For the TRC, this involves thinking about how these themes will play out in practical terms. Here it is useful to cast the net widely. What contributions can scholar-practitioners and educators bring to deliberations about how to create constructive dialogue regarding history and memory in the face of historical trauma? What have they identified as the critical elements that must be part of this endeavour? Linking theory to three studies involving academics in Canada, the United States, and Colombia, I delve into these questions, beginning with a thematic overview that situates these studies in a broad comparative context. Many international experts see apology and reconciliation as critical not only in "developing" countries but for more stable democracies such as Canada, the United States, Australia, and New Zealand.[2] Canada, like other settler nations, is part of what American historian Elazar Barkan identifies as a recent global phenomenon in which "guilty nations" grapple with the unresolved moral and ethical legacies of colonialism. Nations, as architects of past wrongs, negotiate willingly with victims seeking restitution, which may include both monetary and symbolic compensation.[3] Some liberal theorists suggest that, when "indigenous peoples' claims to prior and continued sovereignty over their territories question the source and legitimacy of state authority ... the issue is not simply a matter of how a state came to be, but of how it can be 'morally rehabilitated' even if it began in an illegitimate fashion."[4] Canadian philosopher James Tully argues that the legitimization of systems of internal colonization has deep roots in liberal theory. He notes that governments employ a range of techniques designed to assimilate or accommodate Native people within the larger Canadian polity, in ways that ultimately confirm the state's legitimacy.[5]

With this in mind, it is wise to heed Barkan's caution that restitution is not a panacea, and that there is always a danger that "it might succeed precisely because it enables the appearance of moral action while being burdened only by minimal cost."[6] This is consistent with a neo-liberal agenda in which settler nations have devised various political and legal strategies to resolve the troublesome question of their moral legitimacy, while enhancing their international human rights reputation with regard to oppressed minorities. Moreover, in a new imperial arena of backlash politics, Indigenous people's activism regarding their rights is increasingly categorized as domestic terrorism or criminal activity. Non-violent political dissent is often dismissed as the irrational or reactionary behaviour of a disgruntled minority that stands in the way of progressive socio-economic development.[7] Maori scholar and educator Graham Hingangaroa Smith states that, in the face of these post-9/11 realities, "there is a pressing need to create more positive, durable and robust intercultural relationships to counteract the current climate of fear, intolerance and distrust, in which the racial targeting of the Other works to the detriment of constructive critical dialogue."[8] Not surprisingly, apology and reconciliation are seen by many as viable in generating such relationships. If apology is understood as a catalyst for action, what then are the necessary components of an ethical reconciliation process?

Writing about the need for a national US Indigenous reconciliation process, Chiricahua Apache legal scholar William Bradford argues that reparations alone, by which he means legal remedies such as monetary compensation, cannot adequately address the full range of harms visited upon Native people in the United States or meet Indigenous political demands for self-determination and the restoration of lands, language, and cultures. He suggests that demanding "reparations [alone] would miss a key opportunity to employ moral argument ... Morally central to the Indian claim for redress is the idea that treaties impose upon the parties the ongoing moral obligation to act in fairness and good faith."[9] For Bradford, "the first step in U.S.–Native-American reconciliation must therefore be [the] dismantling of [a] national myth of Indian inferiority and white infallibility through retelling and re-envisioning U.S.-Indian relations."[10] American critical race theorist Eric Yamamoto asserts that interracial justice requires both "material changes in the structure of the relationship (social, economic, political) to guard against 'cheap reconciliation,' [that is] just talk ... [and] the kind of recognition and redress of deep grievances that sparks a joint transformation in consciousness, diminishes enmities, and forges new relational bonds."[11] Thus, apology is a formal recognition by the state that moral wrongs have been committed. Yet ethical reconciliation requires more than words of regret. Such words must be spoken in conjunction with monetary and cultural reparations that support Indigenous self-determination along with a demythification of settler history – a questioning of the moral foundation of settler societies.

Here, it is instructive to consider briefly how apology and reconciliation have played out somewhat differently in Australia and Canada.[12] Overall, the Australian and Canadian visions of reconciliation are flip sides of the same coin: on the Australian side, reconciliation has been primarily a social movement; on the Canadian side, it has been largely a legal remedy. Generally, the Australian reconciliation movement has focused on grass-roots community-based initiatives designed to educate settler Australians about Aboriginals and Torres Strait Islanders, and to improve Indigenous-settler relations. In 1997, the Human Rights and Equal Opportunity Commission issued its report *Bringing Them Home,* which documented the plight of the Stolen Generations, the victims of a government policy that forcibly removed Native children from their families, a practice that continued well into the 1970s. The commission recommended that an official apology be made and monetary compensation be provided.[13] Neither recommendation was implemented, but Australia established the Council for Aboriginal Reconciliation, which, until the end of its mandate in 2000, provided a national focus and public education for various reconciliation initiatives designed to improve life outcomes for Aboriginals and Torres Strait Islanders. The council developed community-based tool kits to assist communities in planning local reconciliation activities.[14]

In 2000, a non-profit organization called Reconciliation Australia was established to take up the work left unfinished by its predecessor, specifically to close the seventeen-year life expectancy gap between Aboriginal and non-Aboriginal Australians. Reconciliation Australia works with a wide range of stakeholders, including corporations, NGOs, and community organizations, to develop reconciliation action plans with specific targets and measures designed to achieve this goal while improving relationships.[15] Perhaps the best-known grassroots reconciliation initiative that has come out of Australia is National Sorry Day and the Sorry Book Campaign. Initiated in 1998, over one thousand Sorry Books circulated throughout the country at churches, schools, libraries, and other public venues.[16] Although the books may have increased non-Aboriginal Australian awareness of Indigenous issues, and may even have facilitated improved relations, in the absence of monetary compensation, substantive socio-economic and political change in Australian society, or a formal state apology, this type of apology was token at best.

Under former prime minister John Howard, the national government focused its efforts on what he called "practical reconciliation," a "forward-looking" policy that was supposed to improve the poor socio-economic, health, and education outcomes of Aboriginals and Torres Strait Islanders. At the same time, he steadfastly refused to apologize. In his view, one that many Australians support, reconciliation does not hinge on an apology, and white Australians should not be held accountable for the harmful actions of their ancestors.[17] However, on 13 February 2008, a newly elected government under Prime Minister Kevin Rudd gave a formal apology on behalf of all Australians with regard to the Stolen Generations but also stated that no financial compensation was being contemplated.[18] In his response to the apology, Tom Calma, Aboriginal and Torres Strait Islander social justice commissioner, Australian Human Rights and Equal Opportunity Commission, called upon the government to fully implement all the recommendations of the *Bringing Them Home* report.[19]

According to a media report published in the *Manchester Guardian* just before the apology, "by far the hottest issue is the question of whether the apology will lead to financial compensation ... The government has said that this will not happen but Aboriginal activists are already saying that sorry is not enough and have talked about a $1bn fund."[20] In the wake of a landmark South Australia case in 2007, in which Bruce Trevorrow, who was forcibly removed from his parents' care, successfully sued the government and was awarded $500,000 in damages, advocates continued to press the Australian government to compensate all members of the Stolen Generations.[21]

In Canada, our vision of reconciliation has been more legalistic, primarily concerned with reconciling Aboriginal and Crown land title, recognizing Aboriginal rights under section 35 of the Canadian Constitution, and paying financial compensation to individual IRS students who have resolved their abuse claims. Unlike in Australia, there has been no widespread grassroots reconciliation movement in Canada, with the notable exception of the National Day of Healing and Reconciliation; spearheaded in 1998 by Dr. Maggie Hodgson and Edward Colley, this initiative provides information and resources to local communities across the country to hold education and commemoration events on 11 June each year.[22] At present, however, when non-Native Canadians talk about reconciliation in other than a strictly legal sense, the tendency is to speak solely of the need for Native people to heal themselves and reconcile with us, so that the country can put this history behind it and move forward. The national benchmark survey mentioned in the previous chapter also canvassed respondents with regard to what part, if any, individual Canadians should take in reconciliation efforts and found that "fully two-thirds (67%) of Canadians believe that individual Canadians have a role to play in efforts to bring about reconciliation in response to the legacy of the Indian residential school system, even if they had no experience with Indian residential schools. Four in ten (42%) feel strongly that this is the case. About one-quarter of Canadians believe that individual Canadians do *not* have a role to play in reconciliation if they were not involved in the residential school system, but only 12 percent feel strongly that ordinary Canadians have no role."[23] It is encouraging that most Canadians recognize that they have a role to play in reconciliation, but when asked to define what reconciliation meant to them in relation to Indian residential schools, only 11 percent identified acknowledgment or accepting responsibility as essential; 16 percent emphasized the importance of achieving closure and moving on.[24] This is highly problematic in light of my argument that an overemphasis on closure and moving ahead will simply gloss over a difficult past. *Webster's Dictionary* defines "reconcile" in two ways: "to restore to friendship or harmony" or "to cause to submit to or accept something unpleasant." Many Indigenous people say that the latter definition most accurately describes current reconciliation efforts.

Despite their various political perspectives, critics of reconciliation agree on one theme – that the Canadian public's ignorance and denial of the ongoing detrimental impacts of colonial history upon Indigenous people are significant hindrances to reconciliation.[25] Taiaiake Alfred argues that, though Canadians talk about restoring good relations, reconciliation in practice is conceptually weak and morally flawed; it assuages settler guilt in ways that benefit the majority population while failing to make any substantive difference in the lives of Indigenous people.[26] Alfred states bluntly that, as currently envisioned, reconciliation is actually a "huge obstacle to justice and real peacemaking." He places the blame squarely on the non-Native majority, those settlers whose "ignorance ... and willful denial of our historical reality detract from any possibility of meaningful discussion on true reconciliation."[27]

Alfred and Tsalagi (Cherokee) scholar-activist Jeff Corntassel reject outright the notion that settlers are peacemakers. Instead, we are "contemporary colonial shape shifters" who continue "to erase Indigenous histories and senses of place," employing forms of violence ever more subtle than those practised by our ancestors.[28] Alfred therefore calls upon those settlers who would be Indigenous allies – those "who are capable of listening" – "to share our vision of respect and peaceful co-existence" and to "creatively confront the social and spiritual forces that are preventing us from overcoming the divisive and painful legacies of our shared history as imperial subjects."[29] In his view, creative confrontation is essential to restoring just relations between settlers and Onkwehonwe (the original people); these should be "based on re-establishing respect for the original covenants and ancient treaties that reflect the founding principles of the Onkwehonwe-settler relationship."[30] Ultimately, as Alfred suggests, this can be achieved only through a decolonizing struggle on both sides.

In a study comparing the efficacy of truth and reconciliation commissions and apologies as mechanisms for addressing human rights abuses, Jeff Corntassel and Cindy Holder conclude that, when the goal of reconciliation is delinked from Indigenous self-determination, states are not held fully accountable for past wrongs or for transforming intergroup relations.[31] The right to self-determination is articulated in historical treaties, reinforced by constitutional rights, and now affirmed at the international level in the United Nations Declaration on the Rights of Indigenous Peoples. As of January 2010, only Canada, the United States, and New Zealand were not signatories to the UN declaration. After initially refusing to adopt it, Australia did so in April 2009. Non-Indigenous

Canadians must understand that the IRS history and legacy cannot be addressed in isolation from Indigenous people's political struggle to live as self-determining, self-sufficient, healthy communities in accordance with their own customs, law, and connections to the land. Placed within this broader context, the residential school system epitomizes colonialism at its most destructive in a way that is both intensely personal and highly political. Thus, the manner in which Canada and Canadians choose to respond to the issue is a powerful indicator of the overall status of Indigenous-settler relations.

Although some material changes have occurred in Canada, because we have done something more than just talk, the reconciliation we offer is parsimonious at best. And, of course, much of what has been stolen – lands, childhoods, families, cultures, and languages – can never be fully restored. We seem a very long way from the substantive restitution, reparations, and social transformation that critics identify as essential to just relations and authentic reconciliation. There is a distinct possibility that we may not only fail to achieve reconciliation but will actually deepen the divide. A superficial understanding of reconciliation has become entrenched in Canadian discourse. Given this reality, and in light of the TRC's five-year mandate, it is both timely and necessary to rethink reconciliation.

On Truth Telling, Settler History, and Myth

Taking full responsibility for the policies and practices that flourished in Indian residential schools entails truth telling. What is truth? Challenging the peacemaker myth and critiquing reconciliation discourse requires us to be honest with ourselves about the actual impacts of colonial policies and practices upon the lives of Indigenous people. The South African Truth and Reconciliation Commission incorporated concepts of truth into its work that encompassed not just factual or forensic truth associated with law and science but personal narratives, social or dialogue truths, and healing or restorative truths that place "facts and what they mean within the context of human relationships."[32] Truth, then, is not singular, objective, or absolute: it is multiple, subjective, and power-differentiated. Canadian legal scholar Jennifer Llewellyn writes that, conceptually and practically, dialogue based on restorative justice principles can help to bridge the societal gap between truth and reconciliation:

Restorative justice places significant weight on truth-telling as a necessary step towards restored relationships ... The process is predicated upon parties telling their truths about the nature and extent of the harms they have suffered, their needs with respect to redress and recovery, their role and responsibilities for what occurred, and their capacity to assist in repairing the harms and restore relationships. It is also through the sharing of their truths that parties come to know and understand one another's experiences, perspectives, and needs ... Reconciliation requires a truth that is able to contain the complexities borne by our interconnectedness and interdependence ... Relational truth is truth with all of its nuances and complexities.[33]

Llewellyn's definition of relational truth is well suited to the everyday work of truth telling and reconciliation, and is also congruent with Indigenous philosophical concepts of law, justice, and peacemaking, which are rooted in holistic ideas of interconnectedness. She points out that inflicting wrongs has a ripple effect that encompasses victims, perpetrators, families, and communities. This ultimately has a detrimental impact on the moral foundation of a society, as these inequities and injustices permeate its structures and institutions:

Starting from a relational view of the world, restorative justice recognizes the fundamental interconnectedness of people through webs of social relationships. When a wrong is perpetrated, the harm resulting from it extends through these webs of relationship to affect the victim and wrongdoer and their immediate families, supporters, and communities. As a result, wrongdoing also profoundly affects the fabric of the society ... Restorative justice then is not about getting parties to hug and make up; rather it strives to create the conditions of social relationships in which all parties might achieve meaningful, just, and peaceful co-existence. Restorative justice identifies respect, mutual concern, and dignity as the conditions of relationships that will assure such co-existence.[34]

Thus, adopting a restorative justice approach entails repairing Indigenous-settler relations not by insisting on forgiveness but by emphasizing a

collective moral obligation to take action to address the underlying societal conditions that precipitated and condoned the wrongs. Truth telling from multiple perspectives not only reveals those situations where
respect for human rights and dignity has been violated but creates space
for dialogue about what concrete steps must be undertaken to rectify
current policies and practices that may perpetuate similar harms into the
future. In *What Does Justice Look Like?* Wahpetunwan Dakota scholar
Waziyatawin writes about the importance of truth telling and about the
role settler myth plays in skewing the history of Indigenous-settler relations
in her homeland. Her analysis is also relevant for Canada, where the non-
Native majority rarely questions the settler version of history:

> To many Minnesotans truth telling may seem an unnecessary educa-
> tional goal because there is no awareness of a denial of truth ... The need
> for truth telling espoused here assumes that what has passed for the truth
> may not be truthful at all. It assumes that the educational system has not
> engaged our history in a satisfactory way and that most Minnesotans
> still operate in the realm of myth making ... For those of us who believe
> in the transformative potential of education, our hope derives from the
> expectation that once people understand the truth, they will be compelled
> to act more justly. Indeed, it has been my experience that the thought of
> harming others disturbs most morally conscious individuals ... Further-
> more, once they reflect on the personal implications of harms perpe-
> trated so their families could build futures in Dakota homeland, they
> also feel compelled to commit some kind of corrective action. Most,
> however, have no idea how to conceptualize or implement such a monu-
> mental project for justice that would rectify historical harms. So, they
> simply continue with their lives, confining the awareness of ongoing
> injustices to the recesses of their minds.[35]

She frames her discussion not as a "Dakota versus White issue, but rather
as a twenty-first century moral issue," and further argues that, "because
Dakota people have been more likely to engage in truth-telling surrounding this historical past, there is a much more pressing need for Whites to
engage in their own truth-telling."[36] Waziyatawin puts her finger directly
on the problems associated with such a truth telling: settlers may respond

to injustice with empathy, but lacking strategies for taking personal and political action, they simply intellectualize and compartmentalize their newfound knowledge and do nothing.

Intercultural conflicts between Indigenous people and settlers are rooted in political, socio-economic, and legal structures that the two groups understand from very different historical and cultural perspectives. These institutional structures are not immutable but can be changed through a resistance that emerges through personal and political struggle. Scholar-practitioners and educators can inform our thinking about how to create pedagogical space for respectful dialogue, recognizing our differences and yet building where we can on common ground. However, in *Red Pedagogy*, Mayan American theorist Sandy Grande argues that the prevailing lack of discourse between Western critical theorists and Indigenous scholars themselves is problematic because it limits our ability to work together as allies and advocates. She proposes developing *"transcendent* theories of decolonization" that push the disciplinary boundaries of critical theory and pedagogy. She insists that Western critical theorists "need to examine the degree to which critical pedagogies retain the deep structures of Western thought," whereas "American Indian authors ... [must] challenge their own propensity to privilege local knowledge and personal experience over the macroframes of social and political theory."[37] She cautions against taking an assimilationist approach that would subsume Indigenous theory and pedagogy into Western theoretical frameworks. Instead, Grande proposes developing a "red pedagogy" that "emerges from a collectivity of critique and solidarity between and among indigenous peoples, other marginalized groups and peoples of conscience."[38] She identifies the "competing moral visions" of Indigenous nationhood versus American liberal democratic nationalism that shape the history of Indigenous-settler relations in the United States, manifested and reinforced in American Indian policy, law, and public education. She argues that not only have Indigenous peoples been victims of colonialism but that they have also

been revictimized at the hands of whitestream history. The lesson here is pedagogical. The imperative before us, as educators, is to ensure that we engage in a thorough examination of the causes and effects of all wars, conflicts, and intercultural encounters. We must engage the best of our creative and critical capacities to discern the path of social justice and then follow it. The ongoing injustices of the world call educators-as-students-as-activists to work together – to be in solidarity as we work to change the history of empire and struggle in the common project of decolonization. To do so requires courage, humility, and love (muna).[39]

Like Bradford, Waziyatawin, and Grande, I argue for a truth-telling dialogue that begins with deconstructing our identity and our myths about the history of Indigenous-settler relations. Within the IRS discourse in Canada, the binary oppositions of colonizer/colonized, oppressor/oppressed, and perpetrator/victim have been reinforced in counterproductive ways. If we are to begin the decolonizing work of breaking down this dichotomy, it is helpful to understand how settler historical consciousness is shaped by myth.

On History and the Power of Myth

More important than the past itself ... is its bearing upon cultural attitudes in the present. For reasons that are partly embedded in the imperial experience, the old divisions between colonizer and colonized have re-emerged ... Are there ways we can reconceive the imperial experience in other than compartmentalized terms, so as to transform our understanding of both the past and the present and our attitude toward the future?

– EDWARD W. SAID, *CULTURE AND IMPERIALISM*

Edward Said reminds us that the links of imperialism, culture, and history bind colonizer and colonized together. Our shared stories – our narratives of nations and peoples – provide clues as to the relational nature of imperialism and our historical experience.[40] In his study of various forms of denial, sociologist Stanley Cohen says that focusing on figuring out "why denial occurs" in societies is not as important as solving the more perplexing "political problem of how to create the conditions wherein people choose to *act* instead."[41] This is the challenge that faces us. Under what circumstances would those who are the beneficiaries of colonialism stop denying and choose to act differently? This conundrum can be explored in many ways, but I focus here on history because, as Barkan suggests, it has become "a crucial field of political struggle."[42] When understood relationally, the history of colonialism – of perpetrators and victims – becomes a "new form of political negotiation that enables the rewriting of memory and historical identity in ways that both can share."[43] The individual strands of our joint history are intertwined. Yet in our attempts to negotiate resolutions to a myriad of conflicts, we remain stuck – even comfortable – in our well-established historical roles. Circular arguments over who is guilty and who is innocent are not constructive. Reassessing our shared history in light of new understanding invites us to work with complexity, intersubjectivity, and multiplicity in ways that avoid binary thinking. Taking this approach does not require achieving consensus or creating a monolithic history.

If the current quest for reconciliation is no different from settler practices of the past – a new colonial tool of oppression – it has now become imperative to challenge Canada's peacemaker myth. Peeling back the layers of myth reveals that we must confront our own repressed and unscrutinized past as a necessary part of our own truth telling. Indeed, scholars Brian Rice (Mohawk) and Anna Snyder argue that "exposing the role that myth and stereotypes play in conflict, past and present, is critical to the reconciliation process."[44] American historian Richard Slotkin provides insight into the invisible power of myth, which people invoke "as a means of deriving useable values from history ... Its primary appeal is to ritualized emotions, established beliefs, habitual associations, memory, nostalgia."[45] *Webster's Dictionary* reveals the paradoxical nature of myths, defining them as "a traditional story of ostensibly historical content that serves to unfold a part of the world view of a people, or explain a practice, belief or natural phenomenon" or as "an ill-founded belief held uncritically especially by an interested group." In *Ritual, Politics, and Power,* American political scientist David I. Kertzer suggests that myth and ritual play a key role in political life whether invoked by conservative forces to maintain the status quo or by those who seek social change.[46] Myths are a powerful yet unacknowledged influence on how we make sense of the world; they shape our individual and collective identity as well as our relationships within our own groups and with others: "Myths condition the public to the powerful symbols used by politicians. Myths underwrite the status quo in times of stability and they chart the course of change in times of stress. In the day-to-day business of politics, myths set the terms for most public policy debate. When mythical themes and myth-related language are stripped away from public discourse, little of substance remains. Most political controversy centers around disagreement over which myth to apply to a particular problem."[47] Given this, we see how myth shapes and reinforces the rationalization of a celebratory history and Aboriginal public policy. The very fact that we unconsciously subscribe to myth while consciously constructing history and public policy speaks to its hidden power.

The conflicts we face today have deep historical roots that can be traced in the stories that we as settlers tell and retell ourselves about our "nonviolent" past, invoking the myth of benevolent peacemaking. Conflict resolution scholar-practitioner Michelle LeBaron tells us that, in addressing such conflicts, "revising myths and unpacking assumptions embedded within them is a powerful way to reimagine history and envision a new future."[48] We should not underestimate the importance of undertaking such a task. Lumbee legal scholar Robert A. Williams Jr. observes that "myths have consequences," and settler myths about Indigenous people's cultural and moral inferiority have been used to justify violence "as simply the extension of the West's enlightened reason upon the 'savage' Indian-occupied frontiers of the New World."[49] Popular myths that shape our historical imaginary extol the virtues of the "pioneer spirit" and the practices of "civilizing new frontiers" and "settling empty lands." Stereotypes of Indigenous people as noble savages, violent warriors, victims of progress, and more recently, as protesters, rich Indians, and undeserving beneficiaries of race-based rights, are deeply ingrained in the Canadian national psyche, reinforced by popular culture and the media. These stereotypes informed policy decisions in the past and continue to do so today.[50] Myths, with their attendant stereotypes, are linked closely to political controversy and legal debate over what constitutes Indigenous cultural authenticity. Not surprisingly, culture has become the benchmark of authenticity, with significant implications for whether oral histories are believed in Aboriginal court cases and in negotiations involving treaty, land, and resource rights.[51]

Canadian historian John Lutz and others remind us of the connections between myth and history in stories of colonial encounters. These narratives continue to have a powerful influence on how Indigenous people and settlers understand and misunderstand each other today. The dominant-culture belief that the settler version is the real history – the factual recounting of what happened – whereas Native history is just a legend or make-believe story is a way of saying that the former is true and the latter is not. Lutz captures precisely the tension that exists between these origin accounts: "Is it a story of progress or one of dislocation? Is it about bringing the gifts of civilization or robbing the wealth of the land?"[52] He notes that contemporary scholars have developed various strategies to "move the European from the centre of contact stories," and he proposes a further strategy of "identifying the mythology and the history embedded in stories that emerge from both indigenous and European contact accounts, treating both as equally credible and incredible."[53] Similarly, literary scholar J. Edward Chamberlin suggests that confronting "contradictory truths" moves us out of binary thinking and into the complexity of our respective stories, "which together help us chart the convergence of reality and the imagination."[54] Thus, textual analysis of historical encounter myths constitutes one form of relational truth telling.

My own approach builds on this work but is positioned in ways that may seem counterintuitive to decentring settlers. If non-Native Canadians are to understand the colonial roots of contemporary practices, we must first, as historians Celia Haig-Brown and David Nock suggest, "begin a process of 'unlearning' whereby we begin to question received truths."[55] My particular focus is on settler truth telling as the decolonization of socio-political memory. This truth telling cannot be about determining the "one truth" of positivism. Nor should it be based on the morally vacant post-structuralist theory of "multiple truths in which all claims are perspectival and partial ... For then how," asks feminist scholar Susan Strega, "can the truths we uncover ... provide us with a rationale for political action?"[56] Nor is it concerned with determining the "legal truth" of plaintiff claims in order to determine the extent of defendant liability.

Canadian historian J.R. Miller writes that, over the past two decades, Indigenous people's history and voice have "come in from the margins" to claim a more prominent place in Canada's national story.[57] Yet despite this counter-narrative, the pull of a unifying monolithic national history that is based on "one truth" remains strong. In a national best-seller, *Who Killed Canadian History?* historian Jack Granatstein clearly struck a deep chord with many Canadians in his lament for a lost, more traditional, and triumphant national history. In his view, history books should teach Canadians and new immigrants about the country's great accomplishments, which have their genesis in the cultural traditions of "the European civilization on which it is founded."[58] Thus, the real history of Canada is rooted in Europe, not in encounters between colonizers and Indigenous people.[59] Although he acknowledges that historical injustices have been inflicted upon various racial groups over the course of the country's history, he thinks making them the focus of our attention is wrong-headed. Such an approach, he affirms, will do nothing to improve Canadians' historical understanding or contribute to making better public policy: "Undoubtedly, thousands were treated shamefully throughout history ... [including] Indian children in residential schools ... But apologies and victimhood do not make for either good current policy or a proper collective understanding of history. Instead, they create cynicism in the silent majority of Canadians who are convinced that certain groups are trying to rip off public funds. We all are aware that Canadians have sometimes acted shamefully. But Canadians in their five hundred years in this most favoured of lands have committed relatively few atrocities when compared with virtually any other society."[60] Granatstein's moral relativism provides a tempting rationale for denial. He claims that he does not want to teach "an airbrushed history" but rather wants "the truth about the Canadian past [to] be presented to our young people."[61] This, of course, raises the critical question – whose truth?

Granatstein's truth is predicated on minimizing the suffering of IRS survivors, equating it with victimhood and implying that it is of no great consequence in Canada's history. Rather, it is part of a now distant past that we should somehow acknowledge, while rationalizing it as an exception to our otherwise exemplary behaviour. Yet, if this were so, how does one explain the fact that the residential schools spanned well over a century in Canada? – hardly a temporary blip in an otherwise unblemished historical record. He argues that "apologies do not make for good policy." In doing so, he ignores the power of apology to repair damaged relationships.[62] He never explains how we would go about formulating good policy, but apparently this does not involve coming to grips with or learning any lessons from the harmful policies of Canada's past. Granatstein's desire for a "proper collective understanding of history" is based on maintaining the self-congratulatory myth of what anthropologist Eva Mackey calls "white settler innocence."[63]

More recently, public intellectual John Ralston Saul presents a vision of truth telling that stands as counter-narrative to Granatstein's version. In *A Fair Country,* Saul argues that the real roots of Canadian society are to be found not in Europe but in the Indigenous societies that were here before us and represent the "senior founding pillar of our civilization."[64] Settlers thus fail to recognize that one of our most deeply held beliefs about what makes us uniquely Canadian – that we are a nation of peacemakers who value consensus building and inclusivity based on consultation and negotiation – has Indigenous roots. In Saul's view, the genesis of the Canadian peacekeeper as a model for Canada's participation on the world stage cannot be attributed entirely to Lester B. Pearson's thinking in the 1950s but was part of a continuum, albeit an unconscious one, of the influence of a much longer unrecognized history of Indigenous diplomatic approaches to peaceful relations among diverse peoples:

> It could be argued that the key moment in the creation of the idea of Canada was the gathering of thirteen hundred Aboriginal ambassadors from forty nations with the leaders of New France in 1701. It was here that the indigenous Aboriginal ways of dealing with *the other* were consciously and broadly adopted as more appropriate than the European. Here the idea of future treaties was born. Here an approach was developed that would evolve into federalism. Sir William Johnson's great gathering of two thousand chiefs at Niagara had been organized in order to cement the Royal Proclamation. In many ways, this was the second act in the creation of the idea of Canada – a continuation of the Great Peace of Montreal.[65]

Viewed from this longer historical perspective, Canadian "peacekeeping in its original form comes very close to a First Nations model."[66] In a similar vein, Anishinaabe legal scholar John Borrows posits that Canadian law has Indigenous roots that have been denied and obscured over time, privileging Western legal narratives.[67] Saul further points out that, though settler Canadians pay token regard to Indigenous groups as founding peoples, "there is no intellectual, ethical or emotional engagement with what their place might be at the core of our civilization."[68] Rather, our fear and denial of Indigenous presence has resulted in the mutation of

Indigenous principles such as inclusivity in favour of strategies of forced and "voluntary" assimilation. Similarly, as I argue in Chapter 3, the settler peacemaker myth privileges a British imperialist legal vision of how one constructs peaceful coexistence, thus representing a colonial perversion of Indigenous philosophies of peacemaking. Ultimately, Granatstein's form of truth telling is more akin to selective forgetting – what Michael Ignatieff has described as the "range of permissible lies" that must be dismantled as part of setting the historical record straight.[69]

Maori scholar Linda Tuhiwai Smith explains why history matters to Indigenous peoples. The strategic reclaiming of history and testimonies that put a human face on the sufferings caused by the colonial enterprise are profound acts of personal empowerment and communal political resistance.[70] At the same time, how we as settlers choose to engage with and understand this alternative history in relation to our own historical narrative can either reinforce colonialism or act as a decolonizing force. Indigenous people have begun the hard work of truth telling and restorying history, but we ourselves have not yet done so.

Breaking Cycles of Colonial Violence: Restorying Public History

> From the perspective of Indigenous people, original violence might
> best be understood as the disruption – and far too often, outright
> destruction – of a people's story. These patterns are found on every
> continent and with every aboriginal group's story ... One cannot go
> back and remake the history. But that does not mean history is static
> and dead. History is alive. It needs recognition and attention ... The
> challenge ... lies in how, in the present, interdependent peoples
> "restory," ... that is ... begin the process of providing space for the story
> to take its place.
>
> – JOHN PAUL LEDERACH, THE MORAL IMAGINATION:
> THE ART AND SOUL OF BUILDING PEACE

Scholars have addressed how structural and symbolic patterns of violence are embedded in the history of Indigenous-settler relations across the globe. Although their analyses may differ somewhat, all propose ways to break free from these cycles of violence. For international peace and conflict studies scholar-practitioner John Paul Lederach, a society's ability to transform "geographies of violence" into "cultures of peace" requires developing personal and structural processes of social change that are rooted in authenticity, the use of moral imagination, and the restorying of history. Accordingly, he argues that "the real challenge of authenticity and the moral imagination is how to transcend what has been and is now, while still living in it. For the moral imagination to make the journey across this terrain it will need to address complexity and support change over time."[71] Vern Neufeld Redekop, a conflict resolution scholar-practitioner, identifies the "mimetic structures of violence" that exist in deep-rooted ethnopolitical conflicts, including those between Indigenous peoples and settler Canadians. He suggests that these violent patterns of behaviour develop their own "mythos or storyline" over time, as the colonizer and the colonized "imitate each other's violent attitudes, rhetoric and behaviour."[72] In Chapter 4, I provide a case study that demonstrates how this mythos influenced the discourse surrounding the IRS claim settlement process. From an Indigenous perspective, Taiaiake Alfred reminds us that, in the past, when Native peoples practised diplomacy "from a position of strength and rooted in philosophies of peace, they negotiated ... real treaties [that] ensured peaceful coexistence and created new relationships that removed our peoples from cycles of violence."[73] Lederach, Redekop, and Alfred each propose holistic pathways to peace that require digging deeply into the cultural, psychological, socio-political, structural, and institutional barriers that perpetuate cycles of violence in order to restory the past within the context of the present.

Public history representations that involve remembering historical wrongs and cultural trauma in highly visible ways that honour victims inevitably disrupt the more laudatory version of national history and its attendant myths. Writing about the many controversies that have characterized American public history and commemoration of the past, American historian Eric Foner notes that, over the past two decades, most liberal democracies have experienced these kinds of "history wars."[74] He concludes that, "among other things, the 1990s debates revealed that the desire for a history of celebration is widespread and knows no political boundaries."[75] Australian historian Bain Attwood remarks that Australia's history wars went far beyond the boundaries of the academy, as the Aboriginal past became relevant to contemporary Aboriginal rights, settler identity, and Australian nationhood.[76] A history that gave voice to Native counter-narrative was thus deeply disquieting and controversial for settler Australians:

> The new Australian history was unsettling for several reasons. Since most people know their country and understand their place in it through narratives such as a national history, a dramatic change in such stories can make what has long seemed familiar unfamiliar, thus undermining a sense of home or belonging ... The story of Australia's colonial past that many Australians now encountered was confronting because it threatened to deprive them of a familiar and comforting map of the past. Most of all, though, the new Australian history unsettled because it drew into question the moral basis of British colonization in the past and so the Australian nation in the present. The significance of this emotionally cannot be gainsaid. In large part, nations are deeply cherished ideals because of their moral status ... Many settler Australians were also unsettled by the way in which the new Australian history changed their position in relation to the status of victimhood. They were used to seeing their forebears as victims, not oppressors, as sufferers, not perpetrators. The new Australian history placed their forebears in a past in which they were responsible for heinous deeds. Most importantly, it called for mourning in respect to another people's historical experience.[77]

Canada has engaged in its own history wars for much the same reasons. This is most evident in the battle of expert witnesses called to testify on behalf of either Indigenous plaintiffs or Crown defendants in Aboriginal title and rights litigation. Canadian historian Arthur J. Ray notes that the litigation process itself destabilizes conventional colonial understandings of "Lockean notions of property, evolutionary models of cultural development, and nation-building historical narratives that glamorized Canada's treatment of its Aboriginal people."[78]

But despite this counter-narrative, Canada's national account remains very much a celebratory settler story. Canadian historian Margaret MacMillan notes that public forms of history are often nothing more than a

comforting escape into a nostalgic romanticized past. Equally importantly, she cautions that, in endeavouring to address historical injustices,
simply talking about and apologizing for past wrongs "can be used as an
excuse for not doing very much in the present."[79] Haitian-American historian Michel-Rolph Trouillot argues that the pedagogical intent of public
history and commemoration of histories of oppression should always be
to challenge the public to confront its own comfortable myths. Holding
onto such myths enables the dominant-culture majority to maintain a
false innocence about a problematic past. For Trouillot, an accounting of
the past involves not just empirical accuracy but establishes an ethical
relationship with that past. He explains that "authenticity is required, lest
the representation become a fake, a morally repugnant spectacle."[80] From
this perspective, public history that fails to link past wrongs to ongoing
racism and oppression may simply provoke the sort of colonial empathy
described in the previous chapter.

In connection with public history, Trouillot argues that academic historians have played a key role in influencing what constitutes legitimate
history, sometimes effectively silencing the disruptive counter-narratives
of oppressed people. History is not neutral. Athabascan scholar Dian
Million holds, for example, that the body of literature on residential schools
written by survivors and their allies constitutes a significant challenge to
mainstream historians who have acted as the "gatekeepers" of knowledge.
Their empirical studies, based on Western research methodologies that are
seen as objective and neutral, are thought to constitute the real or legitimate history of residential schools. Consequently, those who write from a
subjective, anti-oppressive, experiential stance in testimonial voices that
express strong emotions about this history are often dismissed or challenged by more conventional academics who question this methodology:

> Native analyses on the outcomes of aggressive historical policy, institu-
> tional and physical attacks on Native societies did not fit traditional
> academic expectations for History because they seek to narrate and
> analyze effects that admit subjectivity, i.e. the experiential subjective pain
> and social chaos associated with past events that have real effects on
> Indian lives now. These academic historians with their boundaries have
> written histories and find causal patterns and connections within the

larger project of Canadian history. They do not find present liability, or even effect outside their own projects. Furthermore, it is these historians who have definite issues with emotion, with anger and with pain. Native writers who show emotional evaluation or emotional content in "history" oddly provoke many historians' ire.[81]

Million notes that even those historians who are sympathetic to Native perspectives are often hard-pressed to recognize the legitimacy of those scholars who write with passion and conviction about a past that, instead of being remote and therefore safely segregated, is still present in their own lives and communities. Because Indigenous methodology embraces engagement over neutrality and insists on the immediacy of colonialism, it is still viewed with suspicion by many (though not all) academic historians.

The problem is also pedagogical. How we teach this contentious history matters. False innocence – the oppressor's attempts to deny, rationalize, or minimize the impacts of wrongdoing – feeds on sanitized versions of public history. Writing about the controversy that erupted over a proposed public exhibit on slavery in the United States, Trouillot says that the historical presentism that some academic historians have identified as problematic is actually essential to being authentic and morally congruent. He calls on historians to reject "the fixity of pastness" and to "position themselves more clearly within the present."[82] To do otherwise is morally repugnant and it trivializes victims' suffering:

> The collective guilt of some white liberals toward "the slave past" of the United States, or the "colonial past" of Europe can be both misplaced and inauthentic ... What we know about slavery or colonialism ... should increase our ardor in the struggles against discrimination and oppression across racial and national boundaries. But no amount of historical research ... and no amount of guilt ... can serve as a substitute for marching in the streets ... Authenticity implies a relation with what is known that duplicates the two sides of historicity: it engages us both as actors and narrators ... Whether it invokes, claims, or rejects The Past, authenticity obtains only in regard to current practices that engage us as witnesses, actors, and commentators ... Thus, even in relation to The Past our authenticity resides in the struggles of the present. Only in that present can we be true or false to the past we choose to acknowledge.[83]

Viewed in this way, accusations of presentism can be understood as a means of silencing an authentic past. Similarly, Roger Simon argues for an ethical insurgent remembering that is possible only when we allow ourselves to be "touched by the past" – that is, "to become emotionally vulnerable (open to feeling) ... 'Being touched' demands taking the stories of others seriously, accepting such stories as matters of 'counsel' ... stories that actually might initiate ... a potential shifting of our own unfolding stories, particularly in ways that might be unanticipated and not easily accepted."[84] In a critique of Canadian mainstream history, historian Timothy Stanley argues that writing history from an anti-racist stance counters national narratives that have excluded or minimized those aspects of our identity that do not fit with popular myths about Canada as a tolerant country of diversity, equality, and inclusion.[85] Megan Boler says that confronting powerful emotions associated with challenging cherished beliefs and assumptions about the past requires a willingness to "inhabit a more ambiguous and flexible sense of self" in order to "extend our ethical language and sense of possibilities beyond a reductive model of guilt vs. innocence."[86] Each of these scholars emphasizes the ethical implications of historical remembering in public spaces, which are often commemorative in nature and by design. In many instances, history exhibits, commemorative books, park sites, and the like are produced by professionals – museum curators, archivists, and historians – in consultation or collaboratively with the communities whose lives and experiences are being documented. At the same time, commemorative acts may occur more spontaneously, apart from or in reaction to, official sites of commemoration.

Commemoration: The Politics of Historical Memory

Students' emotions about the past can be brought into the present
in order to shape and support their current ethical commitments ...
What we need to teach our students is not simply to remember, as if
history were only a lesson in mnemonic devices, but that memory is
an ongoing social activity, the very process of history-making itself,
to which they are being called to contribute.

– RACHEL N. BAUM, "WHAT I HAVE LEARNED TO FEEL:
THE PEDAGOGICAL EMOTIONS OF HOLOCAUST EDUCATION"

The process of history making, or restorying, involves the public remembering of a contested past. In the context of truth and reconciliation commissions, historical memory as a transitional justice mechanism has evolved as a field of study that explores "how efforts to collectively remember past human rights abuses can contribute to a more democratic, peaceful and just future."[87] Scholar-practitioners seek to understand how commemorating or memorializing past wrongs shapes historical memory. Although commemoration is more commonly understood in terms of memorial structures (monuments, statues, cemeteries, public parks, and so on), memorial practices and the politics surrounding them most influence what and how we remember. For Canada's TRC, tasked with educating the public about the IRS system, establishing a national research centre is meant to be a permanent memorial structure that pays tribute to survivors. Equally important, commemoration of the residential school experience will also occur through written texts, museum and archival exhibits, and various art forms including painting, theatre, film, videography, dance, and song. These ways of remembering are embodied ceremonial and ritual performances that engage our emotions, senses, and imaginations, evoking a moral response. They are also highly political acts in which "public memory speaks primarily about the structure of power in society because that power is always in question in a world of polarities and contradictions and because cultural understanding is always grounded in the material structure of society itself."[88]

As Sue Campbell points out, it will therefore be important for the TRC "to think explicitly about the role of memory in the process ... [and to] weave talk of memory into the representation of the Commission's work, its public face."[89] The Commission must also be mindful of the inevitable tension that will surface between Indigenous people's desire to commemorate collective historical trauma, cultural survival, and resistance versus a national settler imperative that emphasizes a more self-congratulatory version of history.[90] Public commemorations that generate controversy reveal underlying structures of violence and power relations. Commemorations are thus public acts of remembering that can either reinforce or challenge and ultimately transform master historical narratives.[91] As J.K. Olick reminds us, "commemoration is a way of claiming that the past has something to offer the present, be it a warning or a model."[92] Here, it is useful to compare three quite different studies of memorial practices as they relate to the production of historical memory. The first demonstrates the way in which citizens' benevolent intentions regarding reconciliation can work to sanitize a difficult past. The second considers the powerful impact of restorying history on the ground. The third demonstrates how various memory practices are used to work through traumatic experiences associated with violence to process historical trauma and rework identity.

Writing in the Canadian context about the racialized history of Africville, a black community in Halifax, Nova Scotia, which was demolished during the 1960s, Jennifer J. Nelson explains the controversy that continues over the community's obliteration and attempts to memorialize it. Her study reveals how the societal attitudes and world views of well-intentioned people can provide a rationalization for the forced relocation of minority groups and ethically suspect acts of reconciliation. In situating herself as a white woman, she concludes that, despite the recent commemoration of Africville as part of the white community's attempt at reconciliation with blacks, racism remains the defining discourse. Violence, selective forgetting, and denial still prevail in the sanitized version of the Africville story.[93] She attributes this, in large part, to the white community's "unrelenting insistence on their *good* intent, at the time of the forced relocation as well as in the present, [which] diverts serious consideration of the consequences and harm in their action, [and] suggest[s] that the emphasis on benevolence must be tabled and ... investments in innocence must be relinquished."[94] Nelson argues that "to resist forgetting is to refuse the official story of benevolent intent, of 'mistake,' and of reconciliation. It is also to regard the difficult, the painful, the ugly as part of history – to talk about it, to debate it, to move with it, and beyond it at once."[95] We see, then, how the myth of benevolence is manifested beyond the parameters of Indigenous-settler relations to include other minority groups. In both cases, selective forgetting is the norm, whereas admitting complicity raises uncomfortable questions about the values of inclusivity, equality, and justice that form the bedrock of Canadian identity and historical memory.

In the second instance, restorying and commemoration are linked in a historical re-enactment that challenges mainstream interpretations of colonial history. Wahpetunwan Dakota scholar Waziyatawin (Angela Wilson) writes about her participation in a series of commemorative marches held in Minnesota, beginning in 2002, to remember and honour the Dakota people who were forcibly relocated from their homelands at the end of the US-Dakota War of 1862 and whose descendants now live in the United States and Canada.[96] Waziyatawin remarks,

> I was ... incredibly sad that the event had come to an end. I have since had time to contemplate that sadness and to clarify the significance of the Commemorative March for me on a personal level. More than any-thing, I think this experience was about empowerment. We were honoring the ancestors who had not been honored in this way or publicly grieved over; our ancestors had been dismissed in the history books as unfortu-nate casualties resulting from Dakota violence against White settlers. Despite the hardship – or maybe even because of it – we were taking a hold of our past and controlling our history in a powerful, public effort. We were beginning the process of reclamation, steeped for seven gen-erations in the memory and strength of our ancestors.[97]

Writing in the American context, she nevertheless provides key insights that are applicable to Canada as to why commemorative re-enactments of an oppressed people's traumatic history often trigger controversy. Un-official commemorative acts can be important pedagogical strategies for restorying history. Waziyatawin interweaves personal narrative and family, tribal, and state history into a complex, nuanced, and powerful testimony to her people's suffering and also to their strength, courage, and resilience. In a damning indictment of the Wasicu (settlers) who exiled the Dakota from their homelands, she describes the feelings that surfaced as the march-ers retraced the route that her Dakota ancestors had been forced to walk two hundred years earlier. Deep grief and a sense of tremendous loss overwhelmed the marchers as they mourned the women, men, and children who had suffered so terribly. Those who died or were lost to their families were named, prayers were offered, and symbolic markers were placed at historically significant sites along the way. At the same time, she describes the marchers' feelings of deep pride, joy, and restrengthening as they trav-elled on "a journey to reclaim all that was lost with integrity and righteous-ness."[98] In this way, the marchers restoried Minnesotan history.

Waziyatawin also documents how various Wasicu responded to the commemoration march. Some participated as Dakota allies; some were sympathetic observers; and some were indifferent, racist, or openly hostile. On several occasions, the marchers met with Wasicu townspeople whose own ancestors had settled on Dakota lands. She describes in vivid detail how Dakota truth telling encountered settler resistance, denial, and a refusal to engage in a disturbing encounter with a much darker version of Minnesota history than many of the townspeople were willing to hear. At the same time, she indicates that Wasicu can be strong allies of Indigenous people when they undertake their own truth telling about the past in ways that make them more accountable in the present.[99] Thus, the marchers and their allies made a hitherto silenced past highly visible, and in doing so, they publicly challenged dominant-culture versions of a shared but conflicting history. No consensus about this history was achieved, but that was not the point. More importantly, Dakota and Wasicu historical consciousness had been raised, and a critical dialogue had begun. In a real sense, Minnesota's history was being restoried as the marchers walked quite literally in the footsteps of their ancestors.

The third example involves a historical memory project for Colombian urban youth whose lives have been affected by widespread violence. In the aftermath of a massacre in the city of Medellín, youth struggle to make sense of an increasingly violent world. In *Dwellers of Memory*, anthropologist Pilar Riaño-Alcalá situates herself not as a neutral witness to terror but as one whose research and writing incorporates memory practice. Unlike many of those involved in transitional justice endeavours who view their role simply as observers or studiers of violence, she argues for research as ethical praxis. In the face of human suffering amidst violence, she recognizes the need for "more effective, pragmatic and civic responses." In describing the memory workshop she developed for youth, who have multiple roles in the conflicts that envelop Medellín as victims of, or witnesses to, violence or as perpetrators of criminal acts themselves, she explains that she did so because youth needed practical strategies and skills for coping with the violence that had permeated their lives:

> Workshops ... employed a variety of verbal and visual methods – storytelling, mapping, visual biographies, image making, paper quilts, music, and photographs – to explore the multiple embodied and sensory dimensions of the practices of remembering and forgetting ... I carried out several extended walkabouts for the purpose of locating myself in the city environment ... When a group collectively explores its past through the sharing of stories, the practices of memory often cover a continuum

between description, sensorial experience and analytical reflection ... I had to decide how to respond to the manifestations of pain and grief, and the expressions of anger and despair that emerged from the workshop, as well as my own emotional reactions. The key to my response was found in the social context of the memory workshop ... The group and the researcher created a temporary non-violent space of listening, respect and trust where mourning, reflection, meaningful sharing, expressions of strong emotions and a degree of conflict were all possible.[100]

Although these three studies, each from a different country and having its own specificity, constitute an admittedly small sampling, what preliminary lessons about truth telling and reconciliation processes can we take from them? If the case of Africville is a cautionary tale about how official attempts at reconciliation, although well intentioned, can fail, the other studies provide clues as to how unofficial commemorative community-based initiatives that circumvent bureaucracies provide the necessary space and place for giving voice to multiple versions of the past, speaking hard truths, expressing contradictory emotions, healing the wounds of the past, and engendering hope. As the TRC moves forward, it will be important to acquire a deep understanding of the role that memorial practices can play in restorying residential school history as part of a national process that must ultimately be connected to individuals and communities.

3

Deconstructing Canada's Peacemaker Myth

Canada has numerous examples of internal unpeacemaking ... Our teachings [and] learnings ... must become those which promote our understanding of a shared his/herstory of violence and peacemaking and which foster a multiethnic perspective and honesty. Curricula and instruction must consider the sensibility of unconditional love/respect and compassion required for sustainable peacemaking for ourselves and our children in classrooms and other communities. For it is our children who will inherit the future we teach.

– SHARILYN CALLIOU, "PEACEKEEPING ACTIONS AT HOME:
A MEDICINE WHEEL MODEL FOR A PEACEKEEPING PEDAGOGY"

Most Canadians, if asked about the history of our relationship with Indigenous peoples, would not describe it as violent. Rather, we take pride in a cherished national myth that distinguishes between the horrific "Indian" wars of frontier settlement in the United States and the more benign settlement process that we tell ourselves occurred in the Canadian West.[1] In this narrative, we cast ourselves in the role of benevolent peacemakers – neutral arbiters of British law and justice, Christian messengers of the peaceable kingdom – who collaborated together in various ways to negotiate treaties and implement Indian policy intended to bestow upon Indigenous people the generous benefits or gifts of peace, order, good government, and Western education that were the hallmarks of the colonial project of civilizing "savages."[2]

Yet the history of treaty making and Indian policy not only reaffirms that we have not kept our treaty promises but calls into question this emblematic myth of the peacemaker. The language and attitudes of the myth persist, invoked however unconsciously in the public mind and in a myriad of processes established to negotiate modern treaties, to resolve outstanding historical grievances related to Indigenous lands and resources, and to settle IRS claims. Thus, the myth – our identity as a nation of peacemakers intent on solving the Indian problem – begins with the story of colonial treaties and Indian policy, and continues today with a new storyline about achieving reconciliation between Indigenous people and the settler majority. Ultimately, this new quest for reconciliation may be no different from our peacemaking practices of the past.

Many Canadians still believe that Indigenous peoples have been the fortunate beneficiaries of our altruism, although some historians now question Canada's bounty and benevolence. They ask us to reconsider "which treaty partner has been truly kind and generous."[3] Today, these generous gifts to our treaty partners have taken on new forms. Basing its approach on the constitutional rights of First Nations, Métis, and Inuit people, and in the wake of the Supreme Court of Canada's *Delgamuukw* decision in 1997, the Canadian government is attempting to negotiate reconciliation between the Crown and Indigenous people on a number of fronts.[4] Thus, Canada has granted or "bestowed upon" Indigenous peoples limited political recognition and self-government within a multicultural state, has negotiated modern treaties and land claims settlements based on the extinguishment of Aboriginal title and rights, and has implemented a range of policies, programs, and services designed to help Native communities solve the Indian problem that has been created by past policies.[5] All of these actions are highly contested by Indigenous peoples, who point out that trust has been broken on a number of fronts. They seek full political recognition as self-determining peoples and treaty partners.[6] Moreover, they wish to govern their own affairs, including education, justice, health, and social programs – all of which are key to their decolonization and cultural revitalization.[7] These tensions continue to play out as Canada, like other settler nations, grapples with the unsavoury legacies of colonialism.

Treaty Partners or Wards of the State?

Let us have Christianity and civilization to leaven the mass of heathenism and paganism among the Indian tribes; let us have a wise and paternal Government faithfully carrying out the provisions of our treaties, and doing its utmost to help and elevate the Indian population, who have been cast upon our care, and we will have peace, progress and concord among them in the North-West; and instead of the Indian melting away, as one of them in older Canada, tersely put it, "as snow before the sun," we will see our Indian population, loyal subjects of the Crown, happy, prosperous and self-sustaining, and Canada will be enabled to feel, that in a truly patriotic spirit, our country has done its duty by the red men of the North-West, and thereby to herself. So may it be.

– ALEXANDER MORRIS, *THE TREATIES OF CANADA WITH THE INDIANS OF MANITOBA AND THE NORTH-WEST TERRITORIES*

Canada would not be Canada without the Aboriginal peoples ... In fact, the European settlement in North America arose because First Nations were prepared to share their resources ... It is now time for us to renew and strengthen the covenant between us ... Canada faces no greater challenge than those that confront Aboriginal Canadians. It is a challenge of immense consequence ... for the country as a whole ... For too long, we have turned our backs on this moral and economic reality ... Aboriginal Canadians must participate fully in all that Canada has to offer, with greater economic self-reliance and an ever-increasing quality of life, based upon historic rights and agreements that our forefathers signed long ago, but that are not forgotten ... Let it be that ten years from now, people will look back on this day and this Roundtable as an event that marked a truly new beginning for Aboriginal peoples in Canada. One that heralds a brighter, healthier and more prosperous future.

– PAUL MARTIN, IN CANADA-ABORIGINAL PEOPLES ROUNDTABLE, *STRENGTHENING THE RELATIONSHIP*

When juxtaposed, these two visions of Canada, separated by 124 years, reveal a disturbing reality. In his 1880 publication *The Treaties of Canada with the Indians,* treaty commissioner Alexander Morris laid the foundations of a settler story of treaty making that "emphasized government generosity, First Nations passivity, and treaties as contracts that extinguished the property rights of the original occupiers."[8] Morris' words exemplify a dominant theme in settler history that characterizes Indigenous people as victims of progress who must be saved from their own cultural and economic backwardness by superior, wise, and benevolent fathers such as himself. In this version of the colonial story, Indian policy and British justice – treaties, law and order, the creation of Indian reserves, and Western education – would bring peace and progress, the gifts of civilization, to the frontier and salvation to the disappearing Indians. The underlying assumption was that Native people had only to behave as loyal subjects of the Crown, and they would inevitably become happy, prosperous, and self-sustaining members of a new civilized society.

Prime Minister Paul Martin's speech on 19 April 2004, at the opening of the Canada-Aboriginal Peoples Roundtable, confirms that, from Morris' time to the present, Canadians have failed to do our duty to bring peace and progress to Native people, who somehow under our wise tutelage have not become happy, prosperous, and self-sustaining, a fact revealed by the systemic poverty and social dysfunction in their communities today. Nor, as recent demographic studies indicate, are they in danger of disappearing, as Indigenous youth now comprise the fastest-growing segment of the Canadian population. To be sure, Martin's remarks reflect the political sensibilities of twenty-first-century peacemakers – the overt racist and paternalistic language prevalent in Morris' day is gone. Employing a new discourse of reconciliation, we now say that we recognize and value Native contributions to Canada and that we acknowledge our failure to honour the treaties. Although we have previously turned our backs on this moral and economic reality, we claim that we are now ready to take up the challenge of renewing and strengthening our covenant with Indigenous peoples.

In this revised storyline, well-intentioned political leaders and government bureaucrats have transformed from morally and culturally prescriptive nineteenth-century imperialists into newly enlightened, culturally sensitive twenty-first-century partners in solving the Indian problem. Although individuals within dominant-culture political, bureaucratic, and legal systems may indeed be more enlightened, collectively we still studiously avoid looking too closely at the settler problem. The hegemonic structures and practices within bureaucratic systems, and the unequal power relations that define colonial violence, remain for the most part invisible to non-Native people. Concrete examples of how this is manifested can be found at negotiating tables or in claims resolution processes in which preset mandates enable government negotiators to determine whether Indigenous history can be brought to the table and, if so, whose version will dominate the dialogue. The peacemaker myth lies at the heart of the settler problem; it informs, however unconsciously, the everyday attitudes and actions of contemporary politicians, policy makers, lawyers, and negotiators, and it remains an archetype of settler benevolence, fairness, and innocence in the Canadian public mind. To begin the decolonizing work of truth telling and reconciliation, it is useful to first reassess this foundational myth in Canada's settler past.

Failure to gain insight into the historical roots of contemporary settler attitudes and actions toward Indigenous people and to make visible their continuity over time will make Canada's apology to Indigenous people meaningless and reconciliation false.

Accordingly, I approach the peacemaker myth from various angles. I begin by setting the context. The myth's interrelated themes of treaty making and saving Indians, which dominate nineteenth-century public discourse, emerged at a time of significant political unrest and socio-economic upheaval in the West. The basis of the myth can be found in the earlier peace and friendship treaties of Eastern Canada. But as treaty making moved west, the process itself became increasingly policy-focused, bureaucratized, and concerned with limiting the economic expenditures required to implement treaties. Within this milieu, as Indigenous people faced the significant political and socio-economic pressures associated with Western settlement, they were seen less as trade or military allies and more as a moral and economic burden – wards of the state.

Nineteenth-century English Canadians believed that British justice and government systems represented the pinnacle of civilization and would benefit colonized people when administered benignly. As part of the national dream to transform wild prairie lands into a peaceful agricultural garden, government and police officials, as the neutral and impartial arbiters who embodied justice, were tasked with ensuring that violence and unrest would be brought under control through a combination of treaty making, Indian policy, and law enforcement. Despite Morris' confident words, designed to reassure his readers that peace and prosperity would be attained by delivering on the treaty promises of a wise and paternal government, in actuality, various officials were anxious about the possibility of Indian violence, a worry that played out somewhat differently west of the Rockies. My purpose here is to make visible the dominant-culture mythos – the underlying pattern of violent behaviour and denial of Indigenous history, law, and peacemaking practices – that runs through this version of the settlement story. Finally, I look at how the peacemaker myth has been carried forward to the present, in celebratory popular history representations of Canada's past. In some settler circles, the myth remains an underlying rationale for denying historical realities and minimizing responsibility for rectifying historical injustices.

The Peaceful Garden of the West: Settler Visions of Law and Order

> In the middle of the nineteenth century a number of Canadians
> became convinced that the possession and development of the
> Hudson's Bay territories were essential to the future of Canada ...
> Those ideas, in turn, helped to shape the policy of government, the
> attitudes of Canadians, and the history of Canada itself as the nation
> faced the task of opening and settling the West ... Between 1856 and
> 1869 the image of the West was transformed in Canadian writings
> from a semi-arctic wilderness to a fertile garden well adapted to
> agricultural pursuits; subsidiary to this was a new interest in the
> possibilities of mining, trade and transportation.
>
> – DOUG OWRAM, *PROMISE OF EDEN: THE CANADIAN*
> *EXPANSIONIST MOVEMENT AND THE IDEA OF THE WEST, 1856-1900*[9]

In *Promise of Eden*, Canadian historian Doug Owram examines how a group of influential English Canadian men from the east, including politicians, entrepreneurs, government bureaucrats, and various other professionals, were instrumental in reshaping Canadian ideas about the west. The prairies, they claimed, were not an inhospitable wilderness but a potential agricultural utopia that should be opened up to settlement. These leaders of the western expansionist movement were powerful advocates for nation and empire building. Alexander Morris, who later, as lieutenant governor of Manitoba and a former chief justice, would become one of the queen's representatives responsible for negotiating the numbered treaties, declared in 1859 that "the time has come when the claims of humanity and the interests of the British Empire, require that all the portions of this vast empire which are adapted for settlement should be laid open to the industrious emigrant."[10] But this adaptation was not to mirror the chaotic, lawless, and violent settling of the American frontier. Rather, the Canadian West, as an extension of benign empire, was to be a model of British justice and administrative superiority.

Expansionists were primarily concerned with developing an agrarian hinterland that would serve the imperial and economic interests of Eastern Canada and Britain. Native peoples were of secondary concern, viewed as obstacles to settlement that must necessarily be displaced but should nevertheless be helped to adapt to civilization by being encouraged to sign treaties, move onto reserves, and take up farming.[11] They believed that the violence directed at Indians across the border was symptomatic of the moral, social, and political deficiencies of American-style democracy. Canada, on the other hand, armed only with its superior system of parliamentary monarchy and the tenets of British justice, would avoid such violence through treaty making, practical government policy, and the imposition of law and order: "By the 1870s a good many Canadians were convinced that the history of American Indian policy was, as the *Toronto Globe* once said, 'a dark record of broken pledges, undisguised oppression and triumphant cruelty' ... In contrast, Canadians believed that their approach to the Indian, inherited from the British, was both just and practical."[12] Underlying this popular belief was the assumption that British justice was neutral – that is, its practitioners were thought to be fair and impartial, both in negotiating treaties and administering law and policy. Legal scholars have argued persuasively that British imperial justice was never neutral but rather an expression of colonial power enacted upon Indigenous lands and bodies.[13] Yet, as Canadian philosopher David Kahane points out, the neutrality myth remains a powerful force in Canadian society: "In the dominant Western political vocabulary, there is an easily available story about how to resolve disputes between groups over perceived conflicts of interest, aspirations, or access to resources: let each side make its case before a neutral third party, who will objectively decide on a just settlement."[14] From this perspective, Native peoples' acts of resistance before, during, and after treaty negotiations are hardly surprising. Working from their own understanding of law and treaty making, Indigenous political leaders pushed back, asserting their own demands regarding the terms and conditions of the treaties.

As to whether the Canadian approach was in fact less violent than those of other settler societies, Canadian historian Carl Berger notes that in 1936, Western historian George F.G. Stanley argued that, in the clash between civilized and savage, the destruction of Indigenous and Métis peoples on the prairies was not a consequence of the westward push of democracy but the inevitable result of British imperialism, similar to "the fate of other peoples who unsuccessfully resisted the march of white civilization in Africa and Australia."[15] Stanley's work reflects the thinking of his day, in which the divide between civilized and savage was clearly delineated. But he understood that the settling of the prairie west was not exceptional. Rather, it was part of a global imperial process of colonization in which "white civilization" as exemplified in British imperial policy was no guarantee of protection from devastating violence.

In *Contact and Conflict*, historian Robin Fisher points out that early comparative frontier history "produces a smug self-satisfaction with the Canadian example, as if a comparative lack of interracial violence were sufficient evidence of a superior Indian policy."[16] More recently, some Western historians have argued that drawing this sharp distinction between the American and Canadian frontier is misleading at best. Historian Brian Dippie notes that these newer studies have "challenged both national mythologies by arguing that neither West lives up to its mythic billing. That is, Canada's 'mild' West was wilder that the myth allows, while the American West was never as wild as its myth would have it."[17] Drawing on American historian Richard White's concept of a "middle ground," in which various cultures intermingled and adapted in northeastern North America, Canadian legal historian Louis A. Knafla suggests that the North-West frontier constituted a new regional middle ground that was influenced by British, Canadian, and American perspectives on the law that were often at odds with Indigenous law.[18] Although newcomers brought with them "the knowledge of how disputes had been settled at 'home' ... the law ways of the indigenous peoples and the realities of local circumstances precluded the blanket impositions of foreign legal structures."[19] In a study of the ways in which liberalism evolved in the Prairie West and BC from 1887 to 1927 through various surveillance techniques used by government, church, and police officials, historian Keith D. Smith suggests that "liberalism was an exclusionary rather than inclusionary force that allowed for extraordinary measures to be employed to remove Indigenous peoples from the territories of their ancestors."[20] Such measures included treaty making in order to eliminate the legal impediment to settling Indigenous lands as well as legislation and policy designed to regulate and manage Indigenous lives with a view to acculturation and assimilation.

The role of the North-West Mounted Police (NWMP) in the settlement process has also been re-evaluated on several fronts. Roger L. Nichols writes that settlement on both sides of the border was characterized by violence and the devastating impacts of starvation and disease on Indigenous populations. In fact, he says, "Canada's relatively peaceful frontier dealings with its tribal groups lasted only until it sent Mounted Policemen west. Just over a decade after the Mounties marched onto the Plains, the 1885 fighting broke out."[21] As Sidney L. Harring points out, a popular storyline in Canadian history attributes the actions of the NWMP to the Canadian government's desire to avoid the Indian wars that were occurring in the United States. He asserts that, despite this myth, the government was more concerned about Indigenous resistance to settlement. The NWMP, as a national police force, was a "self-contained legal institution organized on a quasi-military model: Mounties arrested, prosecuted, judged, and jailed offenders under their jurisdiction."[22] In Harring's view, what is extraordinary is that the police were delegated such sweeping powers of judicial authority "over a civilian population in peacetime."[23]

As well as creating a police force to impose British law and order on the Canadian West, the government developed other aggressive strategies to pacify Indigenous people. Harring analyzes Ottawa's policy with regard to the rapidly declining buffalo herds and finds disturbing similarities to the American approach. He notes that, by 1874, the dominion government was well aware of the looming crisis; Cree and Blackfoot chiefs had already sounded the alarm. But although its own Department of Justice had prepared a report on the advisability of buffalo protection laws, Ottawa referred the matter to the regional North-West Territorial Council, "which ultimately passed a watered-down ordinance in November of 1877" that was subsequently repealed. Harring concludes that although "some Liberal and Conservative members of Parliament believe[d] that the dominion had a treaty obligation to preserve the buffalo ... the dominion government deliberately failed to take action because it was understood that the buffalo hunt was central to the social orders of Plains tribes; the government knew that destroying the buffalo would force the Indians to reserves."[24]

In a similar vein, Sarah Carter argues that the policies of government officials and the NWMP in the immediate post-treaty era included such actions as deliberately starving Cree chief Big Bear and his followers in 1882, by withholding rations until they agreed to sign a treaty, and the forced relocation of the Assiniboine in the same year, which resulted in starvation, sickness, and death.[25] Carter concludes that "study of the post-treaty years challenges comfortable assumptions about Canada's benevolent and wise Indian policy, as the history is one of broken treaty promises, fraud, and the use of coercive measures, enforced with the aid of the police and later troops."[26] At the same time, more subtle coercive measures were also employed in treaty negotiations and in the implementation of Indian education policy, as part of a Western settlement strategy.

The dominion government followed British imperial policy as set out in the Royal Proclamation of 1763, which decreed that all Indian nations and tribes west of the British colonies retained ownership of their lands. Settlers could not buy these lands directly from Native people, who could only transfer or sell them to the Crown. From the settler perspective, treaty making served primarily as the legal mechanism for extinguishing Native landownership and pre-existing rights that stemmed from Indigenous legal systems.[27] Men such as Alexander Morris perceived that the dominion government had a legal obligation to negotiate treaties. Moreover, espousing the cultural and social imperatives of his time, he believed that government officials were morally obligated to uphold the honour of the Crown in its efforts to acquire new lands and bring "civilization to the savages."[28] Various treaty negotiators and government officials, including Morris, David Laird, and Duncan Campbell Scott, provided early accounts of the treaty-making process and Indian policy. Evaluating Morris' published work, historians Arthur J. Ray, Jim Miller, and Frank Tough note "the treaty commissioner's attitude of complacent self-satisfaction with what he and other government negotiators had done." They observe that "Morris ... depicted Canada's motives as high-minded and wise and its treaty negotiators as paragons of patience, reasonableness and good humour. First

Nations negotiators, on the other hand, come through as high-flying ora-
tors with unreasonable 'demands' in negotiations, unless ... they were
portrayed as amenable and eager to sign treaties."[29] This theme – of government negotiators as upright and reasonable, and Indigenous people as
malcontents or pitiable supplicants – appears consistently in the settler
treaty record. According to Morris, the government maintained a steady
upper hand. The fact that Indigenous negotiators did obtain certain important concessions, particularly regarding the education and agricultural needs of their people, did not deter him from claiming that the
numbered treaties were made possible primarily by the fairness and superior diplomatic and pragmatic skills of the government negotiators.

It is also clear from the historical record that Indigenous peoples west
of the Rockies fully expected to enter into treaties as had other nations in
the east and on the prairies. In 1874, David Laird, who was then minister
of the interior, submitted a report to the Judicial Committee of the Privy
Council in which he set out the "present unsatisfactory state of the Indian
Land Question in British Columbia" after the province entered Confederation in 1871.[30] The peculiar case of British Columbia regarding the absence of treaty making is well documented and remains unresolved today.[31]
Laird reported that the failure to address the well-founded concerns of
Indigenous peoples in the province was contributing to growing unrest
among tribal groups, who knew that treaties were being negotiated on the
prairies "and naturally contrast[ed] this treatment to the policy meted out
to themselves."[32] In a foreshadowing of future federal-provincial jurisdictional wrangling over Indian policy, he was careful to blame provincial
officials for the situation. He raised the spectre of a possible Indian war
and recommended that "the Government of the Dominion should make
an earnest appeal to the Government of British Columbia, if they value
the peace and prosperity of their Province, if they desire that Canada as a
whole should retain the high character she has earned for herself by her
just and honourable treatment of the red men of the forest, to reconsider
in a spirit of wisdom and patriotism the land grievances of which the
Indians of that Province complain, apparently with good reason, and take
such measures as may be necessary promptly and effectually to redress
them."[33] Ultimately, the recommendation was to no avail, but Laird, in
language reminiscent of Morris, urged the province to pattern its actions
after those of the dominion government, whose officials, as he saw it, had

been just and honourable. Therein lay the path to peace and prosperity. Provincial officials, however, had their own version of the benevolent peacemaker – one that saw no need for treaties.

George A. Walkem, BC attorney general in 1875, explained that Indian unrest could be blamed directly on Confederation. Before 1871, Walkem declared, Indian policy in the colony was grounded in principles of equal treatment under the law and encouraging Indians to assimilate into mainstream colonial society. As a result of Victoria's "generous, enlightened and humane policy," Walkem claimed that "the Colony was enabled on the day of Confederation to hand over to the trusteeship of the Dominion, a community of 40,000 Indians – loyal, peaceable, contented and in many cases honest and industrious ... Since Confederation the Indians have undoubtedly become discontented. Hopes of visionary wealth to be acquired without labour, have been excited in the minds of some of the tribes; for it is a notorious fact that 80 acres of land was promised, of course without authority, to each head of an Indian family before the question of Reserves was even laid before the Provincial Government."[34] In Walkem's view, the former colony of British Columbia, when left to its own devices, had developed such a successful Indian policy that adopting the dominion's more extravagant approach simply transformed contented Indians into discontented ones and was therefore to be discouraged. Although the province developed its own regional variation on the peacemaker myth, which, unlike dominion policy, rested on the absolute denial of Indigenous ownership of lands, the messages are the same – government was more than generous, and Indians were the sometimes ungrateful beneficiaries of largesse.

Historian Brian Titley aptly sums up settler attitudes to Indigenous people as an odd mix of contempt, arrogance, denial, fear, and guilt – the hallmarks of colonial Indian and subsequent Aboriginal policy:

> Canadian Indian policy found its principal inspiration in the assumptions of nineteenth-century evangelical religion, cultural imperialism, and laissez-faire economics. The Indians were to be led, by whatever means possible, to "civilization" ... Economic self-sufficiency was also part of this agenda ... [to] ensure that the native population no longer constituted a burden on the public purse ... The intolerant ethnocentrism of the Anglo-Canadian elite, which was closely tied to prevailing notions

of racial superiority, precluded the possibility of the co-existence of culturally diverse peoples within the same political entity. Tolerance ... would have implied a residue of self-doubt ... Instead, the lingering guilt arising from conquest and appropriation was assuaged by the myth of duty and the delusion of parental responsibility.[35]

His assessment is amply confirmed in the records created by government bureaucrats, which reveal the extent to which the administration of a fiscally responsible Indian policy rather than a commitment to nation-to-nation treaty making became the real impetus for colonial government officials. Duncan Campbell Scott perhaps best exemplifies this growing emphasis on bureaucratic and assimilative solutions to the Indian problem that was ultimately to relieve settlers of their moral and financial burden.

In their study of the various bureaucratic mechanisms, economic rationalizations, and accounting techniques employed by successive government administrators of Aboriginal policy, Dean Neu and Richard Therrien point out that, under "Scott's regime, federal government initiatives such as residential schooling and the centralization and rationalization of the Indian department, along with more micro-bureaucratic routines, set the context for subsequent Indigenous/settler relations."[36] Scott, who worked for the federal Department of Indian Affairs, served as a treaty negotiator and eventually went on to direct the department at a pivotal time in settlement history.[37] As he developed and implemented policies that increasingly made Indigenous people the subjects of fiscally responsible social engineering, the language and ritual of treaty making receded into the background and was replaced by a more bureaucratic language.

By 1927, in the long jurisdictional dispute between federal officials and the provincial government over Indian policy in British Columbia, Scott no longer saw the need for treaty making. Appearing before a Special Joint Committee of the Senate and House of Commons convened in 1927 to inquire into the claims put forward by the Allied Indian Tribes of British Columbia, he provided a just and practical rationalization as to why treaties were unnecessary in the province. Titley explains that Deputy Superintendent Scott,

an experienced treaty-maker in his own right, was unable to see the symbolic importance of treaties to native people, and viewed the process purely in monetary terms ... He ... dazzle[d] the committee members with ... examples of Ottawa's generosity ... [and pointed out that] ... the millions spent on the Indians of British Columbia since Confederation were proof that they had been as fairly treated as if they had signed a formal land surrender. Nor would a treaty, even at this late stage, be of much advantage to them. Treaty terms, were, after all, settled beforehand by the government and were not subject to meaningful negotiation.[38]

Scott viewed such treaties as increasingly irrelevant, particularly when public monies could be better spent implementing Indian policy. In the matter of British Columbia, Titley concludes, "the rights and needs of native people were scarcely considered."[39] Scott's primary concern was maintaining administrative control over the Indian reserve lands and leases.

Scott played a significant role in creating the peacemaker myth in political circles and in the public mind. He was a well-known poet and author who shared his views on Indians with the Canadian public in the popular press and in his published works. In both, he reiterated the widely accepted belief that Indians were perilous yet childlike savages in need of strong guidance from government officials and missionary teachers to curb their war-like tendencies. In a December 1906 article published in *Scribner's Magazine,* Scott explained to his readers that "in the early days the Indians were a real menace to the colonization of Canada, [and that] only the cleverest diplomacy ... managed to keep the peace in those dangerous days."[40] Scott is both denigrator and protector of Indians, who are cast in multiple and sometimes contradictory roles as savage yet noble, warlike yet weak. In this, he conveyed the mixed feelings and attitudes of a settler society that was uneasy about its relationship with Indigenous people: "Scott was not only a well-placed bureaucrat with a deep understanding, as an accountant, of the economic basis of his department's actions, he was also a poet, essayist, prolific letter-writer and esteemed member of the Royal Society of Canada ... He recorded history both through his subjective, aesthetic perspective and through his official government record-keeping ... The juxtaposition of D. C. Scott's bureaucratic initiatives with his literary output highlights both the parallels and the tensions between Indian department policies and societal discourses pertaining to Indigenous peoples."[41]

Thus, government bureaucrats such as Morris, Laird, and Scott, who were tasked with addressing the Indian problem, also became the Indian experts of their day among politicians, government officials, and the Canadian public. Their emphasis on their own diplomatic skills, coupled with ethnocentric, racist notions about the traits of Native people, laid the foundation of the peacemaker myth that has become so emblematic of Canadian identity. Through their government reports and public renderings of Indigenous people, the myth crystallizes in the public mind during the western prairie settlement period of the late nineteenth century. Their vision of a wise, paternal, and just government that would fulfill its treaty obligations by helping and elevating Indians toward civilization – a vision shared by their superiors, fellow bureaucrats, missionaries, North-West Mounted Police officers, and the Canadian public – became analogous with settler responsibility for solving the Indian problem. During this period, Scott and others increasingly ignored treaties as a mechanism for fulfilling Canada's obligations. Instead, they focused on unilaterally developing and administering Indian policy based on various prescriptive provisions of the Indian Act. By the mid- to late nineteenth century, Native people throughout the West were treated not as treaty partners but as dependent, childlike wards of the state whose lives, lands, and resources must be regulated accordingly.

In conjunction with the treaty negotiations under way during the western settlement period, various pieces of earlier legislation concerning Indians were consolidated under the Indian Act of 1876. This legislation determined who was a status Indian and therefore a federal responsibility, entitled to treaty and other benefits, and also controlled every aspect of Indigenous people's lives, lands, and finances from the cradle to the grave. Indians could not vote or become professionals without relinquishing their Indian status. Voluntary and involuntary enfranchisement was intended to make adult male Indians full Canadian citizens, thereby removing them from federal responsibility.[42] Adult women who married non-Indian men lost their Indian status and benefits. IRS policy attacked the Indian problem from the opposite end of the generational spectrum – it targeted children. Thus, the seeds of symbolic violence – invisible and seemingly gentle and benevolent – were sown when colonial officials unilaterally created an educational policy and system fundamentally at odds with what their treaty partners had envisioned. Indigenous people in British Columbia were doubly disadvantaged, as they had no treaties and were also subject to the same Indian policy as their Prairie counterparts.

Treaty Promises, Education, and Indian Residential Schools

After treaties were signed on the prairies, officials interpreted their education provisions in ways that justified an aggressive, paternalistic policy of assimilation as necessary to save and civilize Indigenous people. In British Columbia, where only a few earlier treaties existed, the implementation of a national Indian education policy in which residential schools became the cornerstone of civilizing Indians faced even fewer obstacles. Morris' and Scott's accounts of the treaty-making process do not mention that many provisions were added at the insistence of Native negotiators, who were well aware that their people would need to acquire a different kind of learning and new skills in order to survive and flourish in the settlement period economy. Missionaries, many of whom had long-standing relationships with various tribal groups, were "involved in the treaty-making process as facilitators, witnesses, and interpreters."[43] Their motives for encouraging Indigenous people to sign treaties, as well as the quality of their translation skills, are the subject of ongoing debate.

Of particular interest here are the treaty promises related to education. In Treaties 1 to 6, negotiated from 1871 to 1877 across the North-West, it was established that "Her Majesty agrees to maintain a school on each reserve hereby made, whenever the Indians should desire it." However, in Treaty 7, concluded in 1877 with the Blackfoot, the Crown agreed only to "pay the salary of such teachers to instruct the children of said Indians."[44] This difference in wording is significant in that it is "a harbinger of what treaty implementation in general, and honouring schooling promises in particular, would mean for First Nations."[45] Native people had negotiated for schools to be located on their reserves, but as Canadian historian J.R. Miller explains,

> the reasons why Ottawa decided soon after making treaties to use off-reserve residential schools, in violation of commitments in at least six of the treaties, are clear and revealing ... Missionaries and bureaucrats alike were disillusioned with the day schools that existed in Indian communities, arguing that erratic attendance and a continuing influence of home

and community that worked to preserve Aboriginal identity rendered the day schools largely useless ... By the time Ottawa was ready to announce a new educational policy in 1883, Indian Affairs had come out firmly in favour of residential institutions run by Christian missionaries for both pedagogical and assimilative reasons.[46]

In the government's view, education that would encourage the learning of Western skills and assimilate children more easily was a more efficient approach, and officials were convinced that they, not parents and communities, knew what was best for Indigenous children. This unilateral decision making marked the beginning of a growing distrust on the part of Indigenous people toward government officials who ignored treaty promises.

Canadian historian John Milloy, who has documented IRS history in Canada, makes the critical point that "below the rhetoric of duty and civilization ran another motivation that occasionally broke through the surface of church and Departmental texts. It bespoke not a feeling of self-assured superiority in the face of Aboriginal culture but a fear of the unknown Other and of its disruptive potential."[47] As the *Report of the Royal Commission on Aboriginal Peoples* explained, "residential schools were more than a component in the apparatus of social construction and control. They were part of the process of nation building and the concomitant marginalization of Aboriginal communities. The department's inspector of education wrote in 1900 that the education of Aboriginal people in frontier districts was an important consideration, not only as an economical measure to be demanded for the welfare of the country and the Indians, themselves, but in order that crime may not spring up and peaceful conditions be disturbed."[48]

This fear of Native discontent was heightened just before the beginning of treaty talks in the North-West. With the Métis rebellion of 1869 to 1870 no doubt fresh in their minds, treaty negotiators were anxious to find ways to placate and pacify Indigenous people in the North-West and in BC, where no treaty making was under way but the administration of Indian lands and resources was well entrenched. Education was seen as an effective peacemaking tool, one that, if properly used, would ensure harmonious relations on the western Canadian frontier.

In reality, the tool was a weapon, wielded with full force against Indigenous people, who, with good reason, came to deeply distrust government officials and missionaries associated with the residential school system. How could it be otherwise when the entire system, from inception to implementation, was rooted in violence? The *Report of the Royal Commission on Aboriginal Peoples* reveals the extent to which violence permeated every aspect of the IRS experience:

> At the heart of the vision of residential education – a vision of the school as home and sanctuary of motherly care – there was a dark contradiction, an inherent element of savagery in the mechanics of civilizing the children. The very language in which the vision was couched revealed what would have to be the essentially violent nature of the school system in its assault on child and culture. The basic premise of resocialization, of the great transformation from "savage" to "civilized," was violent ... The department aimed at severing the artery of culture that ran between the generations and was the profound connection between parent and child sustaining family and community. In the end, at the point of final assimilation, "all the Indian there is in the race should be dead." This was more than a rhetorical flourish as it took on a traumatic reality in the life of each child separated from parents and community and isolated in a world hostile to identity, traditional belief and language. The system of transformation was suffused with a similar latent savagery – punishment ... In the vision of residential school education, discipline was the curriculum and punishment an essential pedagogical technique.[49]

This chilling vision, enacted upon small bodies, minds, and spirits, had devastating consequences for children, their parents, their extended families, and their communities. To be sure, there were individual missionaries, various government officials, and parents who opposed it. Milloy reports that Scott received many complaints over the years about bad conditions in the schools, poor educational and health standards, abuse, and neglect.[50] Miller states that the majority of missionaries "were an honourable minority in Canadian society in caring about the welfare, both material and spiritual, of Native peoples ... Most ... were decent, hard-working individuals who neither meant to nor did harm Indian children."[51] As David Nock points out, cultural exchange was a two-way street, and some missionaries' beliefs about Indigenous peoples changed over time as they lived in proximity to and developed close relationships with their "religious charges."[52]

But, as Nock and Celia Haig-Brown remind us, we must "never lose sight of the fact that [they] are fully implicated in the process of colonization despite their sensitivities."[53] Although it is undoubtedly true that individuals were well intentioned, it is nevertheless critical to develop a clearer understanding of their long-term complicity in a system that, even by the educational and public health standards of its time, was viewed as deficient.

Settler Non-Recognition of Indigenous Diplomacy and Peacemaking Practices

Historically, gift exchange was integral to diplomacy, treaty making, and spiritual practices among Indigenous nations and was also essential to establishing and maintaining constructive treaty and trade associations with European colonizers. Some traders, government officials, and missionaries were astute intercultural interlocutors who not only recognized the importance of such ceremonial practices to Indigenous people in maintaining good relations but genuinely sought to understand their complexities. But, as the settlement process unfolded across North America, many colonial officials representing the settler majority came to view such exchanges simply as the cost of doing business in the New World in order to access Native lands and resources. Missionaries, in their role as experts on Indian matters, and intent on imposing their own religious beliefs, advised government to prohibit Native spiritual and ceremonial practices associated with the potlatch and sun dance.[54] The NWMP brought the British vision of law and order to the West, and the peacemaker myth became integral to Canada's historical meta-narrative.[55] Secure in the assumption of their own moral and cultural superiority, these various officials ignored and eventually outlawed the teachings offered to them by Indigenous people about the importance of human connection – the necessity of establishing trust and nurturing respectful relations as central to addressing conflict and maintaining peace among diverse peoples.[56]

Under the guise of benevolence and generosity, mid-nineteenth-century treaty negotiators proved the old adage that the pen is mightier than the sword. Speaking a language of peace as they gave chiefs the treaty pen to touch and thus signal their acceptance, these representatives of the settler government needed no weapons except their false words. Indigenous diplomats who had brought their own diplomatic principles and ceremonial practices to the negotiations had no way of knowing that peacemaking as they understood it had been perverted into an act of symbolic violence. In the case of treaties, this was expressed through Western rituals involving "the force of the written document."[57] For government negotiators, schooled in Western political thinking and law, treaties were secured and made legitimate by touching the treaty pen or signing an "x" on documents – not by smoking a peace pipe, giving gifts, or engaging in prayers, songs, or feasting. They tended to see participating in sacred ceremonies as a preliminary nuisance, a token gesture rather than Native treaty-making protocol.

As their military power and economic relevance waned in the eyes of government officials, police officers, and missionaries, people who had formerly been respected as military allies and economic partners were transformed into childlike victims of progress who must now be protected. Colonial officials, who had previously engaged in Indigenous diplomatic practices as a necessary part of the fur trade and empire building, now viewed these old diplomatic alliances as less critical.[58] Government officials and missionaries alike saw little of value in Indigenous spiritual and diplomatic practices. Moreover, the ceremonial life of Indigenous people was seen as highly problematic in the colonial project of transforming savages into civilized citizens. The growing conviction that all things Native must be eradicated reached its pinnacle with the banning of sacred ceremonies such as the potlatch and the sun dance.[59]

Public History Representations: The Peacemaker Myth Lives On

Historian Richard Slotkin suggests that, in the United States, national identity is formed by the frontier myth of regeneration through violence, the means by which progress and civilization advance. Epitomized in the quintessential adventures of heroes such as "Indian fighters" Daniel Boone and Davy Crockett, the myth "became the structuring metaphor of the American experience."[60] In Canada, our national identity is shaped as the antithesis of this violence. The writings of prominent government officials such as Morris and Scott reinforced popular notions of Indigenous inferiority and the chaos and backwardness of tribal life as compared to its British equivalent. Thus, the ways in which Indians and treaty making were portrayed in popular print were highly influential in shaping settler ideas and stereotypes during the settlement period. It was this version of colonial history that came to dominate the Canadian public mind.

Historian Elizabeth Furniss considers the implications of Canadian frontier mythology that is predicated on the theme of benevolent conquest.
Canada's historical heroes, as portrayed in textbooks and popular culture,
solidified the notion that Canada's colonization was a peaceful process
that stands in stark contrast to the unchecked violence of the American
frontier:

> Just as the hero of many American frontier histories is the Indian fighter,
> and just as regeneration through violence is a central narrative theme of
> many American versions of the frontier myth, in Canada the dominant
> heroic figure is the Mountie, and a dominant narrative theme is what
> could be called "conquest through benevolence." Canadian heroes do
> not inflict violence; instead, they impose peace, order, and good govern-
> ment on Aboriginal and non-Aboriginal people alike ... This theme of
> conquest through benevolence ... the continual assertion of history as a
> narrative of paternal domination of Aboriginal peoples – weaves in and
> out of Canadian literature and popular history ... A long-term implica-
> tion is one of silence regarding the realities of Canada's own repression
> of Aboriginal people and a cloaking of forms of domination and power
> as paternalistic expressions of goodwill.[61]

Indigenous people and revisionist historians have revealed the fault lines
of the myth. But for the most part, the celebratory legend persists. A nation
of peacemakers emerged from this popular literature, particularly the
valorization of the North-West Mounted Police in poetry and pulp fiction
produced from the 1880s to the 1940s. Daniel Francis documents how
widely accepted certain aspects of the myth have become. In *The Imaginary Indian,* he comments that, "for many Canadians, the Mounties came
to stand for the very essence of our national character – a healthy respect
for just authority ... The saga of the NWMP 'winning an empire for civilization' soon became as important to the myth of Canadian nationhood
as the Battle of the Plains of Abraham."[62] The peacemaker myth appears
in today's popular history, which is no less stereotypical than earlier works.

Historian William H. Katerberg observes that the popular Heritage
Minutes series that plays on television and in movie theatres across Canada
still presents a storyline in which Mounties and treaty officials are "keepers
of the Queen's peace." As such, they personify "Canadian law and order –

defined in the British North America Act by the motto, 'peace, order and good government' – [which] effectively forestalled the culture of gunplay and violence typical of the American West and its ideal, 'life, liberty and the pursuit of happiness.'"[63] He asserts that the reality was quite different, and "the Canadian West was not so peaceful" if we factor in various manifestations of Indigenous-settler conflict, including the Seven Oaks Massacre, the North-West Rebellions and subsequent execution of Louis Riel, and a prior history of Hudson's Bay Company retaliatory acts against Native people.[64] Moreover, the coercive pressures brought to bear on Indigenous people, including withholding rations, the "benign" failure to deal effectively with the buffalo crisis, the military-like presence of the NWMP, the treaty negotiation process itself, and prescriptive Indian policy, most notably related to residential schools, stand counter to the myth. Nevertheless, we see its power and persistence in the award-winning popular CBC TV series *Canada: A People's History,* which was viewed by millions of Canadians when it first aired in 2000. A best-selling book, video, and website continue to make this version of our national history readily available.

The peacemaker myth first appears in a segment titled "Pioneers Head West: Can Ottawa Settle the Frontier without Bloodshed?" It describes how the "Canadian government had watched the carnage unfold in the American West, when settlers brazenly flocked into the untamed land, provoking bloody and expensive Indian wars ... Canada's answer to the western dilemma; bring peace and order to the West before the settlers arrive." This was done by establishing the NWMP, who "developed good relations with the natives and encouraged them to negotiate with the Canadian government. During the 1870s, the natives signed a series of treaties, which transferred land to the Canadian government and transferred Plains Indians onto reserves." According to the website associated with the series, this conflict prevention strategy was so effective that, "by 1880, the frontier had peace and order and was ready for white settlement."[65] In "Treaties Signal End: Natives Sign Over Land and Watch a Way of Life Slip Away," Native people are depicted as "a dying race ... weakened by whiskey and disease," who are increasingly dependent on a benevolent government that was "eager to arrange treaties with the natives. It wanted to avoid bloody and costly Indian wars as the west opened for settlement."[66] As the immense popularity of *Canada: A People's History* shows, the peacemaker myth remains deeply ingrained in the Canadian mind.

In a critical essay on *Canada: A People's History,* historian Lyle Dick suggests that the myth succeeded so well because it tapped into a deep reservoir in the Canadian psyche: "The story connects with its audience ... [by] characteriz[ing] Canadian history as a story of 'redemption' that, while not explicitly religious, uses narrative devices such as prophecy to suggest a biblical inevitability to the history that unfolds."[67] Dick concludes that "the narrative significance of these assorted negative characterizations ... is to discredit Aboriginal claims to western lands in the nation-building era of Canada's expansion."[68] Thus, the narrative bolsters settler justifications for appropriating Indigenous lands by framing these actions as a "predestined" moral and religious imperative to "claim the land in the name of humanity," as the well-known Prairie feminist Nellie McClung once proclaimed.[69]

Although the creators of *Canada: A People's History* claim to be telling history "from the bottom up," in actuality the narrative is structured along traditional lines, filled with visionary "Great White Man" heroes who must overcome enormous obstacles to fulfill their national dream. Moreover, the story describes a series of epitomizing moments – Confederation, western settlement, the building of the railway – that reinforce the importance of establishing the settler imprint upon the land. Slotkin explains how popular myths, with their idealized heroes, become metaphors that help to explain and justify our actions in the past and into the present: "Myth does not argue its ideology, it exemplifies it ... Myth uses the past as an 'idealized example' in which 'a heroic achievement in the past is linked to another in the future of which the reader is a potential hero' ... The moral and political imperatives implicit in the myths are given as if they were the only possible choices for moral and intelligent human beings ... [Myths transform] secular history into a body of sacred and sanctifying legends."[70] In the Canadian context, we have mythologized historical treaty negotiators, bureaucrats, and police officers as heroes who, as Slotkin suggests, exemplify national values and characteristics in foundational myths that we do not question but simply believe to be true.

The Twenty-First-Century Benevolent Peacemaker

Perpetuation of the peacemaker myth is perfectly consistent with the manner in which non-Native Canadians have come to understand (or misunderstand) the history of Indigenous-settler relations and the settler role in treaty making and Aboriginal policy. As we have seen, academic historians have raised troubling questions about this version of Canadian history, and we now know that the attitudes and actions of nineteenth-century government and police officials were hardly benign. But as John Paul Lederach points out, "we hold fast to myths that what we have created to govern our lives is responsive to whom we are as human beings and to our communities."[71] In other words, we cling to the notion that the institutions we have created are functioning well, even as we see their growing inability to meet the pressing political, socio-economic, health, and environmental needs within our communities, both settler and Indigenous. Consequently, we fail to make the connection between the myths we believe about our history and the abysmal failure of our legal, policy, and governing institutions to make a positive difference in the lives of Native people.

Regardless of where on the political spectrum settlers may stand concerning Indigenous issues in Canada, the peacemaker myth is at the heart of how we justify our actions. On the political right, it is manifested in disingenuous rhetoric about the problem of race-based rights and the need for one law for all, which of course is superior Western law.[72] On the political left, it is the well-intentioned hand-wringing over the plight of "our Aboriginal people," those victims of progress whom we must now help. Either way, cultural arrogance and a denial of colonial history drives both political agendas. Furniss points out that, "in Canada, there has been no radical break with the past: Canadian culture remains resolutely colonial in shape, content, meaning and practice."[73]

In the face of Indigenous people's accusations of genocide, racism, political non-recognition, and the theft of lands and resources, we comfort ourselves with the peacemaker myth, which precludes us from examining our own legacy as colonizers. Within the Canadian historical imaginary, our identity as a nation of peacemakers is predicated on the myth of our innocence regarding the profound extent to which we have erased an Indigenous presence from the consciousness of mainstream North America. For settlers who have long "suspected that we can never be at home in America because we were not Indians, not indigenous to the place," a version of history that declares our innocence and portrays us as heroes assuages a fear that our real identity is not peacemaker but perpetrator.[74]

The peacemaker as a national archetype became even more firmly entrenched in the Canadian psyche as Canada took on an active role in the international peacekeeping arena in countries wracked by civil war and ethnic violence. Historian Jack Granatstein cautions that the idealization of Canadians as morally superior peacemakers in comparison to their American neighbours is actually a "clichéd Canadian myth [that] now appears to be accepted as truth" and is ultimately harmful to the country's foreign policy.[75] But, although Granatstein argues that the myth has its genesis in the 1950s, when Prime Minister Lester B. Pearson promoted an international peacekeeping role for Canadians, we have seen that its origins go back much further, to our relationship with Indigenous people during the settlement period. The *Report of the Royal Commission on Aboriginal Peoples* drew on the peacemaker myth to explain how historical treaty making played a significant role in developing our identity: "The Canada that takes a proud place among the family of nations was made possible by the treaties. Our defining national characteristics are tolerance, pluralism and democracy. Had it not been for the treaties, these defining myths might not have taken hold here."[76] According to one foreign policy critic, our predilection for peace, in rhetoric if not substance, has transformed Canada into a "Boy Scout imperialist" intent on "responding to a missionary impulse which drives us to export our values to the less fortunate peoples of the world ... Value-oriented goals appear consistent with a deeply-rooted, traditional theme in our national psyche, that of Canada as the world's foremost peacekeeper, peacemaker and peace builder."[77]

The myth has become part of the common-sense knowledge that cuts across all segments of settler society and is periodically invoked to propagate the political agendas of both left and right. A leftist critic of Canada's military actions and arms trade in international wars observes that the myth is "integral to our culture" but "like all myths ... has very little basis in reality," so "dismantling the myth of 'Canada the Peacemaker,' is one step toward building a culture of peace."[78] At the other end of the spectrum, conservatives frame the myth as an unfortunate by-product of liberalism. One conservative political columnist describes Canadians as "sold on empty moralizing" and chastises the liberal government for ineffective Aboriginal programs that are simply an "opportunity to highlight our great moral goodness" rather than effect substantive change. Becoming more than a nation of empty moralizers, he says, "will require a profound change in the mindset of the majority of Canadians."[79]

Regardless of whether critics call for its dismantling or chastise us for not living up to its ideals, we do not question the historical roots of the peacemaker myth. However, peace studies scholar and activist Anne Goodman suggests that we must now cast a much more critical eye on "the contradictions and discrepancies of Canada's peacemaker image" not only in our foreign policy but also concerning the historical and contemporary injustices visited upon Indigenous people within Canada.[80] But even when we are confronted with the contradiction between myth and reality, we tend to deny, obfuscate, and minimize the latter. When the Oka crisis erupted in 1990, the images of masked Mohawk warriors and armed Canadian soldiers that flashed across television screens were at odds with our self-image. Canadians were shocked and upset. But as Neu and Therrien point out, "if we, as citizens, had had a better understanding of both the contested histories of settler society and our continuing complicity in genocidal practices directed at Indigenous peoples, the Oka stand-off would not have been seen as extraordinary at all."[81]

In a new twist on the peacemaker myth, some settler Canadians now acknowledge that the actions of our ancestors were morally suspect but cast themselves as morally superior to them. Claiming to have already learned the hard lessons of history, they focus on improving the lives of Indigenous people.

In the face of this unfounded belief, what is the reality? In 2004, after his mission to Canada, Rodolfo Stavenhagen, the former United Nations special rapporteur on Indigenous issues, noted that Canada ranked eighth on the UN Human Development Index, which measures socio-economic indicators related to quality of life. Yet when the same criteria were applied to Indigenous people in Canada, the ranking slipped to forty-eighth on the scale.[82] Moreover, a report published in 2005 by the Department of Canadian Heritage, *A Canada for All: Canada's Action Plan against Racism*, makes it clear that racism toward Indigenous peoples in Canada is the norm, not the exception: "46% of Aboriginal people living off-reserve stated that they had been a victim of racism or discrimination ... [and] 59% of Canadians felt that Aboriginal peoples are discriminated against by other Canadians."[83] In *Facing the Future*, a report published in 2004 by the Centre for Research and Information on Canada, Native people discuss the implications of widespread racism. One woman observes that "Canadians are known and respected for warmth, kindness, and being polite ... [but] Canada can be a hostile, cruel place ... a politely racist experiment for Aboriginal people ... Racism is subtle ... It is so polite, everything delivered with a smile."[84] Indigenous leaders in British Columbia have identified the barriers to improving educational success rates for Native students in the province: "These barriers include a legacy of distrust due to residential schools; unemployment and poverty ... the omission of aboriginal histories and knowledge, and the lack of an aboriginal voice in education decision-making. But without a doubt, the most challenging of all barriers to our students' success is the denial that racism is a problem. It is real and it is alive. When our students can see themselves in the history books, then we may see greater successes."[85] Every year, literally hundreds of reports reach similar conclusions.

It is telling that, in the face of these well-documented realities, we still subscribe to our beliefs about the moral and cultural superiority of Canadians and think that these qualities mitigate any mistakes we have made in the past. We are filled with good intentions, which is, after all, what really matters. This attitude allows us to conclude, conveniently, that we should all just live in the present, where things are so much better. And if they are not yet entirely better, we are working to make them so. Canada is a constant good work in progress, its missionary roots still intact. As we have seen, the Canadian majority has accepted only limited responsibility for the actions of past governments. Nor do we openly acknowledge that we are the primary beneficiaries of colonial policies that marginalized Indigenous people in their own lands. Others admit that some bad things happened to some people and think that an apology would be appropriate. But unless non-Native Canadians are willing to make substantive changes to the status quo, such apologies will ring hollow. Ultimately, the attitudes and actions of the majority population must shift. It is not just the mind and pocketbook of settler society that must be reached, but its heart, soul, and conscience as well.

The peacemaker myth is resilient and flexible. It is manifested today in a new discourse of reconciliation. Despite talk of reconciliation, the underlying structures and behavioural patterns of colonial violence that have shaped our relationship lie just beneath the surface. On occasion, they become more visible. Such was the case in the controversy that erupted over the Alternative Dispute Resolution Program designed to address Indian residential school claims as part of a broader government approach to healing and reconciliation.

4

The Alternative Dispute Resolution Program

Reconciliation as Regifting

REFLECTIONS

In 2002, when I first began working as a claims resolution manager at Indian Residential Schools Resolution Canada (IRSRC), Ottawa was in the early stages of developing the Alternative Dispute Resolution Program (ADRP) to settle thousands of litigation claims filed by former IRS students against the Crown and the various church entities that were responsible for operating the schools.[1] In my academic studies, I had been focusing on the limitations associated with applying alternative dispute resolution (ADR) models, based on a Western concept of the law as neutral, in Indigenous contexts. The government's impetus for using ADR to address residential school claims was threefold: it would move claims out of the adversarial litigation process; it would be more timely and cost-effective; and it would better support healing and reconciliation. In theory, ADR would create real opportunities to deal with the residential school legacy in a fundamentally different way that might mark a paradigm shift in Indigenous-settler relations.

In practice, of course, we encounter significant challenges in trying to move from a culture of litigation to one of reconciliation. Thus, I came to think of this new promise of reconciliation – this gift we offered in an attempt to attend to IRS claims in a kinder, gentler way – as a type of regifting of old settler promises to repair our relationship with Indigenous people. Despite good intentions, the ADRP did not, in and of itself, bring us closer to reconciliation. Indigenous people said it had achieved the opposite, that talk of healing and reconciliation was just pretty-sounding language wrapped around a program that was creating harm, not healing. Ultimately, they rejected this recycled gift, compelling us to rethink our ideas about the meaning of reconciliation. It was this rejection that ultimately led to the negotiated national Indian Residential Schools Settlement

Agreement and the genesis of the Truth and Reconciliation Commission of Canada.

The diabolical nature of symbolic violence lies in its subtlety and invisibility. On one level, it is possible to point to the actions that Canada has taken regarding residential school claims as proof that we are addressing this injustice. Yet, at the same time, if we are honest with ourselves, we must ask why, even as we speak to Native people of healing and reconciliation, they must file litigation claims in an attempt to gain redress. As I learned more about the full horrors of the residential school legacy and the complexity of the issues, it seemed to me that the evolving ADR philosophy was a strange mix of tort-based claims resolution embedded in a discourse of reconciliation that focused on healing, apology, and commemoration. I heard regularly about the need for Native people and communities to heal and reconcile among themselves and with us. Of course, this is true, but the talk made me uneasy because it was so one-sided. What I heard little about was the need for non-Native people to examine what it means to be a colonizer and our own need to heal and decolonize.

At the heart of my misgivings was a growing realization that this reconciliation discourse was actually a living testament to the ongoing dysfunction, violence, denial, and unequal power that characterize Indigenous-settler relations. In this sense, our dialogue contains all the elements of an abusive crazy-making relationship – victims name the abuse, which perpetrators either deny or acknowledge with a promise to reform, while pointing out all the supportive ways in which they are helping victims. It is hard to recognize the perpetrators' manipulative behaviour because, on the surface, their actions seem to verify an intention to conduct themselves decently and honourably. How does this dynamic play out on the ground? The following example is representative.

In March 2004, I attended a conference titled "Residential Schools Legacy: Is Reconciliation Possible?" at the University of Calgary.[2] A diverse group gathered, including Indigenous political leaders, IRS survivors, lawyers, academics, and government and church representatives, to engage in a difficult dialogue about Canada's new Alternative Dispute Resolution Program, which had not been well received by survivors and their supporters. The program was promoted as a more humane, faster way to resolve IRS claims, but it was generating anger, confusion, and distrust. Moreover, Ottawa had recently announced that it intended to appeal the *Blackwater* decision, one of the landmark residential school court cases from British Columbia.[3] This conference was jointly convened by the Assembly of First

Nations (AFN) and the University of Calgary's Faculty of Law to explore whether it was meaningful to even talk about reconciliation in light of these events.

An elder began the conference with a prayer and a welcome song. As the day unfolded, we heard many stories and different perspectives on what the residential school legacy meant for Native people and other Canadians. Various speakers talked about legal issues, the impacts of the schools, and the need for reparations for state wrongs and abuse. An AFN representative told conference participants about the strong feelings generated and the "acrimony that is prevalent now" regarding the ADRP in the many communities he had visited across the country. A non-Native church representative said that, "if I enjoy the privileges created by my ancestors, then I must also accept the responsibilities that come with them." He said that "there is a deep fracture running through Canadian society that must be recognized, and our history is part of this." He criticized the narrow focus of the ADRP and asked, "Whose justice, whose laws are represented? Who is controlling the process?" He called for a broader, more comprehensive process that would address not only sexual and physical abuse but also loss of language, culture, and spirituality. By the end of the day, the depth of dissatisfaction with the program was apparent.

On the second day, the minister of IRSRC made a speech in which he outlined all the programs and services developed by government for Aboriginal people. He referred to the Statement of Reconciliation issued by Canada in 1998, which expressed regret for the harms caused to residential school students. He acknowledged that most Canadians do not know about IRS history, saying that it is "not an easy picture to look at but if we are to move beyond victimization and toward healing and reconciliation, all Canadians must understand this history." A panel of government officials made a presentation on the ADRP, delineating its advantages. As a member of the audience, I saw a wide gap between the positive messaging they put forward and the angry response it received. The minister was stopped in the aisle as he attempted to leave, and angry survivors demanded that he answer their questions. The panel was peppered with statements and questions making it absolutely clear that the audience did not share Ottawa's vision of healing and reconciliation.

On the afternoon of the second day, as the dialogue continued, the atmosphere was intense and emotions ran high as speaker after speaker expressed raw anger, despair, and frustration about the lack of progress on the IRS issue. Some themes emerged: The program focused too narrowly on sexual and physical abuse, and did not address the cultural loss suffered by students who were alienated from their families and communities. The process itself was flawed – a long, complicated form asking for details on abuse had to be filled out, which was dehumanizing. One woman asked non-Native people in the audience, "Would you make *your* grandmother fill out a form like this? It's degrading. These things happened to us. We don't want to be revictimized. Enough is enough!" Several speakers said that the process was not acceptable, because it had been unilaterally designed by white people, and consultation had been inadequate.

A survivor reminded us that the schools damaged the spirit and intent of the treaty that was established between his ancestors and Canada. As he talked about the history of betrayal and cultural genocide that his people suffered at the hands of whites, a Euro-Canadian woman sitting next to me fidgeted, visibly agitated. When the speaker was finished, she leaned toward me and said, "We're here to talk about residential schools. What has that got to do with treaties or genocide?" I turned to look at her, wondering why she saw no connections. "Everything," I said. Over the two days of the conference, the government officials responded respectfully to criticism but kept "on message" about the positive attributes of the program. These are the dynamics of symbolic violence played out on the ground. At the end of the conference, in the face of the anger and frustration expressed, the officials agreed to engage in further consultation with the AFN but made no commitment to change either procedural or substantive aspects of the program.

Later, on the plane back to Vancouver, I thought about how Canadians cringe when they hear words such as "genocide," "betrayal," and "abuse." The image of colonizer as abusive perpetrator is at odds with the peacemaker myth, in which we tell ourselves that our settler ancestors, and by extension we ourselves, have always treated Indigenous people fairly, with a just and generous approach to resolving their problems. Now a new generation of government officials and negotiators, still armed with the cultural and legal superiority of Western neutral justice and the need to save Indians, is tasked by Canadians with "reconciling" a relationship that we failed to recognize, respect, and honour in the first place. Are the new bureaucrats simply a modern, more culturally sensitive incarnation of the benevolent peacemaker? The power of dominant-culture hegemony lies in its very invisibility – violence that is masked in neutral dispute resolution processes in which we claim Indigenous peoples can find justice. The debate that I witnessed over the ADRP revealed the degree to which Native and non-Native people are engaged not in a dialogue but in two monologues, as we talk past each other. We are stuck in old ways of interacting as colonizer/colonized, perpetrator/victim. As I left the conference, I had no easy answer to the question "Is reconciliation possible?" Rather, I came away with a sense of the deep divide that exists when it comes to sharing the disturbing stories of our shared colonial past.

Indian Residential Schools: A History of Violence

> The recollections of George Manuel ... serve as a poignant example of the layering and intertwining of ... various levels and types of violence [in] ... residential schools ... "Learning to see and hear only what the priests and brothers wanted you to see and hear ... even the people we loved came to look ugly" ... In this simple statement, we witness the brutal sophistication and irresistible force of racism, applied bureaucratically and rationalized economically at arm's length, working insidiously as psychological terrorism. The violence, having been turned inward, becomes a toxic and effective self-loathing, culturally and individually. Can there be a more elegant violence than this?
>
> – GEORGE MANUEL AND MICHAEL POSLUNS,
> *THE FOURTH WORLD: AN INDIAN REALITY*

George Manuel's story is a stark reminder for settlers who, if they think at all about Indian residential schools, do so in the abstract as an issue that government and churches are now taking steps to address. In this way, we shield ourselves from hearing thousands of survivor testimonies about the "elegant violence" that Canadian society has inflicted on individuals, families, and communities. The inconsistencies in our national story – the real histories and lived experience of Indigenous peoples – mark the disjuncture between the peacemaker myth and the violence that actually forms the foundation of Indigenous-settler relations. There is perhaps no more compelling example of how colonialism's ongoing cycles of violence and deeply ingrained patterns of perpetrator/victim behaviour and attitudes remain consistent from past to present, than in the IRS discourse of reconciliation. In the contemporary context, traces of symbolic violence can be found in the unilateral creation of a program by government officials who attempted to design a claims settlement process that, from their perspective, was neutral, fair, and cost-effective. The dynamics of symbolic violence are evident in the visceral exchanges between residential school survivors, government officials, and church representatives in public forums and less visibly in the everyday bureaucratic processes and practices that serve to reinforce colonial power relations. This subtle violence is all the more elegant because it is embedded in a language of healing and reconciliation that is seductive to both the colonizer and the colonized, albeit for different reasons.

For settlers, the promise of reconciliation is grounded in a false hope that we can somehow compartmentalize the past without facing the history that is still alive. We are loath to give up our cherished peacemaker myth, with its imaginary Indians who are problematic, in order to unmask the ugly truths about the settler problem. Still casting ourselves as neutral arbiters of justice intent on saving Indians, we now focus on their need to heal themselves and reconcile with us. In this way, we avoid facing the full moral consequences of the unjust legacy we have inherited as beneficiaries of colonialism. I am not suggesting that we should discount or minimize the suffering of residential school survivors but that we must stop pathologizing Native people and focus instead on acknowledging the settler problem and our own dysfunction.

In *A National Crime*, historian John Milloy calls Canadians to account for the IRS history and legacy that we must own, or take collective responsibility for, as part of Canada's history:

> The residential school system was conceived, designed and managed by non-Aboriginal people ... The system is not just someone else's history, nor is it just a footnote or paragraph, a preface or chapter, in Canadian history. It is *our* history, *our* shaping of the new world ... As such, it is critical that non-Aboriginal people study and write about the schools, for not to do so on the premise that it is not our story, too, is to marginalize it as we did to Aboriginal people themselves, to reserve it for them as a site of suffering and grievance and to refuse to make it a site of introspection, discovery and extirpation – a site of self-knowledge from which we understand not only who we have been as Canadians but who we must become if we are to deal justly with the Aboriginal people of this land.[4]

The residential schools were part of a broader assimilationist agenda and the colonial project we devised for educating Indigenous people. We must face the depth and persistence of our violence, denial, racism, and inhumanity. We must then ask ourselves who is really sick and in need of healing, those who were the victims of the system or those who created, implemented, and maintained it for over a century?[5] Cree educator and IRS survivor Stan McKay suggests that both the colonized and the colonizer must heal but that "the perpetrators are wounded and marked by history in ways that are different from the victims."[6]

Indigenous people seek not just legal but political and moral accountability. If Canadians fail to provide moral justice for all those harmed by the residential schools and ignore the need for truth telling, Native people may rightly ask how we can expect to reconcile other aspects of our relationship involving treaties, land claims, and resource rights. We should not underestimate the extent to which the residential school system speaks to the very heart of our troubled relationship. How we as a nation choose to deal with this legacy sends a strong message about the integrity of our intentions. The issue is not peripheral to the larger context of Indigenous-settler relations but rather the pivot upon which all else turns.

In evaluating the ADRP, it is useful to keep this historical context in mind. The program was rooted in a liberal neutrality model based on tort law and personal injury compensation levels. As such, it became subject to all the criticisms of ADR processes more generally. The controversy over Canada's ADRP is representative of the contemporary dynamics of colonial violence. It reveals a significant authenticity gap between the rhetoric of reconciliation and the reality of the process that was developed to resolve individual claims. Thus, it becomes evident that Indigenous peoples and settlers are trapped within a paradox of reconciliation that juxtaposes conflicting visions of history, culture, law, and justice in ways that replicate the cycles of colonial violence.

The Ideological Roots of ADR and the Neutrality Myth

ADR may ... obscure or hide ADR's quest for economic efficiencies, preservation of the status quo, tightening of social control, encouragement of a regressive reaction to legal rights, or continued oppression of the least powerful in society ... The ideology of ADR depends on what is constructed as natural, normal, and essential in disputing and on who does the constructing. Understanding ADR as developing ideology about the disputing world can open up further inquiry, particularly critical inquiry. Careful attention can be paid to the long-term consequences of embracing a movement that promises so much hope but that may actually exacerbate existing inequalities either inadvertently or intentionally.

– ANDREW PIRIE, "COMMENTARY: INTERCULTURAL
DISPUTE RESOLUTION INITIATIVES ACROSS CANADA"

Canadian legal scholar Andrew Pirie argues that the ADR movement as an ideology must be evaluated with a critical eye. It is therefore important to understand the historical roots of contemporary treaty negotiations and the ADRP within this ideological context. These roots lie in ADR methods and techniques that emerged in the United States and spread across North America during the 1970s and 1980s as a viable alternative to expensive, lengthy courtroom litigation. Since then, many Canadian government negotiators, lawyers, and policy makers have received ADR training, including in "interest-based" negotiation techniques. First popularized in 1981 by American conflict resolution practitioners Roger Fisher and William Ury, the philosophy and practice of ADR is based on a Western conceptualization of law as neutral justice and predicated on the belief that a negotiator, mediator, or adjudicator can resolve disputes by getting parties to focus on identifying their underlying needs and interests in order to reach mutually beneficial agreements.[7] The underlying assumption is that the ADR process itself is structured in a neutral way and that its practitioners are impartial conflict intervenors who are able to transcend their own socio-cultural frames of reference.

Writing in 1991, American conflict theorists Sara Cobb and Janet Rifkin offered a thought-provoking critique of the ADR neutrality model in which they look at how hegemonic cultural and power dynamics shape our conflict stories, or narratives. Seemingly desirable characteristics such as neutrality are built into the process with little regard for cultural or political differences or power imbalances. They suggest that, despite the rhetoric of neutrality, practitioners are deeply invested in "the political management of stories" of conflict in which a dominant discourse emerges and is subsequently legitimized by "consensus."[8] Using examples of mediation sessions, they demonstrate how one party's story is accepted as the "truth" about what happened, whereas the other party's version is ignored or discounted. As a result, the consensus achieved does not reflect a shared narrative but represents the colonization or co-optation of the less powerful party's story.[9] Practitioners have developed various approaches to working with conflicting parties, including the use of narrative methods of restorying conflicts in ways that attempt to address cultural difference and unequal power relations.[10]

Conflict studies scholar practitioner and activist David Dyck is scathing in his critique of mainstream ADR practitioners, declaring that "it is the practitioners of this form of mediation who are most in need of deeper reflection on the connections between their craft and the work of nonviolent advocacy activism."[11] He states that these mediators ignore the structural and systemic roots of conflict and instead "naively assume that sharing feelings brings empowerment ... [They] are largely Euro-American, middle class professionals with destructive notions of 'neutrality' that usually serve the interests of the powerful and reduce 'injustices' to problems of communication."[12] Moreover, he argues that mediation training is too narrowly focused because it fails to "emphasize the social and historical context of conflict and power analysis."[13] Dyck's critique is a powerful indictment of the field of conflict resolution, which has been so instrumental in influencing the design and implementation of negotiation and claims settlement processes in Canada.

Conflict Transformation: Moral and Ethnopolitical Conflict

In conflict resolution processes, success is defined as negotiating an agreement that satisfies all parties. Taking a different approach, conflict transformation scholar-practitioners aim to facilitate individual and group empowerment, mutual recognition and respect, and the long-term repair of relationships – seemingly more elusive goals that are nevertheless more congruent with Indigenous approaches. In 1994, American conflict studies scholar-practitioners Robert Bush and Joseph Folger also published a critique of the ADR model. They too argued that mediators are anything but neutral and are in fact highly prescriptive in steering parties toward agreements. According to them, the ADR movement, which had begun as a grassroots quest for social justice, had become increasingly conservative, instrumentalist, and utilitarian. Rather than focusing on resolving conflicts, Bush and Folger proposed to transform them, setting out a model designed to empower people and thereby providing opportunities for moral growth and social transformation.[14]

In 2004, American conflict resolution scholar-practitioner Bernard Mayer picked up on the theme of conflict transformation in *Beyond Neutrality,* challenging practitioners to cast off their role as impartial conflict resolvers and "think about the social role that conflict resolution as a field plays in society and the complicated interplay between conflict resolution as an avenue of social change and as a means of social control."[15] Conflict studies scholar Christopher Mitchell also argues that the ideology of conflict transformation is grounded in a more liberatory social justice philosophy and that, whereas conflict resolution is inherently conservative, conflict transformation attempts to address the deeper social, systemic, and structural origins of conflict. On this front, Mitchell says that "the transformational approach ... begins by assuming that there is nothing sacred about the status quo ... The process starts with an analysis and critique of the existing system and an assumption that it will be necessary to create new systems, structures and relationships."[16] Equally importantly, through critical inquiry and social action, a transformative model has the emancipatory potential to address the structural inequities, systemic racism, and oppression that are the hallmarks of colonialism.

The Genesis of the Alternative Dispute Resolution Program

The abuses and cultural harms perpetrated in Indian residential schools gained more widespread public attention with the publication of the *Report of the Royal Commission on Aboriginal Peoples* in 1996. The royal commission called for a public inquiry into the IRS system. In the same year, the first two hundred litigation claims were filed, and a new Residential Schools Unit was established in the Department of Indian Affairs and Northern Development. In 1998, the Government of Canada issued *Gathering Strength: Canada's Aboriginal Action Plan,* its policy response to the royal commission, in which it rejected the recommendation for a public inquiry. Ottawa also issued its Statement of Reconciliation, acknowledging and expressing regret for the abuse that occurred in residential schools.[17] Although the statement recognized the devastating impacts of the IRS system, it was met with mixed reactions, as many Indigenous people said that the wording was too qualified to constitute a sincere apology. Moreover, survivors said that nothing less than a full apology delivered in Parliament by the prime minister would be adequate. In the face of growing litigation, as thousands of former students filed legal claims against the government and churches, the Department of Indian Affairs and Northern Development began exploring the potential for using ADR as a mechanism to resolve IRS claims outside the courtroom. There is no doubt that the high number of claims represented a significant legal and financial risk for the government.

In 1998 and 1999, a series of exploratory dialogues were held across Canada, involving residential school claimants and their legal counsel, Native leaders, church representatives, and government officials. A set of guiding principles for working together was agreed upon and formed the basis of twelve ADR pilot projects.[18] These foundational principles state that any ADR process developed must be voluntary and "designed to provide for disclosure with safety; validation with sensitivity; remedies with flexibility; commemoration with respect ... Appropriate remedies ... for abuse [must] further the goals of healing, closure, and reconciliation [and] may include: monetary compensation; acknowledgment of wrong done; apologies; creation of funds for healing, education and cultural recovery for survivors and their families; effective access to training and other programs; memorialization and community ceremonies; commitment to future prevention activities by government, churches and communities."[19] The pilot projects (including the one in Hazelton) were a concerted attempt, however imperfect, to give residential school claimants more control over the claims settlement process, enabling them to negotiate packages that could include both monetary and non-monetary forms of compensation. According to the results of an independent evaluation report conducted in 2002, "the projects were intended to enlarge the thinking about what might be possible in resolving abuse cases outside of litigation, and to ensure that survivor groups had a meaningful voice in determining how their stories were told and their redress determined ... Although each of the projects is required to go through a validation phase and provide redress for validated claims, the nature of the process and the components of the redress package are major topics of negotiation."[20]

The pilot projects were, however, still subject to all the limitations of a litigation-driven tort-based approach. Nevertheless, in assessing the overall benefits for survivor participants, the report found that, though Ottawa's restrictions on levels of monetary compensation were highly problematic, the non-monetary aspects of redress were significantly more flexible and beneficial to claimants.[21]

In 2000, the Law Commission of Canada released its report *Restoring Dignity*, a major focus of which was Indian residential schools.[22] The report considered the relative advantages and disadvantages of a range of criminal and civil litigation mechanisms conducted "in the shadow of the law" – that is, with claims ultimately still subject to resolution in the judicial process. These included ADR, public inquiries, and truth and reconciliation commissions.[23] As the report pointed out,

> the desire for another type of process to resolve past cases of institutional child abuse has already led to the creation of innovative "redress programs" ... designed specifically to provide financial compensation and complementary non-monetary benefits to survivors and others harmed by institutional child abuse ... Redress programs have certain affinities with truth and reconciliation commissions in that they seek to develop and provide forms of redress that promote healing and reconciliation. But they are also intended to provide financial compensation to survivors – usually by means of an *ex gratia* payment. They also have affinities with community initiatives that respond directly to the specific needs of survivors, their families and communities. But they have a difference: they are not voluntary grassroots processes, but are official responses to the threat of civil liability. They typically find their legal foundation in a government policy decision and need not be formally established by legislation. Consequently, these redress programs can be as expansive and innovative as the imagination and resources of their creators allow.[24]

The pilot projects were the precursor to the Alternative Dispute Resolution Program. Although they provided the scope necessary for developing innovative, creative non-monetary compensation, not all of them took equal advantage of this flexibility, and there was considerable difference among the various pilot projects. Moreover, although the subsequent ADRP retained some flexibility to include non-monetary aspects of redress such as ceremonies and commemorations, much was dependent on the actions of individual claims resolution managers. Without their support and advocacy, such initiatives often floundered.

In 2001, Ottawa established a new department, Indian Residential Schools Resolution Canada, to deal exclusively with the thousands of residential school legal claims that were filed. In 2002, Canada announced a National Resolution Framework designed to resolve the majority of sexual and physical abuse claims through the new ADRP – wherein claims were presented to a neutral adjudicator who then rendered a decision and, if allegations of abuse were proven, awarded compensation. The Alternative Dispute Resolution Program, grounded in a Western neutrality model, relied on tort and personal injury law rather than a restorative justice model.[25] Writing in 2002, Canadian legal scholar Jennifer Llewellyn cautioned that the program was highly problematic. She outlined the shortcomings of using a corrective justice model – a tort-based approach that focused narrowly on settling individual litigation claims with monetary compensation awarded for damages. In emphasizing the individual nature of residential school claims, the program was ill-equipped to address the significant systemic, collective harms inflicted by the IRS system: "Settling abuse claims is only one (and, in some cases, a minor part) of what the parties seek. The abuse suffered by residential school students was the result of a relationship of inequality, oppression, and disrespect between the Canadian government, its citizens, the churches, and Aboriginal peoples. The restoration of this relationship to one of mutual concern, respect, and dignity is what victims seek first and foremost, and any process must have this as its goal or it will not resolve the conflict between the parties and may, in fact, make it worse."[26]

The Components of the Alternative Dispute Resolution Program

The government's expectation was that most claimants would choose to resolve their claims through the ADRP. Although 90 percent of former students cited cultural loss in their claims, Canada did not provide individual compensation for this, because cultural loss is not recognized as a legal cause of action. Rather, Ottawa developed a policy and program response to the IRS issue. A health support program provided counselling services for survivors involved in either litigation or the ADRP. A commemoration program, designed but never implemented, was intended to fund culturally appropriate community-based initiatives that would

honour and remember former students, support healing and reconciliation, and provide opportunities for apologies to be offered by government
and churches. The IRSRC mandate also encompassed educating the Canadian public about the schools. In 2002, the Department of Canadian
Heritage also announced $172.5 million in funding to create an Aborig-
inal Languages and Cultures Centre to "address issues of the loss of traditional languages and cultures by Aboriginal peoples, including those who
attended Indian Residential Schools."[27] Together, these government programs and initiatives were meant to be a comprehensive response to the
totality of the residential school legacy. Why, then, did the ADRP generate
such controversy, ill will, and anger?

The Alternative Dispute Resolution Program on Trial

The rationale behind the ADRP was that it would be a less adversarial,
more cost-effective, and faster approach to resolving residential school
claims than litigation and that it would also support reconciliation. But
the program, however well intentioned, came under attack on a number
of fronts. On 17 November 2004, the AFN released a report produced by
a blue-ribbon panel tasked with evaluating the program. The genesis of
this report lay in the Calgary conference, where senior federal officials
committed to further consultation with all parties.[28] The report did not
reject the program out of hand as a mechanism for addressing sexual and
physical abuse claims. It noted that the ADRP was better than litigation.
It recommended a two-pronged approach to dealing with the residential
school issue. First, every person who attended residential school should
receive a lump-sum payment; this would be in addition to any compensation awarded for damages related to sexual and physical abuse. Second, a
national truth-telling and reconciliation process was seen as critical not
only for survivors, their families, and communities but for educating the
Canadian public.

The AFN report could have become just another consultation document to be shelved and forgotten, but several other legal and political
factors in conjunction with its release contributed to casting the ADRP
in an increasingly unfavourable public light. Thus, the dialogue regarding
the program shifted from the conference floor to the House of Commons
and from consultation meetings to formal parliamentary committee
meetings. In December 2004, the Ontario Court of Appeal ruled that a

$2.3 billion class-action suit by former students of the Mohawk Institute in Brantford, Ontario, could be certified, allowing it to proceed to the next stage toward trial. In rendering this decision, the court stated that, to meet certification requirements, plaintiffs must demonstrate that a class action is preferable to other "reasonably available means of resolving the claims."[29] Canada argued that the ADRP constituted a preferable method of resolving the claims. The court disagreed, saying that the program was "unilaterally created by one of the respondents in this action and could be unilaterally dismantled without the consent of the appellants. It deals only with physical and sexual abuse. It caps the amount of possible recovery ... It does not compare favourably with a common trial."[30] This decision had implications for a much larger national class-action suit, the $12.5 billion *Baxter* class action, which was also seeking certification. In January 2005, Ottawa appealed the Ontario court decision to the Supreme Court.

In February 2005, against this legal backdrop and in an increasingly volatile political environment, the House of Commons Standing Committee on Aboriginal Affairs and Northern Development held hearings on the ADRP as part of a study on its effectiveness. The program, which was supposed to resolve an injustice, had itself become a source of public conflict. By this, I mean that its critics argued that the broad systemic injustices and harms created by the residential school policy and system demanded a deeper moral response from Canadian society than the program could deliver. We see this clearly in the call for a public apology from the prime minister, for group reparations to compensate all survivors for attendance at a school and for loss of language and culture, and for a national reconciliation process for shared truth-telling and public education for all Canadians.[31]

Although the ADRP was framed in the language of reconciliation – healing, redress, apology, relationship – the AFN report that was submitted to the standing committee in February 2005 concluded that, in substance, it risked "a very real danger that new harms in the relationship between First Nations, non-Aboriginal peoples, and the government will be created ... [and] reconciliation will become impossible for the indefinite future."[32] The report condemned the tort-based program as an inadequate and harmful response not only to residential school survivors, their families, and communities but to all Indigenous people in Canada.[33] The Canadian Bar Association, which also submitted a comprehensive report to the committee, supported the AFN report's recommendations, cautioning that the ADRP was based on "blame and faultfinding, harm, wrongdoing and compensation ... concepts [that] inform tort law ... [and was] not conducive to reconciliation."[34] In its critique, the Canadian Bar Association report captures the essence of the situation faced by all the parties, saying simply that "there are legal arguments and there is justice. It is time for justice."[35]

On 9 February 2005, Conservative opposition MP Jim Prentice stood in the House of Commons to ask for the government's response to allegations that the ADRP was not working, that the costs associated with its implementation were excessive, and that the results were negligible. "Moreover," he said, "it is not working for the victims. Newspapers in this country are replete with stories of residential school victims who feel they are being re-victimized by the process."[36] This media coverage increased public scrutiny on the Liberal government at a time when the high-profile Gomery inquiry into alleged misspending of government funds was foremost in the public mind, and the minority government was in real danger of falling.[37] Simultaneously, the prime minister was showcasing the Canada-Aboriginal Peoples Roundtable, convened in April 2004, as an indicator of the new "transformative" relationship that Ottawa was building with First Nations.

During the standing committee hearings on the ADRP, a number of witnesses in addition to the Assembly of First Nations and the Canadian Bar Association gave evidence, including survivors, grassroots survivor organizations, the Aboriginal Healing Foundation, plaintiffs' counsel, and senior government officials. Analyzing the testimony of various witnesses and media coverage of the issue gives a sense of the complex ways in which ingrained patterns of violence play out in the residential school context. Parliamentary rituals of public debate and committee in the House of Commons created a performance space in which this dialogue could unfold in the public eye. The personal testimony of survivors compelled parliamentarians to transcend partisan politics, however briefly, to recognize the presence and humanity of the survivors, whose stories they could no longer deny.

On 15 February 2005, in eloquent, powerful, and moving testimony, Chief Robert Joseph, representing the Indian Residential School Survivors Society in British Columbia, spoke to an Indigenous vision of reconciliation:

As you can see, I was wearing my ceremonial robes as a sign of respect for your parliamentary traditions and the standing committee, of course ... There are times when we as men and women are called upon to do the extraordinary, times when we must do the honourable thing, times when we are compelled to rise above the accustomed simple solution and to struggle to reach for the hard, principled one. These are such times. We call upon you and Canada to do this with us ... ADR is indeed a better alternative to the courts. Beyond these, ADR falls far short in addressing the majority of survivor needs for comprehensive redress ... For us and Canada to turn the page on this chapter of our mutual history we need a broader response than the ADR can deliver. So here we must heed the survivor voices. For the past ten years over 40,000 survivors ... have told us what that broader response should be: an apology, compensation, funding for healing, and future reconciliation. With respect to an apology, survivors want and need a full apology delivered by the Prime Minister on the floor of the House of Commons ... With respect to lump sum compensation, survivors are entitled to and want financial redress for the pain and suffering – loss of language and culture, loss of family and childhood, loss of self-esteem, addictions, depression and suicide – we've endured ... By neglecting to address residential school survivors and forcing them through an onerous process like ADR, Canada accepts the risk of being accused of institutional racism yet again ... While we struggle with our pain, our suffering, and loss, we know that our culture and traditions are embedded in the need for balance and harmony – reconciliation.[38]

Chief Joseph appeared before the committee wearing his ceremonial robes as a sign of political respect for the rituals of Parliament, but his gesture also sent a symbolic message reminding us that Indigenous diplomacy, law, and peacemaking principles and protocols exist. In calling on parliamentarians to do the hard, principled thing, Chief Joseph asked for leadership and vision, and he asked Canadians to transcend colonialism and to do the honourable thing. In both words and action, he identified our failure to heed the symbolic importance of ritual and apology in addressing the history of racism and injustice, thus preventing any meaningful reconciliation.

On 17 February 2005, the committee heard from several survivors whose testimony reinforced Chief Joseph's message. They described their own experiences in residential schools and with the ADR process. In coming forward, these survivors put a human face on the residential school legacy. In the recorded minutes of the hearings, Flora Merrick, an eighty-eight-year-old elder whose ADR claim was appealed by the federal government, told the committee,

> I cannot forget one painful memory. It occurred in 1932 when I was 15 years old. My father came to the Portage la Prairie residential school to tell my sister and I that our mother had died and to take us to the funeral. The principal of the school would not let us go with our father to the funeral. My little sister and I cried so much, we were taken away and locked in a dark room for about two weeks. After I was released from the dark room and allowed to be with other residents, I tried to run away to my father and family. I was caught in the bush by teachers and taken back to the school and strapped so severely that my arms were black and blue for several weeks ... I told this story during my ADR hearing, which was held at Long Plain in July 2004 ... I was told that my experiences did not fit into the rigid categories for being compensated under the ADR. However, the adjudicator, Mr. Chin, after hearing my story at my hearing, awarded me $1,500. The federal government appealed to take even this small award from me. I was willing to accept the $1,500 award, not as a fair and just settlement, but only due to my age, health, and financial situation. I wanted some closure to my residential school experience, and I could also use the money, even as small as it was. I am very angry and upset that the government would be so mean-spirited as to deny me even this small amount of compensation ... I'm very upset and angry, not only for myself, but also for all the residential school survivors.[39]

Even the dry pages of recorded evidence manage to convey the fact that committee members were moved by the words of Flora Merrick and other survivors, perhaps even temporarily unsettled:

Lloyd St. Amand (Liberal):
If one of your purposes in coming today was to bring alive for all of us these accounts, these memories, if part of your reason in coming was to put a very human, brave face on the abuses of the past, trust me, you

have succeeded beyond your wildest expectations. For me, and I dare say for others, the accounts that you verbalized to us, which to this point we've only read about, are now very much alive. You have very much encouraged us, motivated us, to immediately and quickly get something done to deal with this abuse in the most fair, equitable fashion possible.

Bernard Cleary (Bloc Québécois):

The government refuses to face the facts and raises a thousand and one questions on this issue. The government should recognize it made a mistake. What can I say? It made a mistake, and that is terrible. The primary concern of elders in discussing this matter is that they be offered an apology, if only to comfort them. Money is fine, but the satisfaction it gives someone when what they have been saying all their life is recognized as true is worth much more. It does not cost much for a responsible government to say that mistakes were made and that those were monumental mistakes that the country cannot tolerate ... Let us settle this matter once and for all. What matters most is not an extra $200 million or even an extra $1 billion. What matters most is to ensure that people, like you, who have lost their whole life – When I look at Ms. Merrick and her daughter as well as Ms. Daniels and hers, I see three generations of people who have suffered the same problems. How appalling is that! Three generations have gone through the same problems, suffered the same hardship and had an equally hard time overcoming them. I could have sobbed like a child earlier, listening to this story, because I could feel how terribly difficult it was for the witnesses to recall memories they would rather forget, but are unable to.

Carol Skelton (Conservative Party of Canada):

This is my second term in the House of Commons, and Tuesday's committee and today's committee have been the hardest days of testimony I have sat through in this House of Commons, because I feel the last two days have shown me totally how much injustice has been done to each of you. From the bottom of my heart, I say how sorry I am for that. I do wish the Minister of Indian Affairs and Northern Development and our Prime Minister had been here this morning to hear these beautiful, courageous ladies say what they said. Mr. Troniak said you have been denied justice, that you were prisoners of the system. I'm taking words out of the testimony this morning. What has happened is disgraceful, and I say to the government of the day: Have you no shame? It is totally unfair to have your name changed by a school because they didn't like your name, to be beaten so badly, and to not be allowed to attend your own mother's funeral. My mother, Mrs. Merrick, is your age. She never, ever had to undergo the injustice you had to undergo, and that's not fair. It's not right, and it's the responsible thing for the government to stand up and do what's right.

Pat Martin (New Democratic Party):
The Assembly of First Nations has pointed out how wrong the current process is and that it's not only failing but it's wrong in principle and in concept ... What I'm getting at is that a key part of the proposal from the Assembly of First Nations is not only the money. I think you're getting consensus here that eligibility for compensation should only be based on proof of attendance. If you can show that you were a student during these periods at these residential schools, we can assume that you've been victimized and no one else will make you relive that ... The second thing that the Assembly of First Nations is calling for is a truth and reconciliation healing process, not only for you to tell your story and hopefully tell the world what happened, but for us too, for the general population, for Canadians to be part of that healing process. I think I can safely say that if you could get these stories to average Canadians, you would tap into a great deal of goodwill, because no one in this room will ever forget what we've heard today. If, as you say, there are thousands of those stories, and worse, I think your average Canadian will move swiftly and quickly.[40]

These excerpts give a sense of the power of testimony that is direct, unfiltered by the legal and bureaucratic processes that shape the IRS narrative to conform to their own requirements. In coming forward, Flora Merrick explained that she accepted the original award not because she felt that justice was being done but because it was of some small comfort and assistance to her. Parliamentarians began to understand that financial compensation, though important, was just one component of a much broader response that was needed from Canadian society as a whole.

Government Perspectives on the Alternative Dispute Resolution Program

The committee then heard briefly from Ted Hughes, chief adjudicator for the Indian Residential Schools Adjudication Secretariat, which was tasked with adjudicating the residential school claims in the ADRP. He explained the essence of the independent, neutral ADRP from the secretariat's perspective:

> I think you perhaps know that the essence of it is to expedite the matter, and while files go to Ottawa when the applicant fills out the application form, they ultimately come to our secretariat. I can assure you that insofar as I am concerned and the 48 adjudicators who work with me are concerned, our secretariat is independent of government. Granted, I suppose, we were confirmed by government, by contracts, after those stakeholder groups selected us, but the government doesn't tell us what to do, other than the fact that has been very adequately pointed out here today, that we have to work within the model given to us by the government. Those are the constraints we're under. We can only make awards and so on within the terms of the model that was set out, and we cannot stray beyond that. I think perhaps it's appreciated that the key of our process is that it's a non-adversarial model, where the claimant is questioned only by the adjudicator, and we endeavour to do this in a sensitive and relaxed manner. We will go to the claimant's home if that's the most suitable. We've had hearings in hospitals, on reserves, and in other public facilities in communities and so on. Our whole idea is to try to make the claimant who comes forward to tell a very painful story, along the lines of those we've heard here today, to feel as relaxed as they can. Time doesn't permit me to go into the constraints under which we operate insofar as the areas we can deal with are concerned. You've heard it said today that in the main our mandate is limited to physical and sexual abuse cases, with some claims for wrongful confinement.[41]

Hughes' remarks are of particular interest in light of Flora Merrick's testimony. He indicated that the adjudication secretariat was independent from government but that it was constrained by the terms of the ADR model. As we see in Merrick's case, when the adjudicator stepped outside these constraints after hearing her story, the government appealed his decision, no doubt concerned that it would set a precedent for other claims. When she gave her testimony, the members of the standing committee were moved, as the adjudicator had been. They saw that a profound injustice had occurred, both in the original offence and in her experience within the ADRP, and they knew instinctively as human beings that it must be made right.

Regardless of whether or not the government's actions were justifiable in strictly legal terms, in the court of public opinion, they were now deemed indefensible. Flora Merrick's claim was one of thousands that did not meet the strict criteria of compensability under tort law. If there were any doubt that violence still lay at the heart of Indigenous-settler relations, her testimony was stark evidence that new forms of "elegant violence," made all the more insidious because they were cloaked in a language of healing and reconciliation, were being perpetrated. In responding to Hughes' testimony, committee member Gary Lunn noted that the basic ADRP principles regarding the expeditious settling of claims were not being met:

Gary Lunn (Conservative Party of Canada):
First of all, Mr. Hughes, my questions are all directed at you. We heard the most gut-wrenching testimony this morning that it would make anyone's skin crawl. The only conclusion is that this system has failed miserably. I appreciate that you're saying that once you get the application, you're trying to do it in three months. But these are applications from people who are very elderly. There's the process that the applications go through, whereby they're checked, investigated, etc. I don't know how long it takes before they even get to you. The stories we heard this morning were just horrific. Again, some of the statements that were made by some of the claimants that this wasn't considered abuse at the time it happened just simply aren't acceptable ... In terms of the amount of claims coming forward – and I include the ones that have gone off to the department – I think we're well over a thousand, as you've pointed out. A very small number have actually been settled. As was pointed out by Mr. Faulds, I believe, we're in a crisis. He used the word "crisis." We had better act very quickly to correct that crisis and identify the problems. Not coming up with solutions before people are going to their graves is just not okay. Every single member on this committee, from every single party, will concur about what we heard this morning. I will say that, based

on some of the most credible testimony that I've heard in seven years as a parliamentarian, this process has failed miserably.[42]

After hearing clear testimony from survivors and others that the ADRP was fundamentally flawed, the committee heard a very different story from then minister of IRSRC Anne McLellan, who appeared before it on 22 February 2005, to justify the program's rationale and results. McLellan stated that

> previous governments largely ignored this issue. In response to the Royal Commission, however, the Government of Canada developed a specific and innovative strategy to address, in a comprehensive way, this troubled legacy. Our goals, then, as now, included opening pathways to healing and reconciliation by apologizing, by compensating, and making that process less difficult for those who have suffered. These values are reflected in the priorities this government has set for improving the lives and conditions of all aboriginal people. The round table, hosted by the prime minister ... and our ongoing work with each of the national aboriginal organizations clearly demonstrate this government's commitment to build a partnership with aboriginal people. Together, we will make steady progress toward improving the lives of aboriginal people.[43]

The minister then offered a short history of the evolution of IRS claims policy and the development of the National Resolution Framework and the ADRP. She emphasized the high degree of consultation that had occurred with various stakeholders, including survivors, their lawyers, and senior church officials. She reiterated the need to validate claims in order to be fiscally accountable to Canadians. She described the programs included in the National Resolution Framework and claimed that "our ADR approach is groundbreaking, a culturally based humane and holistic way to provide additional choices for former students who are seeking compensation for sexual and physical abuses." She pointed out that the government was consulting with the Assembly of First Nations concerning the recommendations it had tabled and was "considering the additional costs of the AFN proposal" for a lump-sum payment to all residential school students.

McLellan concluded by saying that "all you have heard from every witness argues in favour of approaches that are flexible and which demonstrate a willingness on the part of all parties to listen."[44] Yet, given the testimony of survivors who appeared before the committee and the negative response to the program in Indigenous communities, one must ask whether the government was truly listening to what survivors were telling it about the best way to address the issue. Rather than promoting healing and reconciliation, the ADRP actually replicated colonial power relations, in which the more powerful party ultimately controlled the framework, scope, design, and substance of the claims settlement process.

A survey of media coverage also provides a sense of the complex political and legal environment in which this debate took place. For example, in "McLellan under Attack over Native-School Redress," *Toronto Globe and Mail* journalist Bill Curry, reporting on the standing committee meetings, wrote that,

> sandwiched between emotional testimony from aboriginals who say Ottawa is taking a heartless approach to compensating residential school victims, Deputy Prime Minister Anne McLellan told a Commons committee that the government's "groundbreaking" program is working well ... In responding to questions about the merits of a lump-sum payment, Ms. McLellan said that any new plan must require natives to prove their claims. "Otherwise, I'd be before another committee responding to an auditor-general's report." Opposition MPs lashed out at the minister, pointing out that previous testimony from former students and organizations such as the Canadian Bar Association, shows that the government's plan does not work and that far more is being spent on bureaucracy than on payouts ... Conservative MP Jim Prentice said Ms. McLellan appears to be the only person who thinks the government's plan works. "What we have heard as a committee has moved us, appalled us and shamed us" ... Other Opposition MPs offered similar comments.[45]

Thus, the article captured the essence of how the debate played out in a convoluted mix of national settler politics, legal complexities, and fiscal accountability to Canadians. Traces of the peacemaker myth were evident in the rhetoric of government officials proclaiming the efficacy of yet another bureaucratic solution to a particularly thorny aspect of the Indian problem. McLellan, clearly on the political defensive, insisted that Canada had developed a superior administrative, bureaucratic solution.

At the same time, she was careful to assure Canadians that the government was still the arbiter of a neutral adjudicative justice in which IRS survivors would have to prove their claims like anyone else. Although opposition MPs expressed empathy for survivors as the victims of historical injustice, they were equally willing to capitalize on the ADRP as yet another example of bloated Liberal bureaucracy and misspending.

In the time leading up to the tabling of the standing committee's report, media coverage criticizing the program kept the issue in the public eye, ensuring that political pressure remained high and reminding Canadians that the residential school legacy was still very much alive. One such article, by *Toronto Star* journalist James Travers, noted that

> survivors' stories ... rip the smugness out of being Canadian ... The cumulative effect of that evidence was so compelling that a compromise Conservative motion was adopted by the committee ... Some witnesses told the committee that process so completely dominates results that the sole-purpose department is spending about $4 on administration for every $1 it pays victims. Martin's way out of a mess that is also a national shame is relatively painless. As almost everyone with intimate knowledge of the system advises, the solution lies not in wasting millions to ensure that no one gets one cent more than warranted but in righting a wrong, on healing and reconciliation.[46]

All the signposts indicated that the standing committee report would not look favourably on the program. Given the volatile political climate in which the Canadian public was growing increasingly angry over alleged Liberal government misspending, waste, and duplicity in a range of programs, it seemed obvious that changes would have to be made.

Consequently, it came as no surprise that the committee was unconvinced by the minister's reassurance and that its report, tabled in the House of Commons on 7 April 2005, was scathing in its condemnation of the ADRP. The report made eight recommendations, the primary one being the termination of the program. It stopped short of supporting the lump-sum payments suggested by the Assembly of First Nations and the Canadian Bar Association. Rather, it proposed that court-supervised negotiations be undertaken "to achieve a court-approved, court-enforced settlement for compensation that relieves the Government of its liability." The report was silent on the issue of an apology but did recommend "that the Government, to ensure that former students have the opportunity to tell their stories to all Canadians in a process characterized by dignity and respect, cause a national truth and reconciliation process to take place in a forum that validates the worth of the former students and honours the memory of all children who attended the schools."[47]

In producing the report, the committee itself became embroiled in political wrangling, as Liberal committee members refused to endorse the report and the NDP fought to have lump-sum payments and an apology included. Thus, the final version represents a compromise on the part of opposition members who, despite their political differences, agreed that the issue must be brought before the public in the House of Commons.[48] The committee relied upon the comprehensive reports submitted by the AFN and the Canadian Bar Association, and made clear the relative weight it accorded the testimonies of survivors and others who spoke, compared to that of the minister:

> The Committee took particular note, in formulating the recommenda-
> tions below, of the written and oral evidence of the former students and
> the representatives of former students and survivor organizations re-
> garding their personal experiences in the residential schools and in the
> Indian Residential School Resolution Canada ADR process. The wit-
> nesses were compelling for their candour and integrity about their ex-
> periences as inmates in the residential school system and fair, frank and
> persuasive on matters of public policy ... The Committee took particular
> note, in formulating the recommendations below, of the written and oral
> evidence of the Minister ... The evidence was contradictory with respect
> to financial and case-resolution performance numbers of the Indian
> Residential School Resolution Canada ADR process ... More discon-
> certing, however, the Minister's evidence was unapologetic and self-
> congratulatory with respect to both the underlying framework and the
> results of the ADR process. It disclosed her apparent disconnectedness
> from the experience of the survivor witnesses, for whom she has a par-
> ticular duty of care and to whom she is not listening.[49]

The report also concluded that the ADRP was "strikingly disconnected from the so-called pilot projects that preceded it," that it used "a model of

dispute resolution that ... revictimize[d] former students," that the application process "impose[d] an egregious burden of proof on the appli-
cants," that the consultation process was inadequate, that the program was
too exclusionary and too slow, and that compensation was insufficient –
"an arbitrary administrative solution that is subject to political whim."
Equally importantly, the committee said that "former students do not trust
the process."[50] The report was concurred in the House on 12 April 2005.
That such a strong condemnation of the program was now a matter of
public record put the government under increasing pressure to respond
substantively to the criticisms levelled against it.

In May 2005, as the governing Liberals clung to power with the threat
of a non-confidence vote looming, the AFN and Inuit and Métis organizations prepared for a policy retreat with Cabinet that came out of Prime
Minister Paul Martin's Canada-Aboriginal Peoples Roundtable commitments to develop a new, transformative relationship with First Nations.
The agenda involved discussions on housing, health care, and education.
Expectations were running high that a major announcement would also
be made regarding changes to the government's handling of residential
school claims. On 12 May, the Supreme Court rejected Canada's appeal of
the *Cloud* class-action lawsuit, clearing the way for it to proceed. The decision significantly increased the government's legal risk regarding IRS
claims.[51]

Thus, there was every indication that the Cabinet retreat would mark
a major turning point on the IRS issue. On 14 May, the *Toronto National
Post* reported that NDP MP Pat Martin "anticipates a potential $1-billion-
plus announcement from the Liberals within days that would offer one-
time lump sum compensation payments to all 87,500 former students of
Indian residential schools."[52] On 27 May, the *Vancouver Sun* stated that, at
the upcoming Cabinet retreat, a political accord would be signed, by which
"Ottawa will attempt to defuse anger over its approach to compensating
survivors of physical and sexual abuse at residential schools via a commitment to work with the AFN on a proposal for lump sum payments to all
former students ... a truth-telling commission ... [and] a formal apology
for the sorry chapter in Canadian history."[53]

On 30 May 2005, with media gathered to record the ritual, the Government of Canada and the Assembly of First Nations announced that they
had reached a political agreement regarding the residential schools issue.

The event was solemnized symbolically in two ways, the smoking of a peace pipe and the signing of an agreement in which both parties "are committed to reconciling the residential schools tragedy in a manner that respects the principles of human dignity and promotes transformative change." Furthermore, the parties "recognize[d] that the current ADR process does not fully achieve reconciliation between Canada and the former students of residential schools."[54] The immediate action on compensation that some had anticipated was not forthcoming; instead, Canada announced that it was appointing the Hon. Mr. Frank Iacobucci, former Supreme Court judge, as the federal representative tasked with negotiating with all parties and making recommendations to Cabinet by 31 March 2006. According to Minister McLellan, Ottawa was taking this action in response to the work of the AFN, which had been "instrumental in helping to highlight the need to recognize the residential school experience of all former students." Canada acknowledged that, "over the last year, advocacy from many sources, most notably from the Assembly of First Nations, has brought into focus the need to recognize the adverse impacts of the Indian residential school system."[55]

Given the legal and political complexities involved, the choice to appoint a negotiator rather than to proceed with immediate action was perhaps predictable, as was the fact that the announcement met with mixed response. Not surprisingly, both the AFN and the National Consortium of Residential School Survivors' Counsel welcomed the appointment.[56] However, two grassroots survivors' groups, the Indian Residential School Survivors Society and the National Residential School Survivors' Society, issued a joint press release saying that they were "very disappointed that Survivors will have to wait even longer to start receiving compensation" and that "the much-hyped and eagerly anticipated announcement ... failed to formally recognize the suffering of Survivors across Canada by not delivering a comprehensive compensation package."[57] The organizations were concerned that survivors whose expectations had been raised would suffer negative impacts as a result of more delay.

The political accord also received mixed reviews in the national media. It is important to note that some of the coverage presented a sympathetic view, profiling survivors' stories. However, other articles were unsympathetic or even hostile. On 31 May 2005, the front page of the conservative

Toronto National Post declared "Billions for Natives." The lead story played to Canadians who were resistant to providing a lump-sum payment to each person who attended a residential school, believing that only sexual and physical abuse warranted compensation:

> The accord ... marks a significant departure from Ottawa's long-held stance that it would not pay compensation to any of the 86,000 former residential school students who were unable to demonstrate they suffered concrete physical or sexual abuse ... After a ceremony at the national press theatre that began with an aboriginal elder passing around a "reconciliation pipe" to Mr. Fontaine, Ms. McLellan, Justice Minister Irwin Cotler and Indian Affairs Minister Andy Scott, Mr. Fontaine extolled it as a historic and "healing" moment that commits the government politically to begin negotiating many of the key demands contained in a recent report by the AFN ... The key players in the legal talks will be the AFN, the lawyers for the former students, including the legal consortium that is conducting a national multi-billion-dollar class action ... as well as lawyers for the defendant churches that ran most of the schools.[58]

Don Martin, an editorialist in the same newspaper, viewed the accord as simply one more example of how effectively First Nations leaders had learned to "extort" money from the federal government with the threat of political embarrassment. According to his account, Chief Phil Fontaine threatened to withdraw from the upcoming high-profile Cabinet policy retreat unless significant progress was made on the IRS issue. As a result, "a full retreat on settlement policy and a compensation resolution with a potentially massive price tag were rolled out yesterday to the triumphant smoking of a peace pipe for the cameras. Retired Supreme Court Justice Frank Iacobucci was appointed to drag out, oops, continue negotiations for a final compensation package scheme with a multitude of class-action lawyers. Gosh. More legal wrangling for another 10 months. Just what a process already overwhelmed with too many lawyers needs while clients die off at a rate of five victims per day."[59]

In the *Toronto Globe and Mail*, national columnist Jeffrey Simpson's condemnation was even more cutting. He claimed that, by appointing Justice Iacobucci, the federal government essentially threw up its hands and opened its pocketbook ... abandon[ing] important principles ... on which it had based previous positions – notably that not every Indian who ever attended a residential school deserved payment ... The Chrétien government had created a $250-million healing fund for communities ... The government also issued a statement of reconciliation and acknowledged responsibility. This wasn't apparently enough. The government has now committed the country to some sort of "apology." In addition, there will be some kind of "truth and reconciliation" process. Ottawa had previously resisted both ideas ... The alternative dispute resolution process recognized that not all residential school students were treated the same ... These judgments must not be examined in the light of what was thought appropriate at the time. They must be calculated and analyzed by today's standards – the classic "presentism" in historical analysis, whereby yesterday's events are viewed exclusively through today's prism. That kind of analysis, deeply contested by many professional historians, has also been resisted by Ottawa and some courts. Not any more.[60]

These particular media accounts provide some insight into the rationale behind the criticism of group reparations and a truth and reconciliation commission. They chastise the government for "backtracking" on a previous policy that rejected group reparation payments based on the dubious argument that perhaps not all students had a negative experience at school. They reject any notion that survivors should be compensated according to contemporary standards of acceptable human behaviour toward children, decrying the so-called presentist agenda of manipulative Native leaders and their supporters. There is no sense of civic responsibility to compensate for bad government policy in its own right, an ethical stance that makes irrelevant whether or not any one individual had a harmful experience at a residential school.

The tone of the articles regarding the use of Indigenous diplomatic protocols is equally revealing. The *National Post* lead story uses distancing quotation marks to refer to "an aboriginal elder passing around a 'reconciliation pipe,'" and Don Martin describes the announcement of the political accord as being "rolled out yesterday to the triumphant smoking of a peace pipe for the cameras." The writers insinuate that such ceremonies are not to be taken seriously but are simply a theatrical display performed for the media. They are not interested in understanding why the pipe ceremony is being held. Rather, much like their colonial ancestors, they dismiss it out of hand.

Lessons from the Alternative Dispute Resolution Program Controversy

On 23 November 2005, an agreement-in-principle on a comprehensive compensation package for IRS survivors was announced, and the negotiated Indian Residential Schools Settlement Agreement was finalized in 2006 and subsequently approved in all Canadian court jurisdictions in 2007.[61] What lessons can be learned from the ADRP controversy? The conflict over the program played out at various levels – in communities and survivors' gatherings, in policy consultation meetings between government officials, lawyers, and survivor advisory groups, and finally in high-level political negotiations that eventually played out on Parliament Hill. The government vision of reconciliation was primarily designed to achieve legal certainty by settling litigation claims in a program based on tort law and administered in a neutral adjudication process. In calling for a broader, more holistic restorative approach, survivors, Native leaders, and settler politicians and groups subscribed to an Indigenous vision of reconciliation. This vision was articulated in the call for group reparation payments, an apology from the prime minister, and a truth and reconciliation commission – all of which were deeply important to many survivors.

As we have seen, the ADRP was limited in its capacity to address the concerns expressed by Chief Robert Joseph and other witnesses at the parliamentary committee hearings. Even if claims are "resolved," if we fail to restore the humanity to our relationship and ensure that Indigenous peoples feel that justice has been done according to their criteria, how are we any closer to the healing and reconciliation we say we are seeking? Chief Joseph understood the symbolic power of ritual as he appeared before the standing committee in his ceremonial robe. Both government and Indigenous politicians invoked ritual and history in the public ceremony that gave legitimacy to the settlement agreement – the smoking of the peace pipe, the signing of the document. Moreover, the committee minutes reveal the power of story – the testimony of residential school survivors – to move us even in the midst of political machinations and legal concerns. Although media coverage indicates that some segments of the Canadian public are a long way from agreeing that truth telling and reconciliation are necessary, the response of the standing committee to survivor testimonies marks a pedagogical moment. Reconciliation as envisioned in the Alternative Dispute Resolution Program was inherently flawed, representing a regifting – a new variation on the peacemaker myth that promised to bring neutral justice to Indians in order to save or heal them. Like the peacemakers of the past, government officials did not really listen to Indigenous visions of law, peace, and justice. Rather, they created legalistic, bureaucratic solutions to IRS claims that simply replicated colonial power relations in a new form of violence. In essence, they fashioned a strange hybrid model of reconciliation that reflected the Western capacity for separating rational interests from the emotional/somatic, experiential engagement required to restore human dignity. This model's imperative to manage legal risk and implement policy through bureaucratic practice failed to address the importance of restitution, truth telling, and apology, which recognizes the dignity of people who have suffered traumatic harm.

In the midst of political controversy, all those involved invoked myth, ritual, and history to legitimize their visions of reconciliation, whether in public forums, in the formal setting of House of Commons committee meetings, or in the media. The controversy over the ADRP also reveals the power of survivor testimonies to break through the silence of our denial, compelling us to listen in ways that support truth telling – the restorying of Indigenous-settler history. The various remedies put forward by all parties to address the IRS legacy provide insight into the complex challenges we face in attempting to transcend cycles of violence even as we live within them.

5

Indigenous Diplomats
Counter-Narratives of Peacemaking

REFLECTIONS

Ironically, I have come to the Canadian War Museum in Ottawa seeking peace. That is, I am curious to see how Indigenous peoples' long history of diplomacy, law, and peacemaking is portrayed in Canada's national museum dedicated to commemorating Canada's role in war and peacekeeping at home and abroad. I am mindful of John Ralston Saul's question "Where did the concept of peace-keeping come from?"[1] He argues that the real roots of Canadian peacemaking are Indigenous and that Native leaders over the past four hundred years have consist-ently offered a vision of reconciliation to Canadians that is based on respectful coexistence and just relationships but that "we just don't listen."[2] My own view is that, in this country's national historical narrative, not only have settler Can-adians ignored this reality but we have appropriated the role and identity of the peacemaker as integral to our own version of colonial history. We have mytholo-gized the settler role in treaty making and nation building to reassure ourselves of our peaceful intentions, effectively masking the underlying violent consequences of our actions. Yet, even as I challenge the settler peacemaker myth, I find it harder to disown this heroic archetype than I had imagined.

Upon entering the exhibition hall, I look through the first gallery, titled "Battleground," which documents the sophisticated strategic manoeuvres and weapons used in pre-contact Aboriginal warfare. The Iroquois, who have long been portrayed in Canadian history as fierce warriors, figure prominently in the display, which features a reconstructed pre-contact Iroquois palisade. In the post-contact period, Indigenous peoples are described as strategically important military allies for either the French or British as empires clashed during the Seven Years' War. One exhibit features a French soldier and his Native ally. A plaque entitled

"Peace and Security" commemorates the Great Peace of Montreal in 1701, nego-tiated between the Iroquois League and the French. The Battle of the Plains of Abraham, the American Revolution, and the War of 1812 are highlighted as defin-ing moments in Canadian history, as are the Riel Rebellions and the role of the Métis in Western resistance. Throughout the displays, the stories of individual chiefs and warriors are juxtaposed with those of various colonial officials, em-phasizing that Indigenous peoples were skilled warriors and military allies who made a significant contribution to Canada's war history in the colonial period. Subsequent galleries pick up this theme, noting that, despite the high number of Native soldiers who served with distinction in both world wars, First Peoples were ultimately disappointed that the democratic ideals they had fought for failed to translate into fair treatment and equal opportunity back home in Canada in the post-war period.

Despite the fact that considerable effort has been made to include Indigen-ous history and honour veterans in the museum's exhibits, somehow Native peoples remain peripheral players in the master Canadian narrative. Certain stereotypes are still reinforced – the savage warrior or the faithful ally. As the history of Canada's wars and peacekeeping unfolds in the post-war years, Indigen-ous peoples gradually disappear from view. A gallery entitled "A Violent Peace" highlights the evolution of Canada's international peacekeeping role, which is said to have begun in the 1950s, seemingly devoid of any historical context.[3] I think about the great gap that still exists in the public's consciousness with regard to Indigenous peoples' history of diplomacy, law, and peacemaking, and about the consequences of that gap.

As I leave the museum, I note that a series of questions are posed, designed to encourage thoughtful reflection and action – What do you think? What do you fear? What do you hope? What will you do? There are inviting spaces for people to write their thoughts, and pre-addressed postcards to various political leaders, government officials, and non-government organizations make it easy for people to share their opinions, ideas, and calls for action. From a pedagogical perspective, I am impressed that the immediacy of the museum experience and the emotions this engenders are linked to the concept of taking action. From a personal per-spective, I am shaken by the sheer immensity of empire's destructive forces over the course of human history. Is it feasible to believe that the West and we as set-tlers are really capable of learning from Indigenous visions of law and peace without reappropriating and perverting them yet again? Most Canadians don't even know this history. How do we avoid the token adaptation of Indigenous legal traditions? My gut instinct and experience tells me that the answers lie partly in taking responsibility for our own decolonizing education when we are invited into Indigenous pedagogical space.

History from the Other's Side: Indigenous Visions of Law and Peace

> Throughout the treaty literature, Indians insist on acts of commitment from their treaty partners – signs that human beings, in a world of diversity and conflict, can learn to trust each other. Smoking the pipe of peace, taking hold of a treaty partner by the hand, exchanging hostages, and presenting valuable gifts were just some of the ways human beings could demonstrate their steadfast commitment to upholding their treaty relationships.
>
> – ROBERT A. WILLIAMS JR., *LINKING ARMS TOGETHER*

> On September 5, 1876, Lt. Governor Alexander Morris arrived at Fort Pitt to continue Treaty 6 discussions. The people gathered there included some Cree and Saulteaux known as the River People, as well as some nearby Dene. Unlike the Cree who signed treaty at Fort Carleton, many River People were not Christians. In the area around Fort Pitt, some chiefs such as *wihkasko-kiseyin,* had adopted Christianity, whereas others wanted to keep their traditional lifestyle, centred on the buffalo ... Morris provides more details about *wihkasko-kiseyin*'s actions and words during the signing: "Placing one hand over my heart and the other hand over his own, he said: May the white man's blood never be spilt on this earth ... When I hold your hand and touch your heart, let us be as one."
>
> – NEAL MCLEOD, *CREE NARRATIVE MEMORY*[4]

> Eagle down is sacred among the Gitksan and Witsuwit'en peoples and is a symbol of peace. It is used, for example, to sanctify the beginning of our peacemaking process. In addition, eagle down is used ritually in our system of conflict resolution and mediation. Restitution and compensation are key features in any ceremony in which eagle down

is used. A prerequisite in any peacemaking process is the willingness of the parties to make peace and to commit themselves to keep the peace "until the heart is satisfied." It is a living process. It's an ideal. The Gitksan and Witsuwit'en have yet to use eagle down in their dealings with the Crown in Canada. The Gitksan and Witsuwit'en have been waiting almost two centuries to make peace with the Crown ... We have kept the eagle down for thousands of years because it works. Eagle down is our law.

– FOREWORD, MAS GAK (DON RYAN),
IN ANTONIA MILLS, *EAGLE DOWN IS OUR LAW*[5]

The first of the three quotes above comes from Lumbee legal scholar Robert A. Williams Jr.'s *Linking Arms Together,* in which he deconstructs Western interpretations of North American treaty-making history to reveal Indigenous visions of law and peace during the Encounter era in what is now the northeastern United States and Canada. For Indigenous peoples throughout the region and beyond, culturally specific laws expressed in diverse languages through oratory and peacemaking ceremonial practices established trust between treaty partners. The second quote, from Cree scholar Neal McLeod, describes how the powerful Cree chief Mistahima-skwa (Big Bear), who wanted to preserve the old ways, was excluded from Treaty 6 negotiations, which were conducted in his absence by Wihkasko-kiseyin (Old Man Sweetgrass). Although the latter had adopted Christianity, according to Morris' account, he still used Cree peacemaking practices – the same taking of his treaty partner's hand that Williams describes – and invoked a language of kinship and alliance building: "When I hold your hand and touch your heart, let us be as one." The third quote comes from Gitxsan Mas Gak (Don Ryan), who explains how the eagle down ceremony is still used today to mediate conflict, provide restitution, and make peace among parties. He reminds us that the Gitxsan and Wet'suwet'en, who have always lived in the territory now known as British Columbia, have yet to make treaties with Canada. Together, these quotations demonstrate that, despite immense cultural and linguistic diversity, in different times and places across Turtle Island, Indigenous diplomacy, law, and peace-making practices share common spiritual and political philosophies and traditions that are well suited to resolving conflicts, building trust, making restitution, and facilitating peaceful coexistence.[6]

Readers may wonder how this treaty-making counter-narrative is relevant to truth and reconciliation processes generally, and more specifically with regard to the work of the Truth and Reconciliation Commission of Canada. For my purposes here, I focus on three interrelated principles in the TRC mandate. First, the mandate's preamble states that the TRC process itself is "a profound commitment to establishing new relationships embedded in mutual recognition and respect that will forge a brighter future." Second, one of the TRC's goals is to "promote awareness and public education of Canadians about the IRS system and its impacts."[7] Third, in exercising its powers, the commission "shall recognize the significance of Aboriginal oral and legal traditions."[8] As I point out in an earlier essay, "the critical question that lies ahead is this: how will the work of the TRC be conducted in ways that live up to the spirit and intent of these fundamental principles? ... For reconciliation to be an authentic truth-telling process, it must profoundly disturb a dominant culture history and mindset that 'misrecognizes' and disrespects the oral histories, cultures, and legal traditions of Indigenous peoples, including their histories of peacemaking ... The TRC must provide critical pedagogical space wherein Indigenous peoples reclaim and revitalize the cultures, laws, and histories that colonizers attempted to destroy in residential schools."[9]

An extensive survey of the history of Indigenous diplomacy, law, and peacemaking is beyond the scope of this study, and moreover, quite rightly belongs with Indigenous communities and scholars, but it is nevertheless necessary for settlers to educate ourselves about how the benevolent peacemaker myth has subsumed this history. To do so, we must first gain a sense of just how deeply Indigenous visions of law and peace differ from the colonial vision of law and order that came to dominate the nineteenth-century treaty-making process in Western Canada.

These conflicting visions played out in various ways on the prairies and in British Columbia, and they continue to influence the present. We see this most clearly in the current BC treaty process and in the courtroom where Indigenous history and law have been challenged in Aboriginal title and rights litigation. But the TRC now has an important opportunity to help Canadians understand that the recognition of Indigenous oral and legal traditions is not only integral to creating ethical truth telling and authentic reconciliation processes but to the restorying of Canada's national narrative as well. At the same time, this restorying has important implications for Native communities as they recover from the impacts of colonialism, including the loss of languages and cultures engendered by the Indian residential school system. Thus, the reclaiming of history and the renewal of their customary laws and cultural practices is essential to their self-determination, nation building, and community decolonization.

As Indigenous peoples construct a counter-narrative history of treaties and peacemaking from the Encounter era to the present, drawing upon their own epistemologies, they also provide a corrective to the peacemaker myth. In emphasizing the peacemaking role of Indigenous diplomats, I do not aim to essentialize or romanticize them. The historical record shows clearly that intertribal warfare and family conflicts as well as clashes with settlers occurred on a regular basis. But what remain consistent over time are distinctly Indigenous approaches to creating just and peaceful relationships that are rooted in spiritual and pedagogical practices of storytelling, rhetorical oratory, gift exchange, and ceremony. Historian Arthur J. Ray makes this point in his study of Cree trade and treaty history in Western Canada in which he "emphasize[s] the continuity that existed between the diplomatic and economic protocols that the Cree and their neighbors established with the Crown through the Hudson's Bay Company and thought they had continued through treaties with Canada in the 1870's."[10] Williams also makes a powerful case for studying the long history of Indigenous diplomacy in its own right because its unique and rich legacy holds teachings for finding peaceful solutions to today's global conflicts.[11] These teachings can also inform the design of truth-telling and reconciliation processes as part of the greater decolonization project. Is this simply utopian wishful thinking, or is it a viable strategy?

In an assessment of the current BC treaty process, environmental studies scholar Ravi de Costa argues that, though he agrees with Williams' thesis in principle, he is not confident that historical Indigenous visions of law and peace can be used in contemporary treaty making. De Costa points out that the treaty process itself is deeply flawed and that within Indigenous communities themselves, "structures of legitimacy and authority are radically different than they were in previous centuries."[12] He says that the sheer complexity of modern treaty negotiations, which involve legal and technical documents, is a barrier to incorporating Indigenous legal traditions:

> In British Columbia discussions at treaty tables provide neither Native nor settler communities with models of exemplary behavior, other than perhaps the common-sense principle that it is good for people to talk to one another. In fact, the new treaty negotiations are highly technical blueprints for future systems of rule, the codification of exemplary be-havior rather than its performance. It could be no other way. Compared with the early colonial examples cited by Robert Williams ... both "sides" are far less homogeneous than they were. The locus of authority in each case has been transformed such that when elders perform handshakes today there is as much skepticism as celebration. The hope that senior figures might enact a performance (or text) that is wholly representative, widely supported, and yet aspirational seems utopian amid the complex-ity of modern life ... Shorn of their rhetorical boilerplate and corporate dressage, modern treaties look nothing like the indigenous vision retold by Williams.[13]

Like Andrew Woolford, he views the quest for certainty in treaty making as problematic and concludes that "it makes more sense to encourage a permanent culture of negotiation" than to seek for certainty.[14] Although I agree with de Costa's overall critique of the BC treaty process, I question whether the use of Indigenous diplomatic and legal traditions and peace-making practices should be so readily dismissed as utopian thinking.

De Costa assumes that, though Indigenous legal traditions may have been well suited to simpler times when both Indigenous and settler societies were more homogeneous, they cannot be utilized in more complex con-temporary contexts. This is at odds with an extensive body of revisionist treaty literature, including Williams' work. These authors argue that, in both past and present, Indigenous-settler relations were incredibly complex, reflecting a multiplicity of cultures, languages, and conflicting ideas within both communities about how best to achieve peaceful relations. The greater homogeneity that de Costa says existed in earlier times was never the reality. Writing about the problems associated with framing

Indigenous knowledge as "traditional" knowledge, Anishinaabe scholar Perry Shawana notes, "the 'tradition-based' or 'traditional' language used in domestic and international intellectual property regimes has tended to result in the treatment of Indigenous knowledge as though it were static, developed in the distant past and handed down from generation to generation. One assumption derived from this line of thinking is that Indigenous peoples are not actively engaged in the discovery and creation of new knowledge. Nothing could be further from the truth."[15]

Moreover, Mas Gak's observations about the continuing relevance of Gitxsan law and my own experience with its contemporary application at the Hazelton feast suggests that Indigenous legal traditions and peace-making practices are dynamic and flexible, with the capacity to continue adapting to new circumstances despite the ravages of colonialism.

Although de Costa concludes that "the memory of earlier treaties as moments of recognition and esteem might still be a source of inspiration ... it can no longer be an example," I would argue that the making of space for Indigenous legal traditions in current treaty making would provide precisely the sort of principled framework required for creating the culture of negotiation that he advocates.[16] Interestingly, de Costa alludes to this himself: "In light of the democratic imperatives of decolonization, I concur with the Canadian anthropologist Michael Asch who ... has argued that treaty making as consent-seeking should be 'an uninterrupted process of reciprocal gifts, which effects the transition from hostility to alliance, from anxiety to confidence, and from fear to friendship.'"[17] In referring to reciprocal gifting and emphasizing the importance of building trust and constructive relationships, Asch is essentially calling for a treaty-making process that is grounded in Indigenous approaches. But oddly, de Costa appears not to make this connection. Ultimately, because he falls into the trap of thinking of Indigenous visions of law and peace as static and essentially "frozen in time" rather than as dynamic living traditions, he fails to see their continuity despite colonial disruptions or to perceive their ongoing relevance for today.

Here, it is helpful to look more closely at North American treaty literature. I draw on a historiography that reflects the geographical realities of various Indigenous nations whose territories extended across what would later become the Canada-US border. While keeping in mind that the treaty histories of Canada and the United States evolved quite differently in many respects, multidisciplinary scholars from both sides of the border are now turning their attention to the importance of transnational analyses of American and Canadian treaties with Indigenous peoples. For example, in a recently published multidisciplinary volume *The Power of Promises*, American historian Alexandra Harmon points out that,

> when scanning the historical background and subsequent fates of particular Indian treaties, a wide-angle geographical lens is also useful. Certainly, if treaties made in the northern United States are in the foreground, Canada should be within the range of vision. Not only are the practices of early English colonists and the Royal Proclamation of 1763 part of Canadian history as well as U.S. history, but also and more important, Indian policies in British-ruled Canada continued to affect American expansion even after the United States won independence in 1783. Well into the nineteenth century, Britons carried on with colonial activities in places that would ultimately belong to the United States, including Washington Territory. Consequently, some contemporary American and Canadian tribes or indigenous nations include people whose ancestors dealt with more than one colonial government ... And when the two nation-states finally agreed to divide that region roughly in equal parts at the forty-ninth parallel, the boundary they drew did not follow the boundaries of indigenous peoples' territories and movements.[18]

In a similar vein, critical race theorists and legal scholars have posited that imperial notions of race and culture transcended national borders as colonial administrators moved from one jurisdiction to another, exchanging ideas and developing practices that reinforced the particular "racial truths" of white superiority on a global scale.[19]

During the 1970s, revisionist studies began to emerge in the United States and Canada as Native people continued to articulate the spirit, meaning, and intent of treaties, diplomacy, and peacemaking from their own perspectives, and non-Native scholars explored new theories and methodologies in a reassessment of Indigenous peoples' role in the political, economic, and social relations of the new empire.[20] Earlier American and Canadian national histories that portrayed colonial officials as omnipotent actors were re-examined with a view to uncovering the complexity of early colonial relations in which all sides had various degrees of political agency. In rejecting the stereotypical themes of early historical writing that depicted Indigenous peoples as either savages without civilization or victims of colonial progress, these works reveal a rich oral and documentary archive in which they are full proactive participants in colonial diplomatic and political life.[21]

The Early "Middle Ground" of Northeastern North America

Indigenous diplomacy formed the foundations of a unique North American society, which American historian Richard White refers to as the "middle ground" – a polyglot meeting place, where interactions between Algonquians and Europeans were often violent but also "created new systems of meaning and exchange."[22] White writes that the middle ground

> was not a creation of European savants or distant imperial administrators
> ... Because neither side could gain their ends through force, Europeans
> and Indians had to attempt to understand the world and reasoning of
> others ... Particularly in diplomatic councils, the middle ground was a
> realm of constant invention, that once agreed upon by all sides, became
> convention. The central and defining aspect of the middle ground was
> a willingness born of necessity, for one set of people to justify their ac-
> tions in terms of what they perceived to be their partners' cultural
> premises. In seeking to persuade others to act, they sought out congru-
> ence, either perceived or actual, between the two cultures. The congru-
> ences arrived at often seemed – and indeed, were – the results of
> misunderstandings or accidents.[23]

White's middle ground emerged in a particular place and time – the Great Lakes region prior to 1812 – after which it disappeared as the balance of power shifted. But at this juncture, he says, power relations in the region were balanced, agreement was reached through consensus, and mutually agreed-upon conventions were created to establish and maintain treaty relationships. Treaties formed the framework for undertaking intercultural negotiations in which power relations and representational authority were key determining factors in establishing, maintaining, and repairing relationships.

The Encounter era literature with regard to the Iroquois Confederacy is also particularly interesting. Williams suggests that, because the Iroquois capacity to influence treaty negotiations was especially strong during this period, colonial officials were compelled to negotiate with Iroquois diplomats on relatively equitable terms: "No one group's narratives occupied a privileged dominant position ... Throughout the treaty literature of the period ... indigenous and European can be found negotiating with each other at arm's length about competing visions of peace and justice that would govern their relations ... These groups, more often than our histories might suggest, agreed to create multicultural alliances of law and peace."[24] These alliances, Williams suggests, created a "window of opportunity" wherein a new North American society was profoundly influenced by Iroquois law, diplomacy, and peacemaking. Treaties are paradigms for multicultural connections that are expressed metaphorically through story, ceremony, and ritual.

Here, it is instructive to look briefly at the Iroquoian vision of law and peace. In a study of Iroquois diplomacy in the treaties of the Six Nations, Francis Jennings points out that, although earlier scholars might have failed to recognize Indigenous law and governance systems, the "kings' agents in America knew how to distinguish between theory and practice. They understood very well that Indians were organized in communities, with functioning governments that exercised real powers of control over trade, territory, and military activity. These agents called the Indian governments 'nations' and made treaties with them. The treaty documents refute the no-true-government myth."[25] Thus, nation-to-nation treaty making between the Crown and various Indigenous nations contradicted the popular belief that Native peoples were uncivilized. Equally importantly, William Fenton, Michael K. Foster, and Daniel K. Richter emphasize the flexibility and adaptability of Iroquois diplomats, characteristics that they say continue into the present. Fenton argues that, "not only are key parts of the paradigm of condolence performed in some of the earliest treaties, but the negotiations are embellished by the metaphors in which the later [modern] ritual is couched."[26] Williams provides an example of this continuity, noting that, in 1988 at Geneva, an Iroquois diplomat gifted a wampum treaty belt to the United Nations Human Rights Commission Working Group on Indigenous Populations, which was drafting the UN Declaration on the Rights of Indigenous Peoples. In doing so, Williams writes, "the Iroquois were renewing a centuries-old indigenous North American legal tradition."[27]

In 1976, Foster interviewed Cayuga chief Jacob Thomas of Six Nations as part of his study on the function of wampum in treaty diplomacy; the interviews revealed that Thomas understood the meanings of various wampum belts and could recall the terms of past agreements. He also "had a detailed grasp of the procedures for conducting a council with White government officials ... [in which] one must be prepared to actually renew these agreements which, as far as the chiefs were concerned, were still in effect."[28] The Iroquois had protocols to establish and renew treaty relationships over time, which are reflected in the rituals and metaphors of the condolence ceremony: "We see this in the emphasis in council protocol upon clearing obstructions from the path, polishing the covenant chain, building up the council fire, and the procedures at the Wood's Edge. The metaphors of the fire, the path and the chain reveal ... the Iroquoian view [that] the alliance was naturally in a state of constant deterioration and in need of attention." The importance of renewal, within the context of structural continuity and change, is reflected not only within Iroquois society but in the relationships it established with colonial officials, who, with Western understandings of political protocols and law, viewed treaties as contracts that, once signed, remained in effect until specifically changed.[29]

Revisionist scholars attempt to understand how the treaty institution actually worked, and they recognize the significant influence of Iroquois political structures, language, ritual, and metaphor in colonial treaty diplomacy and negotiations: "Iroquois diplomats adapted the language and rituals of the Great Peace to create the protocol of intercultural diplomacy ... The projection of Great Peace ceremonial practices to Iroquoian-European diplomacy seems to have begun with the Mohawks ... in 1645. From that date forward, words of peace, rituals of condolence, and exchanges of gifts dominated the practice of European-Indian diplomacy in the Northeast."[30] Thus, we begin to see a very different picture of treaty making in northeastern North America – one that reveals the extent to which the condolence ceremony, wampum belts, the covenant chain, and the imagery of linking arms defined Encounter era diplomacy and treaty protocol.[31] Colonial officials were compelled to accommodate and adapt to Indigenous traditions. These scholarly studies provide a critical corrective to earlier historiographical writing. Works by Williams and others also mark a dramatic theoretical and methodological shift toward a much deeper understanding of Indigenous diplomats' motivations. Together, these scholars provide a different perspective on the history of Iroquois diplomacy, one that is far removed from the violent, dehumanizing myths and denigrating stereotypes. Thus, counter-narrative history sets the settler peacemaker myth on its head.

Although revisionists do not deny that trade and military alliances were important, they argue that Indigenous diplomacy was guided by a much deeper philosophical and spiritual vision of law and peace. They view Iroquois diplomacy as an extension of the philosophical and spiritual tenets and moral imperative set out by the prophet Deganawidah in the Great Law of Peace and enacted in the condolence ceremony. According to Williams, "the good news of Deganawidah's message envisioned a multicultural community of all peoples on earth, linked together under the sheltering branches of the Great Tree of Peace ... The sacred rituals of the Condolence Council ... thus became part of a diplomatic language that regarded the negotiation of treaties with different peoples as the fulfillment of a divine command ... Offering strings of wampum and performing other rituals of condolence as instructed by the prophet Deganawidah, Iroquois diplomats situated their treaty relations with each other in the realm of a transcendent, sacred vision of all humankind as one."[32]

American historian Matthew Dennis confronts the old image of the imperial Iroquois as savage warriors to suggest that "historians should attempt to shift the angle of vision and examine the view from Iroquoia in order to understand Iroquois culture and its deep appreciation of peace."[33] His cultural history concentrates on seventeenth-century relationships between the Iroquois, French, and Dutch. Iroquois diplomacy was conducted through the extension of kinship relations, and new people were brought into the longhouse as adopted family members. This was a natural consequence of extending the principles of the Great Law of Peace to outsiders. Dennis asserts that, ultimately, as the Iroquois were unable to create a lasting peace with the French, they adjusted their actions accordingly: "Holding firmly to the essence of Deganawidah's dream, and forging new mechanisms to make it manifest in their world, the Iroquois began to develop a new *foreign* policy. Accepting fictive, or symbolic, over literal kinship, and social separation rather than amalgamation, the Five Nations increasingly expected less of their allies, and sought more self-consciously to preserve their own autonomy."[34] Dennis suggests that Iroquois diplomats grew more cautious as they came to recognize that, though colonial officials participated in condolence protocols and ceremonies, they did not share the Iroquoian vision of law and peace.

Taiaiake Alfred's 1999 *Peace, Power, Righteousness* brings us full circle in our thinking about the continuing relevance of Iroquois diplomacy, when, as a Kanien'kehaka (Mohawk) scholar, he uses the structure of the condolence ceremony in his writing as a metaphor to guide the reader through a transformative process of acknowledging anger and loss, promoting healing and empowerment, and restoring clarity of reason and vision: "The Condolence ritual pacifies the minds and emboldens the hearts of mourners by transforming loss into strength. In Rotinohshonni culture, it is the essential means of recovering the wisdom seemingly lost with the passing of a respected leader. Condolence is the mourning of a family's loss by those who remain strong and clear-minded. It is a gift promising comfort, recovery of balance, and revival of spirit to those who are suffering."[35] Thus, he explores the themes of his book: the impacts of colonization, Indigenous political traditions and leadership, self-conscious traditionalism, and the rebuilding of Indigenous governance and self-determination. In doing so, he delivers a powerful message by drawing upon the traditions of a long line of diplomats who believed that "leadership consists in invoking the power of reason, and that the human capacity to achieve harmony is best developed through pacification and persuasion."[36] In Alfred's work, the condolence ceremony is invoked in a new literary form, thus reinforcing its adaptability over time.

In a reassessment of the Royal Proclamation of 1763, Anishinaabe legal scholar John Borrows rejects the conventional belief that it was created unilaterally by British colonial officials. Rather, he argues that Indigenous people played an active role in negotiating its ratification. He says that the proclamation can be fully understood only when juxtaposed with the Treaty of Niagara of 1764. It then becomes evident that the proclamation represents only one side of the story. It is simply the written text of a treaty that was negotiated between various nations, using Indigenous diplomatic practices: storytelling, gift giving, and wampum. Borrows points out that the subsequent narrow legal interpretation of the Royal Proclamation of 1763, which is seen to assert British sovereignty even as it required the Crown to make treaties, had significant material and social consequences for Indigenous nations. They themselves viewed the proclamation as the framework for an ongoing relationship that "mandates colonial non-interference in the land use and governments of First Nations ... [and] affirmed their powers of self-determination."[37] Given these differing inter-pretations, Indigenous-settler relations sometimes deteriorated into what Matthew Dennis describes as a "discourse of confusion."[38]

In later years, Indigenous peoples would find it increasingly difficult to make their voices heard or their history and presence visible as the set-tler version of history became the dominant storyline. But delving into this treaty literature reveals that Indigenous diplomacy, law, and peace-making practices, often described by colonial treaty negotiators as "exotic or quaint customs," were actually expressions of a profound spirit-ual, philosophical, and political understanding of how to make peace. As Borrows reminds us, "Indigenous law originates in the political, eco-nomic, spiritual, and social values expressed through the teachings and behaviour of knowledgeable and respected individuals and elders. These principles are enunciated in the rich stories, ceremonies, and traditions within First Nations. Stories express the law in Aboriginal communities, since they reflect the accumulated wisdom and experience of First Nations conflict resolution ... They can be communicated in a way that reveals deeper principles of order and disorder, and thereby serve as sources of normative authority in dispute resolution."[39]

Fulfilling Indigenous visions of law and peace involved resolving con-flicts by establishing and maintaining socio-political relationships of mutual trust and benefit using metaphorical storytelling, ceremonies, and symbolic acts such as smoking the pipe, taking a treaty partner's hand, spreading eagle down or feathers, feasting, and gifting. This approach, which required participants to engage each other as human beings capable of rational thought, emotional connection, and ethical behaviour, was at odds with the colonizer's vision of establishing peaceful relations by im-posing neutral British law and order.

The "Middle Ground" Moves West
Building on White's thesis in her study of Indigenous-settler relations in Western Canada, Sarah Carter argues that, during the early years of the

prairie settlement period, there was potential to create a new Western version of the middle ground. She points to several conducive factors: the Manitoba Act was supposed to accommodate the Métis, and treaties were being negotiated with the stated intent, if not the reality, of sharing lands and resources in an emerging agricultural economy. Moreover, through intermarriage between the growing settler population and Native or Métis people, technologies and cultural customs were freely exchanged.[40] But unlike the Iroquois of the Encounter era, Prairie Indigenous groups were already suffering from the devastating consequences of colonialism and the decline of their traditional economy. Consequently, they were more vulnerable to the coercive measures and divisive negotiation strategies employed by government officials. Moreover, it would be a mistake to think that Encounter era colonial officials were more enlightened than their nineteenth-century counterparts with regard to understanding or appreciating Indigenous diplomacy, law, and peacemaking. According to Williams, from the earliest days of encounter,

> Europeans, with their attitudes of cultural superiority, regarded the drawn-out naming ceremonies, rituals, and gift giving that Indians routinely performed at treaty councils as time-consuming diversions from the conduct of vital matters of trade, diplomacy, and survival on the colonial frontier. The European scribes who produced the voluminous treaty literature of the Encounter era rarely commented on the visions that animated their treaty partners in giving a tribal name to a colonial official, smoking of the calumet of peace, or presenting a gift of eagle feathers. For Europeans, these were the "usual ceremonies" that had to be tolerated ... But for Indians, the relationships established by both sides according to this language of connection constituted what has been called the "sinews" of their diplomacy. In American Indian visions of law and peace, the connections sustained by kinship terms, name-titles, and rituals were what held treaty relationships together.[41]

As we have seen, during the prairie settlement period, Morris and his fellow treaty negotiators, along with various Indian Affairs bureaucrats, had similar attitudes and viewed treaty making simply as the legal mechanism required to access Indigenous lands for settlement purposes. In undertaking treaty negotiations, they went through the ceremonial motions required of them but with no apparent understanding of, or appreciation for, these sinews of diplomacy.

Despite the ravages of disease, starvation, and the disappearance of the buffalo, Prairie Indigenous peoples were astute diplomats, able to negotiate provisions, such as that relating to education, which did not exist in earlier treaties. In British Columbia, Indigenous diplomats representing the multiplicity of nations west of the Rockies demanded, albeit unsuccessfully, that government officials negotiate treaties that would protect their lands and resources from settler encroachment. In some cases, these demands came in the form of petitions addressed to the British monarch and written on behalf of tribal groups by missionary or legal allies who had developed strong relationships with Native political leaders:

> In British Columbia from the 1860s on, various groups, denied any other mode of redress short of making war, wrote petitions and sent delegations to local, provincial, federal, and imperial officials and, significantly, to the King himself. Although signatories to petitions did not necessarily appreciate the subtle legal differences between a legislature and a court, or between an elected and an appointed official, they definitely made a distinction between the Crown and the local authorities, and between those who represented the Crown and those who did not. This was largely because it was clear to them that colonial legislatures and, later, provincial premiers did not have their best interests at heart. "The Queen," on the other hand, had always been represented to them as the guarantor of their rights.[42]

Once the BC First Nations were pushed onto small reserves, with no redress for lands illegally taken from them, their lives, much like those of their Prairie counterparts, became increasingly circumscribed by repressive legislation that prohibited the very ceremonial activities that expressed their laws and reaffirmed their spiritual connection to their homelands. Nevertheless, Indigenous peoples persisted, and though their sociopolitical, legal, and governance systems have been weakened by colonialism, they still exist, evident in the stories and ceremonies that have survived into the present.

Broken Treaty Promises, Residential Schools, and Indigenous Reclaiming

If the literature on Iroquois diplomacy provides some insight as to how Indigenous traditions might help to create a more just and peaceful co-existence among diverse peoples, the Blackfoot Treaty 7 elders describe the obstacles that stand in the way. Encounter-era treaty making illustrates how trust forms the basis for a principled relationship; the numbered treaties show us how colonial practices broke that trust. The controversy surrounding the history of Treaty 7 is representative of what happens when opposite visions collide: law and peace versus law and order. We know that Indigenous peoples and governments have conflicting ideas about the spirit and intent of the numbered treaties. The consequences of this debate, however, go far beyond the pages of academic publications or legal arguments in courtrooms. They play out in the hearts, minds, and lives of the Blackfoot, who continue to inhabit their traditional territories in Alberta.

The elders tell us what went wrong in the treaty relationship they established with Canada, of how treaties that were negotiated according to their diplomatic protocols were subsequently dishonoured as Indian policy and legislation overrode the spirit and intent of the treaties. In publishing a Blackfoot history of Treaty 7, the elders want Canadians to hear the whole story about the negotiations that occurred at Blackfoot Crossing in 1877. Contemporary conflicts over treaty, land, and resource rights are based on our historical understanding or misunderstanding of the treaties. The Blackfoot elders emphasize that their nation signed a peace treaty with the British Crown. Peigan elder Tom Yellowhorn sums up the feelings of the Peigan, who are part of the Blackfoot Confederacy:

> The Peigan's initial enthusiasm for the peace treaty grew into bitterness when the seriousness with which they took the agreement was later not reciprocated by the government. In subsequent years, the Peigan were "sorry that they made this treaty." For the Peigan the ceremony of peace-making was solemn, undertaken with much gravity, especially when they smoked the peace pipe ... [We thought] that the Queen "was going to treat us good" ... [but] in the wake of the treaty "they put up the Indian Act to punish Indian people and protect the White man." In fact, the Indian Act of 1876 had already been enacted.[43]

One of these punishments was the breaking of treaty promises made to the Blackfoot and other Indigenous nations with regard to education. The promised on-reserve schools were quickly phased out in favour of residential schools, a decision made unilaterally by Indian Affairs bureaucrats, without the knowledge or consent of their treaty partners. Consequently, thousands of small children were shipped off to schools at great distances from their homes and families. Forbidden to speak their language and deprived of their cultural traditions, many forgot how to be Blackfoot-speaking people, or Siksikaitsitapi.

In *Blackfoot Ways of Knowing*, Blackfoot scholar and former IRS student Betty Bastien describes the many forms of overt and symbolic violence to which her people were subjected after the buffalo disappeared from the prairies. Like several other scholars who have examined the systematic government policies and bureaucratic practices designed to coerce Indigenous peoples into assimilating into mainstream Canadian society, she concludes that the severe disruption of Blackfoot lifeways, kinship ties, and spiritual connection to the land constituted genocide:

> The concrete relationships of the *Niitsitapi* [all Indigenous peoples] are to the land, animals, time, stars, sun, and to each other, but hundreds of years of Europeanizing history have colonized these relationships and they have become abstractions. Detachment and disassociation are evident in the despiritualization of these concepts and relationships. They make genocide possible and allow denial afterward ... Abstracted definitions as used in laws, policies, schools, and social science theories legitimize the despiritualized perception of the natural world ... The colonizers who formulated racist theories and designed genocidal policies were and are detached from the conditions of Aboriginal people. Such distance is a characteristic of ordinary genocide ... Such acts of genocide [are] polite and clinical.[44]

For Bastien, reclaiming her own identity involves a deeply reflective, transformative pedagogical journey of coming to know Siksikaitsitapi, or Blackfoot, ways of understanding and experiencing the world. By reconnecting with the language, ceremonies, and stories of her people as taught by her elders, she learns about the strength of kinship alliances and the principles of reciprocity and interdependence that form the foundation of Blackfoot identity and culture. Bastien's journey is one example of the many ways in which Indigenous people are reclaiming and revitalizing their histories, languages, cultures, and laws through the practices of ceremony and storytelling.

Similarly, Neal McLeod documents a Cree counter-narrative history from treaties to the present. Cree narrative memory is the collective history of his own family and the Cree people as told through stories. McLeod explains that "Cree narrative memory emerges from the worldview and spirituality of the Cree people, and is grounded in the names of both ancestors and places ... Cree narrative memory is ongoing, and is sustained through relationships, respect and responsibility."[45] He describes the spatial and spiritual exile imposed upon those who attended residential schools, removed from their homeland and the families that sustained their spiritual and cultural well-being:

> Exile is both physical and spiritual; it is the move away from the familiar toward a new and alien space. This new space attempts to transform and mutate pre-existing narratives and social structures ... Spiritual exile was the internalization of being taken off the land. A central manifestation of this was the residential school system which was established as a way of "educating" and assimilating Indigenous people ... Instead of being taught by their old people, they were taught in an alien environment that attempted to strip away their dignity. The process amounted to cultural genocide. Once put away, in both a spiritual and spatial sense, many children never came "home." Instead, they spent their lives ensnared in alcoholism and other destructive behaviours.[46]

Like Bastien, McLeod sees the future of his people as rooted in the stories and ceremonies of the past not as a nostalgic, backward-looking longing for an irredeemable era but as a way of reconnecting with living Cree philosophy, epistemology, spirituality, law, and political traditions that are integral to sustaining Cree identity and well-being. These works reveal that the reclaiming of Indigenous history and culture is critical for individual and collective identity, and for Indigenous nation building. At the same time, because settlers have denied this history, particularly as it relates to lands and resources, some Indigenous nations have taken their history and law into Canadian courtrooms in an effort to protect their traditional territories.

Indigenous History and Law in the Courtroom

In British Columbia, Native peoples' long struggle for recognition of their rights has always been highly political, and there is no consensus as to the best course of action. Some nations are involved in the BC treaty process, whereas others reject it as imbued with fundamental political, legal, and socio-economic flaws. Aboriginal litigation has played a key role in BC with regard to unresolved historical claims. Within this context, it is important to consider how myth and history play out in the courtroom. British Columbia's 1991 *Delgamuukw* trial is one example of how Indigenous peoples have attempted to share their history with the courts. It also reveals, through Chief Justice Allan McEachern's judgment, the persistent strength of settler denial, replete with its own myths and rituals. The late Joseph Campbell wrote extensively about the hidden power of myth and ritual. He identifies four functions of myth in societies – mystical, cosmological, sociological, and pedagogical – and suggests that the sociological function, which "supports and validates a certain social order," now predominates in North America. Like David Kertzer, he asserts that myth is reinforced by ritual.[47] Rituals evoke the energy of myths, and their power compels us to behave and think accordingly. But the role of myth and ritual in political relations and legal institutions is not well understood.[48] Western rituals are often invisible to the public and simply taken for granted as customary practice. Campbell describes, for instance, the ritualized environment of the courtroom as public performance. The judge, dressed in a robe and armed with a gavel, is a visible, symbolic, and mythical representation of Western law.[49] Less visible are the ways in which law, embedded in a myth of neutrality, interprets history in the courts in ways that question Indigenous authenticity and deny or minimize the legitimacy of Indigenous knowledge systems, history, and law.

If we look at the *Delgamuukw* case as a representative example, we see more clearly how history and the law are implicated in the colonial project. Although many aspects of litigation are problematic, the adversarial process has precipitated the development of new theoretical frameworks and research methodologies in the discipline of history, resulting in new interpretations of the past. And Indigenous peoples themselves have been at the forefront of pushing these boundaries.⁵⁰ But *Delgamuukw* also demonstrates how difficult this endeavour has been and how high the cost for them, both in terms of legal risk and the human and financial resources required to engage in litigation.⁵¹ Nevertheless, the Gitxsan and Wet'suwet'en entered the courtroom hoping to educate the judge about their histories, laws, diplomatic protocols, and governance systems. As two nations asserting their jurisdictional authority over their unceded lands and resources, the Gitxsan and Wet'suwet'en took a great but calculated risk in adopting a litigation strategy. They brought their "treasure boxes of histories" – their *adaawk* and *kungax* – into a Western courtroom intending to express them in the usual way, through the stories, ceremonies, songs, and rituals of the feast hall. In doing so, they opened them up to settler scrutiny. Skanu'u (Ardythe Wilson) explained their reasons for doing so:

> There was great reluctance when we saw the history of the courts in our territories – we were always on the losing end. But in considering this situation, the Chiefs said, what other choice do we have? Even though they realized that this was a course of action that had to be taken, there was great uncertainty. We knew that in order for the courts to understand ... it was necessary for us to show them our histories, our laws, our practices, our customs, our obligations, our responsibilities. And in order for that to happen, we had to open up our Houses and our families to people who had no understanding or respect for who we are. I think what we dreaded most was what McEachern did.⁵²

In the Address of the Chiefs, delivered on 11 May 1987, Delgam Uukw, a Gitxsan chief, explained his view of history and law: "My power is carried in my House's histories, songs, dances and crests. It is recreated at the Feast when the histories are told, the songs and dances performed and the crests displayed ... In this way, the law, the Chief, the territory and the Feast become one."⁵³ There were clear indications during the course of the trial that this unorthodox and unprecedented approach presented a challenge for the judge, whose own legal training reflected totally different historical and legal cultural paradigms.

Justice McEachern's sense of history, law, and culture was firmly based in a Western colonial mindset that was ultimately impossible to dislodge. When elder Antgulilibix (Mary Johnson) wanted to sing a song – part of her House history – for the court, the judge preferred that it be written down because "to have witnesses singing songs in court, is ... not the proper way to approach the problem." Clearly uncomfortable with this breach of court decorum, he asked the plaintiffs' counsel to explain "why it is necessary to sing the song" and reminded him that "this is a trial, not a performance." In a final effort to dissuade the elder, McEachern claimed that, regardless, he would not hear her song: "I have a tin ear ... So it's not going to do any good to sing it to me."[54] The judge's intercultural deafness – his unwillingness to listen – reveals the depth of the cultural divide between Western and Indigenous knowledge systems, historical understandings, and legal practices.

As embodied in Justice McEachern, the court was unwilling to recognize the authority of the Gitxsan Feast Hall or the legitimacy of the histories presented in court. In his reasons for judgment, McEachern made a distinction between history as "facts" and the "beliefs," or myths, that the elders had relayed to him. Yet, in making his ruling, he relied on a few settler myths of his own:

> The territory is a vast emptiness ... The Indians of the territory were, by historical standards, a primitive people without any form of writing, horses, or wheeled wagons ... The Gitksan and Wet'suwet'en civilizations, if they qualify for that description, fall within a much lower, even primitive order ... Being of a culture where everyone looked after himself or perished, the Indians knew how to survive ... But they were not as industrious in the new economic climate as was thought necessary by the newcomers in the Colony ... They became a conquered people, not by force of arms, for that was unnecessary, but by an invading culture and a relentless energy with which they would not, or could not compete ... It became obvious ... that what the ... witnesses describe as law is really a most uncertain and highly flexible set of customs.[55]

After 374 days in court, listening to the evidence presented by the Gitxsan and Wet'suwet'en elders and chiefs, McEachern's reasons for judgment are entirely consistent with settler denial. Nor is the judgment an example of the false innocence or ignorance of history that is often exhibited by settlers and our institutions. Instead, as historian Adele Perry points out, his denial was "a willful one constructed in spite of, rather than in the absence of, meaningful contact with Gitksan and Wet'suwet'en peoples."[56] History and myth are deeply implicated in the judge's problematic construction of the past.

Although the Supreme Court subsequently ruled that the evidentiary value of oral history must be given equal weight to that of the documentary record, the 1991 record of "colonialism on trial" remains a valuable pedagogical tool. In *The Pleasure of the Crown*, Dara Culhane offers an in-depth analysis of *Delgamuukw*, in which she notes that Justice McEachern relied on the positivist history, ethnocentric attitudes, and racist stereotypes that were put forward by Crown expert witnesses. She argues that his "'findings of fact' did not arise purely out of thin air, or his own imagination. They echoed the Crown's legal arguments ... [and drew] on the unreflected upon 'common sense' of Canadian colonial culture."[57] Within this context, the level of resistance to the counter-narrative presented by the Gitxsan and Wet'suwet'en was predictable.

Following the *Delgamuukw* decision, academics, primarily from the disciplines of anthropology and history, published responses to what they saw as the judiciary's lack of understanding about the theoretical and methodological constructs of their respective disciplines and of ethnohistory.[58] With regard to oral histories specifically, the courts have adopted the principles that were laid down in *R. v. Van der Peet* and expanded upon in *Delgamuukw v. British Columbia*.[59] In the latter decision, the Supreme Court of Canada ruled that, with regard to oral history, "the laws of evidence must be adapted in order that this type of evidence can be accommodated and placed on an equal footing with the types of historic evidence that courts are familiar with, which largely consists of historical documents."[60] Nevertheless, more recent case law indicates that the courts still interpret oral histories in problematic ways and that elders who testify as witnesses are not afforded the "expert" status that is given to academic scholars.

In *Victor Buffalo v. Regina*, for example, the court preferred the Crown experts' methodology wherein the oral history testimony was subject to comparative review in much the same manner as historical documents.[61] In contrast, the plaintiffs' expert emphasized the importance of local community credentialing of elders and the need to observe proper protocols. The judge stated that, though the latter approach "may suit scholars, [it] is simply not feasible, nor is it realistic, for a trial judge. The Court cannot

embark upon independent, fact-finding investigations into evidence tendered at trial ... and while [the expert] offered some interesting insights
into the nature of oral traditions and oral histories, she did not present
the Court with any analysis of the oral traditions tendered at trial."[62] What
the judge failed to understand is that the documentation and legitimization
of Indigenous narrative memory differs from that of Western scholarly
works, which use bibliographic footnoting. Neal McLeod explains that,
"in oral cultures, 'footnoting' is done by acknowledging how one came to
know a story."[63]

Ray points out that, in *Buffalo*, "the trial judge gave little weight to [the
plaintiffs'] line of evidence because he concluded that the Cree lacked a
systematic way of establishing the veracity of their stories."[64] This raises
important questions about how the courts treat the testimony of elders
who are witnesses. The issue at stake was not credibility (though this can
also be a factor) but the reliability of the oral history, and by extension, of
the elders who testified due to their experience as carriers of special
knowledge about the history of the community. The *Buffalo* judge made
a clear distinction between protocol and the process of authentication by
which elders are legitimized in their communities. As he put it, "the oral
history tendered in *Delgamuukw* appears to be far more formal and regi-
mented than that which was tendered in the present case. Protocol was
used in these proceedings, including presenting the elders with gifts of
tobacco. I accept that the use of protocol indicates that the elder was
relating something serious and sacred; however ... protocol does not, by
itself, ensure validation."[65] Thus, in this instance, the court used the cultural differences between various Indigenous nations as a rationale for
discounting Cree oral history and law.

Nlaka'pamux lawyer and legal scholar Ardith Walkem describes Aboriginal litigation as characterized by a "methodology of suspicion" in
which "Indigenous oral tradition evidence ... [is] systematically misunder-
stood, devalued and subject to an analytical framework that naturalizes
suspicion about its ability to accurately or reliably relay information."[66]
From the view of Native peoples who have been historically oppressed, this
discounting of oral history evidence is rationalized by a non-Aboriginal
legal majority who say it is biased and subjective. But as David Kahane
argues persuasively, liberalism's ideal of a "neutral" justice – "the Western
story of justice as neutral adjudication" that can be attained through

"objective, rational analysis" – is also suspect.[67] Not only does settler denial of Indigenous history and law run deep but we fail to see how our own "story of justice" as a neutral vision of law and order can rightly be challenged as the product of a colonial mindset with its own hidden biases.

As the courts become more educated about Indigenous history and law, there is a growing awareness that litigation, although sometimes necessary, is not the preferred path toward renegotiating Indigenous-settler relations. In the 2007 Supreme Court of BC decision *Tsilhqot'in Nation v. British Columbia,* Justice Vickers observed that, "in order to truly hear the oral history and oral tradition evidence presented in these cases, courts must undergo their own process of decolonization."[68] He cautioned that the court was "ill-equipped to effect a reconciliation of competing interests" and reminded us that, historically, Indigenous-settler differences were resolved through treaty negotiations.[69] Relying on the courts to achieve reconciliation is ultimately an inadequate mechanism for correcting historical wrongs or protecting the rights of Indigenous peoples: "The result is that the interests of the broader Canadian community, as opposed to the constitutionally entrenched rights of Aboriginal peoples, are to be foremost in the consideration of the Court. In that type of analysis, reconciliation does not focus on the historical injustices suffered by Aboriginal peoples. It is reconciliation imposed by the needs of the colonizer."[70] An imposed reconciliation is one in which settlers remain the primary beneficiaries of the institutional and systemic legacies of colonialism. As Justice Vickers astutely observes, the "Tsilhqot'in people have survived despite centuries of colonization. The central question is whether Canadians can meet the challenges of decolonization."[71] Thus, he speaks to the crux of our current dilemma.

Indigenous Self-Determination, Reconciliation, and Residential Schools

To conceive of an apology or truth commission as a way for polities to neutralize a history of wrongs is to set it up to fail for Indigenous peoples and to neglect an opportunity for transforming existing relationships that go beyond hollow, symbolic gestures ... We contend that decolonisation and restitution are necessary elements of reconciliation because these are necessary to transform relations with Indigenous communities in the way justice requires. Whether the mechanism attempting to address injustice to Indigenous peoples and remedy wrongs is an apology or truth and reconciliation commission, it must begin by acknowledging Indigenous peoples' inherent powers of self-determination.

— JEFF CORNTASSEL AND CINDY HOLDER, "WHO'S SORRY NOW?"

Indigenous peoples are reclaiming space on a number of fronts in their ongoing struggle for self-determination. Within this context, neither truth-telling and reconciliation processes nor apologies are sufficient in and of themselves to right historical wrongs. Writing in the American context, Chiricahua Apache legal scholar William Bradford argues that "both Indian and non-Indian peoples [will benefit] if U.S.-Indian relationships advance on the basis of a recognition of, and respect for, mutual sovereignties ... A new era of domestic peace with justice ... will follow." He notes that, "fittingly, the ancient Indian method of dispute resolution known as Tribal Peacemaking ('TPM') can guide this restorative journey toward reconciliation." Like Corntassel and Holder, he says that the majority population must fully support Indigenous self-determination.[72] In Canada, scholars Marie Battiste (Mi'kmaq) and James Sa'ke'j Youngblood Henderson (Chickasaw) remind us that Indigenous knowledge systems, languages, and cultures are also constitutionally protected rights. Thus, "little doubt exists that language ... and ceremonies are an integral and distinctive part of Indigenous knowledge and heritage."[73] Within the residential school context, there are strong connections between the issue of cultural loss, this political reclaiming of culture, and First Nations' aspirations to protect and revitalize their knowledge, governance, and legal systems as integral to nation building, community well-being, and intergovernmental diplomatic and political relations.[74]

Examining the links between healing and governance, Canadian anthropologist Wayne Warry observes that cultural revitalization cannot be understood apart from this context. He notes that, though "direct participation in healing ceremonies can be important for individuals, the process of community healing is much broader: it is about the protection and preservation of language, political rights, and nationhood."[75] The complex issues related to culturally appropriate community building and inter-governmental relations are not the focus of this study, for such work rightly belongs with Indigenous peoples. Nevertheless, settlers need to understand how the regeneration of Indigenous governance and legal systems is directly related to the overall well-being of individuals, communities, and nations. At the same time, we must keep in mind that widespread cultural and language loss as well as disconnection from family, community, and nation exists as an intergenerational consequence of the IRS legacy.

In a discussion of the reconciliation issues that the Gitxsan are exploring within their own communities, Val Napoleon states that community and political relationships are marred by the violence and dysfunction that are a direct consequence of the colonial experience. She says that, though the Gitxsan governance and legal system has "remained intact ... its function has been seriously undermined."[76] These same circumstances are replicated in many other First Nations communities. Taiaiake Alfred tells us that "many, if not most, of the spiritual ceremonies and practices of Onkwehonwe have been destroyed or lost."[77] But he also reminds us that there has always been and still is a philosophical unity to the stories and ceremonies that weave connections among all Indigenous peoples and nations.[78] This speaks directly to the disruption and persistence of Indigenous political philosophies and legal orders over time.[79]

One of the many unfortunate by-products of litigation-driven settler understandings of Indigenous culture is that, like Justice McEachern, some settlers become obsessed with the issue of what is "traditional" and therefore "legitimate" and what is not. Linda Tuhiwai Smith observes that "problematizing the indigenous is a Western obsession ... The indigenous can be perceived as a problem because many are considered 'inauthentic' and too ungrateful."[80] In a culture of denial, settlers search for ways to prove that Indigenous cultures no longer exist as they once did years ago. In an ethics of recognition, we acknowledge that all cultures change, adapt, and regenerate themselves. The continuity resides, Alfred says, in the "basics of this Onkwehonwe spiritual and philosophical belief system ... inter-dependency, cycles of change, balance, struggle, and rootedness."[81] This is the foundation of Indigenous cultural resurgence and regeneration.

6

The Power of Apology and Testimony
Settlers as Ethical Witnesses

REFLECTIONS

I begin with a story about the giving and receiving of testimonies. On a wintry morning in Hazelton, BC, a northern community far from Vancouver, I am about to begin my first day as claims resolution manager. I will spend many months in this place, listening to IRS survivors as they talk about what happened to them as children at the residential school. Although I will participate in the settlement negotiations, I am not there to determine whether these claims meet the legal criteria for compensation – that is a job for legal counsel. Rather, I am present to listen to the testimonies of survivors, to acknowledge their experiences, and to try to "humanize" this process. As the "face of Canada," a government representative, I can no longer avoid experiencing the visceral impacts of colonialism by distancing myself from them. The living survivors of colonization will be sitting right before me. In their eyes, I am not an ally but a perpetrator. Carrying this identity does not sit well with me.

On the way to the meeting place, I find myself recounting all the reasons that I am not a colonizer: I am working for social justice and change from within my own dominant-culture institutions; I am enlightened and empathetic; my intentions are good; I am committed to finding a just solution to these claims; I have Indigenous colleagues and friends; I grew up in a single-parent, low-income family in an ethnically diverse East Vancouver neighbourhood; I am not one of those racist white upper- or middle-class people raised in insular privilege! But, I also know that, despite my family's poverty and relative lack of privilege, no one came to my home as a matter of government policy or religious imperative to remove me from my mother's care. My fair skin and colouring protected me from racism, if not gender and class-related biases, at school and later in the work world. So I now find myself in the uncomfortable position of being a Euro-Canadian woman trying to figure out what it really means to bear this unwanted identity of colonizer, oppressor, and perpetrator while attempting to do my work in a way that is congruent with my own principles, beliefs, and sense of integrity.

I already know that the anger, pain, and loss that I will surely hear expressed by survivors will evoke my own emotional responses – not just empathy for what they have been through but strong feelings of denial, guilt, shame, anger, and fear. I have no idea what I will do with all these feelings. I know that, as a government representative, I am expected to put on a "neutral face" as I listen respectfully. I also know that it would be disrespectful to survivors for me to wallow self-indulgently in my own emotions, thus making the process "all about me." I have spent a restless night worrying about how I can possibly do justice to the testimonies I will hear. I cannot even begin to imagine what the night has been like for the survivors I will meet this morning. My stomach is in knots and my heart is pounding, as we arrive at the meeting place. I feel slightly ill. We begin with a ceremonial smudge to clear our minds and cleanse our hearts – to ready us for the hard work ahead. An eagle feather, Indigenous symbol of peace and justice, is passed around, drawing each participant into the circle as we introduce ourselves. By accepting the feather, I understand that I have committed to conducting myself with honour and truthfulness. I am much calmer now. The process has begun.

Back in Vancouver, I had prepared for this day. I had read binders filled with documents about the school itself and had reviewed the individual claims of the survivors. I'd learned a lot – or so I thought – but the real learning will happen in this circle. As an elder begins her testimony, I stop thinking about myself, about what I will say to her afterward, about anything other than entering into the space of her story – to listen. She takes me back with her in time, as she remembers, through the eyes of a frightened, shy, and lonely little girl, all that happened to her. In my mind, I can see a five-year-old sitting with other scared and confused children on the train that took them away from their families and homes. She tells me about the horrific sexual and physical abuses she suffered, and of how the seemingly small acts of cruelty, humiliation, and deprivation that were part of her everyday life were so unbearable. She also talks about how some of the children banded together for comfort and protection, whereas others became bullies and abusers themselves. She describes one teacher who was always kind to her as she struggled with her lessons. She remembers the terrible food and the sheer pleasure of eating the occasional treat. Understandably, it is incredibly hard for her to talk about these things, so we take a break and she is comforted by the counsellor who is there to support her. When she is finished, it is my turn to speak, to try to find the words that let her know that I have truly heard what she has told me and to honour her courage in some small way. Her testimony has brought home to me the full impact of the residential schools in an utterly compelling way that no document ever could. I do not remember now exactly what I said to her and would not share this in any case. What I do remember is that my words had nothing to do with the "validity" of the claim or reciting some rote formula created in an office somewhere by people far removed from this day, this person, and this place. I spoke from my heart, with humility and a vague sense that I had been given a gift – one that I would somehow carry with me when I left.

Fast forward. It is late afternoon on the final day. We gather again in the circle to mark an ending. A community elder has come to smudge us – to prepare us to leave the circle and find our ways home. We are all exhausted, but we talk about what this experience has meant to us. It is a deeply moving moment. Many feelings have been shared in this small room – pain, sorrow, loss, regret. Sharp words of anger and distrust have been spoken. But there has also been laughter, and at times a gentle camaraderie settled upon the room as testimonies unfolded, told with dignity and listened to with respect. I am humbled in the face of the survivors' courage and strength in their determination to call government and church to account. Their life stories are not just of their victimization but of their courage and resilience. In this circle, I have learned something about myself, about the limitations of the ADR process, and about the destructive consequences of denying and silencing history. Equally important, I have felt the power of apology and experienced how the giving and receiving of painful stories can restore human dignity.

Apology and Testimonial Exchange as Decolonizing Acts

Stories enlisted within and attached to a human rights framework are particular kinds of stories – strong, emotive stories often chronicling degradation, brutalization, exploitation and physical violence ... Some stories, formerly locked in silence, open wounds and re-trigger traumatic feelings once they are told. Some stories recounted in the face of oppression and repression, of shame and denial, reinvest the past with a new intensity, often with pathos, as they test normative conceptions of social reality. All stories invite an ethical response from listeners and readers. All have strong affective dimensions for both the tellers and their audience, affects that can be channeled in negative and positive ways, through personal, political, legal, and aesthetic circuits that assist, but can also impede, the advance of human rights. Whether or not storytelling in the field of human rights results in the extension of human justice, dignity and freedom depends on the willingness of those addressed to hear the stories and to take responsibility for the recognition of others and their claims.

> – Kay Schaffer and Sidonie Smith,
> *Human Rights and Narrated Lives*

In describing one of many interactions that occurred between myself and survivors, I am mindful that my apology, although heartfelt and sincere, was offered within the constraints of the ADR pilot project. My words were spoken in private within the context of a claims resolution process that, though more informal in nature, was still bound by legal convention. Yet, residential school experiences are particular kinds of stories that, as Schaffer and Smith point out, chronicle a litany of human rights abuses that cry out for moral justice. In the face of this reality, listeners encounter a moral and ethical dilemma in which they must choose how to respond to each survivor's story. Vicarious trauma, the cumulative effect of listening to many stories of violence and trauma over several years, can inevitably take its toll, tempting listeners to disengage.[1] But such a difficult listening, which is integral to ethical testimonial exchange and authentic apology, constitutes a decolonizing act in its own right when understood as a critical element of truth telling that takes Indigenous self-determination and human rights seriously. Keeping this in mind, how might the TRC, over the course of its lifetime, teach settlers to listen not with colonial empathy but more ethically with a compassion born from our own liberatory struggle?

Truth and reconciliation commissions provide a mechanism for testimonies of trauma to uncover systemic human rights abuses within a broader socio-political framework. Writing in a global context, Rhoda E. Howard-Hassmann and Mark Gibney note that the politics of apology and testimony as social movements "have affected how people perceive oppression and how they remedy it." They point out that "all these trends

– social movements for liberation, indigenous demands for apology, and the politics of multiculturalism – stressed personal suffering and feeling ... In academic and policy discussion, a new focus on personal narratives began. Scholars and practitioners recognized that personal narratives were a strong route to empathy ... Apologies were one means that states and other social institutions could use to show empathy to those they had harmed."[2] In intercultural contexts, there are often conflicting ideas about how testimony is legitimized and what constitutes a genuine apology. For the TRC, incorporating the principle of witnessing as practised in Indigenous oral and legal traditions opens up new possibilities for ensuring that what Howard-Hassman and Gibney characterize as "genuine acts of contrition" are not misinterpreted as acts of hypocrisy or disrespect because they fail to take Indigenous criteria and protocols into account.[3]

On Testimonial Exchange and Settler Listening

In the context of the commission, I use the term "testimony" in its socio-political meaning, not in a legal sense. Cultural and historical trauma theory in the literature on truth and reconciliation commissions has focused primarily on testimony's therapeutic implications for victims or perpetrators of mass violence who speak out in public forums, but the role of the listener is less understood. However, as Megan Boler reminds us, "the listener's work is crucial. The absence of a listener, or a listener who turns away or who doubts, can shatter testimony's potential as a courageous act in truth's moment of crisis."[4] Testimonial exchange may well be healing for certain people, and to some degree the very concept of healing has become analogous with decolonization. Within this context, one can talk about healing individuals or a nation. But the healing metaphor has been used almost exclusively with regard to Indigenous peoples. We have heard far less about the settler need to heal. Although decolonization involves healing aspects, we should not lose sight of the ultimate need for substantive changes to existing economic structures, political institutions, and legal systems. Given these realities, the TRC's educative potential to weave together the personal and political aspects of decolonization is substantial.

Although settlers may be inclined to greet survivor testimony with skepticism, the sheer volume of historical evidence accumulated by the commission will make maintaining this stance far more difficult. In

Unspeakable Truths, Patricia Hayner notes that, in reflecting on the impact of the South African Truth and Reconciliation Commission, South African anti-apartheid activists "argue that the commission's most important contribution was simply to remove the possibility of continued denial."[5] The value of overcoming systemic denial should not be underestimated as a means to generate wider societal support for Indigenous peoples' struggles for self-determination and human rights. Public truth-telling and reconciliation events related to Indian residential schools may be traumatic, certainly for survivors but also for settlers. Writing about the psychosocial aspects of cultural trauma, Neil J. Smelser explains that, when a people's history, culture, and identity are disrupted through acts of remembering that are highly emotional, cultural trauma results. He suggests that "before an event can qualify as a cultural trauma ... it must be remembered, or made to be remembered. Furthermore, the memory must be made culturally relevant, that is, represented as obliterating, damaging, or rendering problematic something sacred – usually a value or outlook felt to be essential for the integrity of the affected society. Finally, the memory must be associated with a strong negative affect, usually disgust, shame, or guilt ... Cultural traumas are for the most part historically made, not born."[6]

For survivors, remembering residential school experiences gives rise to a host of negative emotions involving multiple losses – of self, family, community, language, and culture, along with the devastating intergenerational effects of abuse. At the same time, such remembering can also invoke healing memories of courage, strength, and cultural resilience in the face of extreme adversity and its aftermath.

For settlers, coming to grips with the IRS experience involves thinking about and working through the difficult emotions associated with the various ways in which we are implicated. The sacred memory that will be obliterated in this case is the much cherished peacemaker myth. American law professor Martha Minow argues that involving only victims and *direct* perpetrators in truth telling is not enough: the process must also encompass "bystanders ... who often experience guilt because they avoided harm or else participated, through ignorance and denial, in the regimes producing collective violence" so that they can confront this reality in order to make amends.[7] In the Canadian context, where many direct perpetrators are no longer living, the role of the bystander is especially relevant for those who, like me, have served as representatives of perpetrator institutions as well as those with no direct involvement in residential school issues. Accordingly, a Canadian society of perpetrators and bystanders must re-remember itself not as "innocent" but as complicit. The false innocence of the perpetrator/bystander is revealed in the silence breaking that occurs during the giving and receiving of testimony. As Indigenous peoples *restore* their own sense of human dignity as self-determining groups, settlers must *recognize and respect* that inherent dignity, thereby restoring our own.

The acknowledgment of injustices and harms takes various forms. Stanley Cohen identifies four of these: The first is self-knowledge, the critical reflection that comes with facing truth but which alone is insufficient. The second is moral witness, in which bystanders take an active role in witnessing unjust acts or bearing witness to victims' testimonies, and in the process, create their own testimonies of accountability. The third response is whistle blowing, wherein the person reveals an "open secret," a heinous wrong previously ignored or colluded in, which can no longer be ignored or rationalized. Fourth is living outside the lie, in which a person "begins to say what he really thinks and supports people according to his conscience ... [to] discover that it is possible to live inside the truth, to find a repressed alternative to the inauthentic ... People become committed, driven, unable to return to their old lives or shut their eyes again."[8] This coming to consciousness, or living in truth, that Cohen describes can occur for individual perpetrators or bystanders but can also shift the historical consciousness of whole societies as people grapple with the after-effects of collective violence and cultural trauma.

Apology as Partial Settler Truth Telling

From a pedagogical perspective, official apologies by their nature may act as a catalyst in that they increase public understanding of the historical origins of Indigenous disadvantage. This in turn compels citizens to rethink their civic and political responsibilities with a view to fulfilling a moral obligation to right historical wrongs.[9] Settler Canadians now stand at a critical crossroad in our relationship with Native peoples. The reader will recall that, on 11 June 2008, the prime minister stood in Parliament to offer Canada's formal apology to IRS survivors, their families, and communities, followed by opposition leaders, who did likewise. Their words were duly witnessed by Indigenous political leaders who gathered in a circle on the floor of the House of Commons, by survivors sitting in the gallery or clustered around television screens in their communities, by government and church officials, and by ordinary Canadians across the country. For a brief moment in time, the country as a whole experienced a rare moment of public truth telling about Indian residential schools. After some political wrangling, House leaders had agreed to break with parliamentary convention so that Indigenous leaders could respond directly to the apology, which was entered into Hansard as part of the official record. Given that apologies have tended to reinforce the colonial status quo rather than support Indigenous self-determination, official apologies constitute a partial truth telling that must be followed by concrete action.

Although Canadians might agree in principle that, as a country, we must learn from our past so that history does not repeat itself, most of us fail to "connect the dots" between this problematic past and current attitudes and policies. An Angus Reid poll conducted in March 2008 found that, in the wake of Australia's official apology to Native people in that country for the "laws and policies of successive parliaments and governments that have inflicted profound grief, suffering and loss," only 42 percent of the respondents thought that Canada should offer a similar apology here, whereas 39 percent did not agree. At the same time, however, the vast majority felt that Ottawa should do more to help Aboriginal communities: 70 percent wanted it to do more to address their poverty, and 72 percent wanted a speedier resolution to Aboriginal land claims.[10] Subsequently, in May 2008, Angus Reid found that 53 percent of Canadians thought that the government should offer an apology, an increase of 11 percent from the previous March. In that same poll, two out of five, or 39 percent, of Canadians thought that "reconciliation between Aboriginals and non-Aboriginals is possible, while 32 percent disagreed."[11] Finally, post-apology in August 2008, Angus Reid reported that two-thirds, or 67 percent, of Canadians agreed with the prime minister's apology, whereas 17 percent disagreed; 65 percent of respondents wanted Ottawa to do more to deal with Aboriginal poverty, and 62 percent wanted land claims resolved more quickly.[12]

The fact that a significant number of Canadians saw no need for an apology until after it was delivered, and many are skeptical as to whether reconciliation is possible, suggests that despite Prime Minister Harper's words, many are reluctant to take up the burden of responsibility for the

IRS experience. At the same time, a high percentage of Canadians believe quite strongly that Ottawa must do more to address Aboriginal poverty and to resolve land claims. The poll results confirm the persistence of settler attitudes that I have already described.

If we offer an apology, what makes it genuine? Sociologist Nicholas Tavuchis tells us that an apology requires us to be vulnerable, to risk offering it without expecting or demanding forgiveness in return.[13] He distinguishes between offering an "account" in which "we necessarily attempt to distance ourselves from our actions," thus denying responsibility, versus an authentic apology that "requires *not* detachment but acknowledgment and painful embracement of our deeds, coupled with a declaration of regret."[14] A true apology, then, is a "remedial ritual" – an "enacted story" that is performed with a humility that must be *spoken* – an act by which we seek readmittance to a moral community of human decency whose bounds we have transgressed.[15] As Tavuchis remarks, "it is not surprising, therefore, that although an oral apology may be supplemented by the written word and symbolic tokens of conciliation, the latter, by themselves, are rarely considered to be sufficient or satisfactory ... There is, quite simply, nothing as effective and unsettling as having to address in person someone we have wronged, no matter how much a culture stresses writing, print, or electronic communication to the detriment of speech."[16] But Tavuchis does not suggest that the documentary record is unimportant, particularly with regard to official or "many-to-many" apologies as opposed to those that are personal. A collective public apology is distinct from private apology, where words alone "have the power to seal an apology." Accordingly, a formal apology for the official record is qualitatively and substantively different. In the public realm, he says, "an unrecorded representative speech has no representational authority ... The apology is fashioned for the record and exists only by virtue of the record."[17] This is why formal political apologies, as opposed to informal private apologies, are understood quite differently by recipients.

Scholars who have undertaken comparative analyses of official apologies made by various governments argue that whether an apology is offered and how it is received are indicators of broader political tensions that play out between nations and oppressed minority groups seeking to advance their reparations claims. In *The Politics of Official Apologies*, American political scientist Melissa Nobles compares apologies from Australia,

Canada, New Zealand, and the United States, observing that they make a moral claim upon society and assign collective guilt that is based on a fundamental reinterpretation of settler national history:

> Although national histories are sometimes vigorously disputed ... these histories are essential to my argument in two ways. First, governments have apologized for (or have been asked to apologize for) specific acts and for the larger policies of which these acts were a part. Second, the past terms of national membership have, to a great degree, shaped both the ways in which indigenous groups have mobilized and the claims they have made ... Apologies politics should be understood as part of this ongoing dynamic of negotiation, where state officials and indigenous groups have each sought to structure and restructure the terms of membership, usually in diametrically opposed ways. State officials built nation-states, at the expense of substantial indigenous political, economic, and social autonomy. Indigenous peoples, in turn, have fought to preserve and regain some measure of autonomy to shape their collective futures.[18]

In reinterpreting national history by virtue of the admission of wrongdoing, an official apology can fuel further discontent, both on the part of Indigenous groups who believe that it does not go far enough and neo-conservatives who think that it goes too far. Political apologies thus constitute a particular form of testimonial exchange, and their texts are carefully scrutinized as are other salient details regarding who delivers them and under what circumstances, and what protocols and ceremony are observed.

Comparing the prime minister's official apology to the earlier Statement of Reconciliation delivered by the minister of Indian Affairs in 1998 reveals why the former may be considered more genuine. Analyzing apologies and quasi-apologies in several countries, political scientist Matt James builds on the work of Nicholas Tavuchis and others to identify eight criteria for an authentic political apology: "(1) [it] is recorded officially in writing; (2) names the wrongs in question; (3) accepts responsibility; (4) states regret; (5) promises non-repetition; (6) does not demand forgiveness; (7) is not hypocritical or arbitrary; and (8) undertakes – through measures of publicity, ceremony, and concrete reparation – both to engage morally those in whose name apology is made and to assure the wronged group that the apology is sincere."[19] James concludes that Canada's Statement of

Reconciliation is a "quasi-apology" that, when measured against these scholarly criteria, fails to stand up as a full apology. He observes that, although it addresses the IRS legacy, it does not express regret for the policies and actions of the government, referring only to the sexual and physical abuse that occurred. The monetary reparations offered in the form of funding for the Aboriginal Healing Foundation were inadequate to meet the needs of survivors, their families, and communities. Finally, James concludes that the statement is only a quasi-apology because of "improper ceremony (as evidenced by the prime minister's absence)."[20]

As mentioned previously, ceremony and ritual play a key role in the historical, political, and moral life of society, and must follow proper protocols to be taken seriously. Thus, the public ceremonies that mark political apologies send a strong message to both recipients and the general public. James asserts that the 1998 ceremony held in Ottawa to deliver the Statement of Reconciliation was problematic on several fronts:

> At a lunchtime ceremony in a government meeting room on Parliament Hill, Minister of Indian and Northern Affairs Jane Stewart sought to address this shameful past. Although Prime Minister Jean Chrétien was in Ottawa that day, he did not attend the ceremony. The event featured performances by Aboriginal singers and dancers, and concluded with Minister Stewart presenting the Statement of Reconciliation, which she read aloud, in the form of ceremonial scrolls to five Native leaders. The Statement of Reconciliation does not form part of Canada's official parliamentary or legal record; it is merely posted on the Department of Indian and Northern Affairs website ... With the important exception of Grand Chief Phil Fontaine of the Assembly of First Nations, the Native leaders present dismissed the Statement as an inadequate response both to Canada's unjust treatment of Aboriginal peoples in general and to the legacy of the residential schools in particular.[21]

The Statement of Reconciliation received a similarly negative response from many Indigenous people across the country. Journalist Andrew Coyne, writing in *Time Canada,* observed wryly that "for all the misty-eyed rhetoric of the Minister of Indian Affairs ... the government is in fact engaged in a bit of plea bargaining, less out of a desire to right old wrongs than to limit its own damages. That may account in part for the tepid, even hostile response the statement received from most of the native leaders gathered for the formal presentation."[22] We know that apology and ceremony have the potential to heal and transform relationships. But when this symbolic ritual is perceived as an act of tokenism, performed without proper recognition and respect, it conveys a stronger message about who has power and is in control than it does about making amends. Those present at the ceremony did not miss the message. Nor did Native people across the country, who rejected the statement not only as inadequate but deeply insulting in light of the harms they have suffered as a result of historical dispossession. Thus, the Statement of Reconciliation set the tone for subsequent dialogue with regard to the residential schools that, for all the talk of reconciliation, remained embedded in the historical violence of colonial relationships played out in a contemporary context. Consequently, when the minister of IRSRC referred to the statement at the Calgary conference that I described in Chapter 4, he probably intended to remind the audience of something good. But in fact, he may have achieved just the opposite effect. Many in the audience would remember the statement only as a symbol of continuing denial and disrespect – a further painful affront to their dignity.

Tavuchis cautions that a public apology is essentially "an act of diplomacy ... And the wording and tenor ... typically the product of anonymous authors must be carefully crafted ... to avoid ambiguity or further offense ... As public representatives, those who convey apology must conform to conventional standards of decorum and protocol ... An apology offered without proper credentials, that is, lacking the moral imprimatur of the group, amounts to no apology at all."[23] He emphasizes the importance of the written record as integral to this proper credentialing. Thus, a formal apology from the prime minister, made in the House of Commons, becomes part of the official parliamentary record, whereas the Statement of Reconciliation lacked the appropriate criteria. Against the backdrop of the IRS Settlement Agreement, Canada's formal apology to IRS survivors thus becomes an act of political diplomacy similar to the apologies delivered in Parliament to Japanese Canadians for their internment during the Second World War, and the more recent apology to Chinese Canadians for the head tax they were required to pay in order to enter Canada. Tavuchis' and James' analysis helps us to identify the characteristics of genuine apology, to distinguish between personal and collective apologies, and to determine what constitutes a public formal apology according to Western criteria. But what are Indigenous criteria for making restitution and apology?

Indigenous Criteria and Practices for Making Restitution and Apology

> Restitution is purification. It is a ritual of disclosure and confession in which there is acknowledgment and acceptance of one's harmful actions and a genuine demonstration of sorrow and regret, constituted in reality by putting forward a promise to never again do harm and by redirecting one's actions to benefit the one who has been wronged.
>
> — TAIAIAKE ALFRED, *WASÁSE*

How can settlers learn to respect Indigenous criteria for making restitution and apology? We know that Western forms of restitution involve monetary compensation that may or may not include apology. Tavuchis and James note the importance of Western documentary and ceremonial protocols that political apologies must meet in order to be seen as legitimate. But within the environment of Indigenous-settler relations, we should also consider how Indigenous criteria for making, legitimizing, and documenting acts of restitution and apology may involve material reparations while also entering a more spiritual realm as sacred acts. Using storytelling, ceremony, and ritual, Indigenous records of restitution and apology are inscribed in the oral traditions of the feast hall, the big house, or the circle.

We have seen how the prime minister's apology constituted a more genuine apology than the Statement of Reconciliation. The latter failed to provide a full admission of specific wrongs, and no permanent official parliamentary or legal record of it exists. These are both essential Western criteria for official apologies. Moreover, even by Western standards, proper ceremonial protocol was not followed. If the statement constitutes only a quasi-apology according to Western criteria, it was equally improper in terms of Indigenous criteria. There were "performances by Aboriginal singers and dancers" that, removed from any meaningful diplomatic, legal, and cultural context, seem superficial at best. What was their significance? Native participants may have understood their meaning, but how did the other participants regard them? Of course, we have no way of knowing. In this instance, the attempt to integrate Indigenous ceremony into an intercultural context is an example of token use that raises concerns from both settler and Indigenous perspectives, albeit for different reasons.

In a critique of restorative justice models (which would include, for example, sentencing circles), Western legal scholar Annalise Acorn questions whether justice, healing, or righting relationships between victims and perpetrators is possible. Part of her critique is the argument that the use of Indigenous restorative justice practices is predicated on romanticizing a mythical harmonious past to support "the political push toward Aboriginal self-government and a more general renaissance of traditional Aboriginal culture."[24] For her, the inclusion of these ceremonial practices in courtrooms, classrooms, and at conferences is nothing more than a lesson in intercultural political correctness. There is no recognition of the long history and practice of Indigenous diplomacy, law, and peacemaking. Acorn questions the authenticity of such ceremonies, seeing them only as a cynical political device used by Native people to compel their non-Native counterparts to "act" respectfully, in spite of what they may privately think about such ceremonies:

> It may be, then, that the goal for Aboriginal people is achieved merely by getting these self-satisfied (and possibly racist) lawyers and judges in a position of having to stuff whatever it was they were really thinking about the ritual and act respectfully. The recent acquisition of the power to determine the aesthetic of ritual in these arenas of white authority – the courtroom, the classroom, and the conference room – may then be an important victory, in and of itself, for Aboriginal people. Of course, it may also be a sop to Aboriginal people inspired by white liberal guilt. And it may be, that by granting this virtually costless-to-the-whites perk, whites find it easier to avoid having to cough up more tangible and useful rights. But whether getting white people to behave here is more of a gain for Aboriginals than it is a balm for white guilt or the window-dressing of esteem – either way – a white show of obeisance to Aboriginal ritual is not, and cannot be required to entail, authentic respect.[25]

Acorn's points are valid enough. Indigenous people do exercise symbolic power in this instance, although the significance of this is far greater than she suggests. Settlers who make a show of respect that costs nothing rather than addressing the issues of compensation and treaties are also guilty of practising cheap reconciliation that is the hallmark of denial. Moreover, the intent she ascribes to settlers reveals the high level of resistance that exists in Canadian society with regard to making *any* space for Indigenous peoples. Essentially, Acorn is saying that Native people can make her go through the motions, but they cannot *make* her respect their ceremonial practices. Of course, this is true. If her *intent* is not to recognize or respect their protocol and ceremony but to be dismissive, how could it be otherwise?

Cree Saulteaux Dunne Zah legal scholar Val Napoleon also finds the widespread use of Indigenous law and ceremony in intercultural contexts problematic. She questions the sincerity of non-Indigenous people who *talk* about healing and reconciliation, and who engage in ceremonies but, in the end, provide nothing of substance. She says that, "if reconciliation for Aboriginal people in Canada is ever going to move beyond rhetoric, reconciliation discussions must include substantive societal and structural changes that deal with power imbalances, land and resources."[26] For her, the danger is that, divorced from their political, governance, and legal systems, stories, ceremonies, symbols, and rituals are reduced to nothing more than "rhetorical window-dressing – or a pretty band-aid on a gaping wound" in processes that remain essentially Western and do nothing to shift the colonial status quo.[27]

Acorn and Napoleon present flip sides of the same coin as they identify both the existing cultural divide and the challenges we face in attempting to bridge it as intercultural interlocutors. Each rejects the tokenism of using Indigenous ceremony as a superficial and ultimately meaningless nod to Indigenous knowledge systems, world views, and beliefs. But Acorn's stance reflects a cultural arrogance coupled with historical ignorance that is similar to the attitudes expressed in the *National Post* article on the smoking of a peace pipe at the signing of the IRS political accord, which I described in Chapter 4. It may well be that this ritual act is another example of the window-dressing that Napoleon criticizes. Did the politicians who smoked the pipe truly understand its legal and symbolic meaning? We cannot know, but both the scholarly analysis and the media account underline the high level of disrespect for Indigenous ceremonial protocols that cuts across all sectors of the settler population.

A first step in addressing the problem in relation to truth-telling and reconciliation processes is to build on the work of scholars who focus on intercultural conflict and peace studies. Michelle LeBaron, for example, calls on practitioners to develop "core cultural competencies" that help to identify how our cultural biases influence the design and substance of various intercultural conflict resolution processes.[28] However, LeBaron and others also point out that simply making Indigenous practices visible and developing cultural sensitivity is insufficient. David Kahane argues that "it is not enough for those in power to commit, with goodwill, to be reflexive about their cultural values, elicitive in process design, and so on; accounts of training for intercultural sensitivity have to incorporate an analysis of social power, and therefore to be explicitly political."[29] Thus, in thinking about the design of truth-telling and reconciliation measures, we can take some lessons from critiques concerning North American conflict resolution models.

By doing so, we can clearly see how process design is affected by entrenched power relations and settler attitudes of disrespect for and non-recognition of Indigenous diplomatic and legal ceremonies. Julie McFarlane observes that, "historically, one culture (Western legal-adjudicative culture) has swallowed all others (including Aboriginal conflict resolution traditions) by imposing its own criteria of substance and process."[30] On this point, we must distinguish between "integration" and "making space" for Indigenous diplomacy, law, and peacemaking. The ideological foundations of Western ADR neutrality models reinforce the attitude that assimilation is unproblematic, even desirable.[31] John Borrows cautions that "care should be taken that intercultural dispute resolution does not become colonialism's leading edge, erasing cultural difference in the guise of sharing."[32] Like Kahane, he views ADR ventures that are dominated by Western cultural understandings of conflict resolution as highly suspect within the realm of Indigenous-settler relations. He argues that the power imbalances that result in assimilation and appropriation are best addressed by creating separate Indigenous legal institutions to provide appropriate checks and balances on mainstream ADR.[33] Indigenous legal scholars say that non-Native people must become more knowledgeable about Indigenous law and legal practices, just as Native people who work in Canadian legal contexts are conversant with both systems. This is a call for the political recognition of Indigenous law. Mohawk legal scholar Patricia Monture states that non-Native ignorance of such law results in "an imbalance in the sharing of responsibility that reconciling two legal systems requires. It is also a recognition of who holds the power and who does not."[34] As we have seen, the non-recognition of "other-culture" methods of dealing with conflict is highly problematic in Indigenous-settler relations.

Natalie Oman provides a historical example that nicely illustrates this point. In a study of an intercultural conflict and subsequent negotiation between the Gitxsan and the colonial government regarding a blockade in 1872, she demonstrates how cultural misrecognition – our faulty assumption that we understand the Other – can have disastrous results or, at the least, unintended consequences. She notes that, although both Gitxsan oral history and colonial documents agreed on the details of what happened, each party had different understandings about the *significance and meaning* of the event. In this instance, each party brought its own ideas about how to resolve conflict and right wrongs. This cultural understanding is embedded in the protocols and practices that we use to recognize other cultural groups – politically, legally, and socially – which may lead to misunderstanding. Oman tells us that the Gitxsan invited government officials to a feast where they employed their legal practices of story, song, ceremony, and ritual to recount the conflict. They acknowledged the government's admission of wrongdoing and its recognition of Gitxsan jurisdiction, accepting the proffered gifts as restitution. An agreement was signed and witnessed in which both parties agreed to respect their respective jurisdictional authorities, after which they celebrated the agreement. In sharp contrast, government officials interpreted the same event as one in which they met with the Gitxsan wrongdoers and were obliged to hear a recitation of the grievance that prompted the roadblock, listen to songs and stories they did not understand, and pay the offenders in return for a signed agreement that they would refrain from blockading again. Finally, the officials reaffirmed their superior jurisdictional authority by firing a gunboat cannon to intimidate the Gitxsan.[35]

Thus, Oman reveals the significant cultural divide that exists between Indigenous people and governments, who have different criteria for how to acknowledge wrongdoing, provide appropriate restitution, and make an apology. Drawing on philosopher Charles Taylor's work, she argues that, in developing intercultural understanding that is based on the *recognition* of other cultures, exchanges between dominant and other-cultural interlocutors must involve more than "just talk." These exchanges entail a performative aspect. She suggests that there are points of congruence between Western and Indigenous theories of intercultural understanding and dialogical practices that can help to develop more effective intercultural conflict resolution and negotiation strategies:

> For Taylor, the dialogical method must extend beyond dialogue itself to *participation* in other-cultural practices. Dialogue alone cannot be the sole means of communicating the standards of value of one culture to members of another, because the language of each cultural group limits the concepts that can be conveyed ... Precisely because I draw primarily upon familiar language and concepts when I attempt to forge an understanding with another person who is shaped by many of the same cultural influences, what Taylor describes as a "fusion of horizons" occurs when we succeed ... However, in the more complex cases on intercultural understanding ... the extent to which our horizons are common ... is correspondingly smaller ... The dialogical process that gives rise to a meta-language of negotiation in this situation provides the participants with the opportunity to discover a broader (shared) horizon ... This notion of sharing horizons seems to express the animating principle of traditional Gitxsan and Wet'suwet'en strategies of international relations as well ... And the path to *inter*cultural understanding ... is through the formal recognition of other-cultural interlocutors and the activity of engaging in ritualized but highly meaningful dialogue with them in the medium of the feast.[36]

Oman's insights help to further explain how the transformative shift from a settler culture of denial to an ethics of recognition might occur in public performative space that is experiential, subjective, and emotionally engaged. Such spaces enable us to create shared horizons of cultural understanding in which "sharing is not distinguished by the interchangeability of the experiences of the partners ... but by the quality of invitation, and of possibility, that each brings to the relationship."[37]

From this stance of invitation and possibility, settlers approach intercultural dialogue with a more conscious intent to recognize rather than deny Indigenous diplomacy, law, and peacemaking in the rearticulation of stories of peoplehood – the histories of Indigenous self-determination and nationhood. But in doing so, we must be mindful that this sharing is explicitly attuned to addressing power differentials between those who have been marginalized and dominant-culture representatives. Kahane points out that, "in treating the dispute as *intercultural*, the focus should be on shifting authority ... in ways that resist particular sorts of domination and marginalization."[38] Decolonization is not "integration" or the token inclusion of Indigenous ceremony. Rather, it involves a paradigm shift from a culture of denial to the making of space for Indigenous political philosophies and knowledge systems as they resurge, thereby shifting cultural perceptions and power relations in real ways. In this, one must remain cognizant that Indigenous criteria for restitution and apology are situated within oral and legal traditions in which those who receive testimonies are required to fulfill particular responsibilities as witnesses.

Indigenous Testimonies: Storytelling, Witnessing, and Listening

Coast Salish scholar Qwul'sih'yah'maht (Robina Thomas) provides a compelling example of how Indigenous scholars write about a history of the residential schools that is still very much alive, giving voice to resistance, survival, and renewal, and reflecting on the responsibility of bearing witness to the stories – the histories of Indigenous lives. In her study documenting the experiences of three IRS survivors, Qwul'sih'yah'maht writes about her own community, using storytelling as her methodology. She describes her own ethical struggle to get the stories right, to make sure that she honours and respects the storytellers, the telling and the listening – the giving and receiving of testimony as witnessing. She discusses her personal discomfort and emotional responses as she weaves her own story into the text. This is not an "objective, neutral" residential school history based on archival documents but an honest, searing, and life-affirming history of people who attended a residential school and a people's collective will to exist – to live as Coast Salish. She explains the importance of struggling "to learn to listen, not simply hear, the words that storytellers have to share ... because they give us teachings that allow us to continue to hear and document these counter-stories – our truths."[39]

Storytelling and listening, or witnessing, Qwul'sih'yah'maht explains, are embedded in the cultural practices of the Coast Salish big house. Witnesses must learn to listen acutely: "Witnessing is a huge responsibility because you are asked to pay attention to all the details of the evening ...

[This] highly sophisticated process of witnessing continues to be central to our traditional ceremonies."[40] Relating this to her witnessing of survivors' stories, she states, "I never dreamed of learning what I learned. I never dreamed of learning to listen in such a powerful way. Storytelling, despite all the struggles, enabled me to respect and honour the Ancestors and the storytellers while at the same time sharing tragic, traumatic, inhumanly unbelievable truths that our people had lived. It was this level of integrity that was essential to storytelling ... When we make personal what we teach, as I see storytelling doing, we touch people in a different and more profound way."[41] Qwul'sih'yah'maht gives a sense of what it means to listen, as an Indigenous person, to survivor testimonies, and in doing so, she conveys a strong message about the power of bearing witness as more than just listening to a story. Drawing on Coast Salish traditions that are enacted in the ceremonies and protocols of the big house, her storytelling methodology stands in stark contrast to that of Western academic traditions, with their more circumscribed capacity to teach us experientially. Similarly, Sto:lo educator Jo-ann Archibald (Q'um Q'um Xiiem) describes the principles and protocols that are integral to Indigenous storytelling as pedagogical practice: "respect, responsibility, reciprocity, reverence, holism, interrelatedness and synergy." These principles constitute a "Sto:lo and Coast Salish theoretical framework for making meaning from stories."[42] Like Qwul'sih'yah'maht, she emphasizes the importance of listening properly to stories, which "requires the concomitant involvement of the auditory and visual senses, the emotions, the mind and patience."[43] Together, their insights formed a catalyst for my own thinking about the settler acts of witnessing that raised different questions. What are the pedagogical implications of the role of the settler as an ethical listener?

How do settlers bear witness? That is, how do we listen and respond authentically and ethically to testimonies – stories of colonial violence, not with colonial empathy but as a testimonial practice of shared truth telling that requires us to risk being vulnerable, to question openly our accepted world views and cherished assumptions about our colonial history and identity? How do we learn to listen differently, taking on our responsibility to decolonize ourselves, making space for Indigenous history and experience? How do we move beyond denial and moral indifference toward acknowledging a history of violence? For settlers, the stories about residential schools are deeply *unsettling*. They are filled with experiences that overturn our cultural identity as a nation of peacemakers. They chronicle violence and dispossession that we do not want to hear, because they shake us to the core. But they are also potentially transformative.

Here, it is important to remember that *how* we listen can be transformative or can simply reinscribe the patterns of colonialism. Roger Simon provides a powerful example of this in describing reader reactions to a book published by the Sayisi Dene about their experience of relocation by the Canadian government in the 1950s. Many non-Indigenous readers asked why the Sayisi Dene did not simply refuse to board the plane that took them away from their home. Simon points out that the Sayisi Dene may perceive this question not only as "impolite or even cruel, but [as] violent and obscene" because the story is told as part of their healing from trauma. Thus, the question "may actually be experienced as a return of physic violence."[44] Consider then, how IRS survivors might react to questions posed by government or church officials, the media, or ordinary Canadians about their school experiences. But these obscene questions, if attended to, contain important clues about settler resistance to hearing uncomfortable truths, and Simon draws our attention to their transformative possibilities:

> Thus a responsible listening to the testimony ... may require that we face up to the question of how to hear accounts of Aboriginal-Canadian history that bear witness to displacement, death and degradation ... It is for this reason that symptomatic obscene questions asked in the face of testimony hold enormous pedagogical potential ... A responsible listening thus may require a double attentiveness, a listening to the testimony of the one who is speaking and, at the same time, a listening to the questions we find ourselves asking when faced by this testimony ... We must pose questions to ourselves about our questions.[45]

Viewed in this way, settlers' questions, especially the difficult ones that spring to mind as we listen and that we might try to suppress, are precisely those that most urgently need our attention. Settler responses to Indigenous testimonies, our questioning, may reveal themselves not only, or even primarily on an intellectual level, but in the feelings and physical reactions that such testimonies engender. Thus, learning to listen involves engaging our whole being, using silence not to deny but to welcome and recognize the transformative possibilities of the stories we do not want to hear. LeBaron describes this act of making ourselves silent in order to receive testimony as a deep listening that is intellectual, somatic, and spiritual:

> The first step in truly listening is silence, not just refraining from speaking but "being silence." Being silence is not an action or inaction; it is a state that engages our bodies, minds, feelings, and spirits. When we are being silence, we are concentrating, still and calm. Our thoughts are silent. Our attention is in the present ... When we are willing to enter a space of listening ... we will hear, know and sense things both spoken and unspoken ... We don't know how this happens, but we know that it does happen. It is as though the stories that are shared are doorways into many other stories ... Once we enter that world with another ... this can lead to many things. One of them is change.[46]

Indigenous scholars suggest that the Western world has much to learn from Native peoples about the art and practice of making restitution and apology. This involves a subtle but important dimension of authenticity that has to do with our intention. How do we demonstrate that we recognize and respect Indigenous history, diplomacy, law, and peacemaking? Are we able to comprehend restitution as a sacred act of purification that is rooted in Indigenous philosophy, world view, and cultural values of justice and peace? How do we honour principles of witnessing and criteria for making, legitimizing, and recording acts of restitution and apology that use story, ceremony, and symbolic ritual in sacred spaces? How do we participate appropriately if (and only if) we are invited to do so by Indigenous people? These questions lie at the heart of unsettling the settler within.

7

An Apology Feast in Hazelton
A Settler's "Unsettling" Experience

Invitation to a Feast

Canada and the United Church of Canada will host a potlatch, to be
organized by the Gitxsan, beginning 1:00 PM, Saturday, March 20,
2004 at the Gitanmaax Community Hall, Hazelton, BC to formally
and publicly apologize to the Gitxsan for the internment of Gitxsan
children at Indian Residential Schools ... The theme for the potlatch
is "Hla Gwxhs Bekg'um" ... a Gitxsan term that characterizes ...
symbolically reinstating the survivor into Gitxsan society. Although
the apology will be to the Gitxsan as a whole, a special focus will be
on the 25 survivors of the Edmonton Indian residential school who
piloted a recently completed alternative dispute resolution program
between the Gitxsan, Canada, and the United Church ... The anticipated 400 guests will not only include dignitaries from Canada and
the United Church, but also VIPs from the 40 Gitxsan extended
families, the local bands, local Gitxsan service organizations, regional
and provincial aboriginal political and services organizations. The
program will include a welcome from the Gitanmaax Simgigyat, the
serving of traditional Gitxsan feast soup, the usual giveaway and
gifting, traditional Gitxsan drummers and singers ... and responses
from the Simgigyat of the Gitxsan after they hear the formal apology
from Canada and the United Church. As a commemoration to the
internment of the Gitxsan, the entire event will be filmed, edited and
produced for distribution locally and abroad.[1]

– Gitxsan Chiefs' Office,
"Apology to Gitxsan for IRS Internment"

REFLECTIONS

What is the story behind the day that Canada and the United Church of Canada came to Hazelton to host a potlatch in the Gitxsan Feast Hall? Most importantly, it is a story of IRS survivors whose courage, strength, and dignity teach us humility and respect. It is a story about a nation welcoming home Gitxsan men and women who as children were torn from their families and communities, who were unable, through no fault of their own, to learn the Gitxsan language, their nation's laws, and their people's ways of being in the world. It is a story of Gitxsan elders, *simgigyat* (male hereditary chiefs), and *sigid'm hanaak* (female hereditary chiefs) who gave their permission for non-Gitxsan to host this feast because it was what the survivors wanted and because this is how one speaks to truth, makes restitution and apology. It is how justice is achieved, according to Gitxsan law. The decision to bring Canada and the United Church into the feast hall not as guests but as hosts with particular responsibilities to fulfill is a powerful act of diplomacy and leadership that demonstrates the resilient capacity of the Gitxsan to use their oral and legal traditions creatively in the face of new circumstances. The story is a testament to the people of the Gitxsan Nation, who stand strong in their commitment to truth and justice for IRS survivors, their families, and communities.[2] It is also a story about institutions – about government and church accepting responsibility for the assimilationist policies and abuses whose irreparable harms continue to reverberate through Gitxsan families and communities. A very small part of the story is also mine. I was one of the non-Indigenous government officials who worked on the Hazelton Alternative Dispute Resolution Pilot Project and who participated in the feast that marked its end.[3]

The day of the feast began very early, long before the guests were due to arrive. Many final preparations were still to be made. The previous day there had been a rehearsal. Gitxsan representatives met with media to distribute press kits and review protocol, visiting dignitaries flew in, and briefings were held. Today, the hall itself was a flurry of activity; trucks filled with food and other supplies rolled up to the door, and the film crew was busy setting up cameras to capture the event for the Gitxsan. There were tables and chairs to be set up, and throughout the day, any number of small logistical crises needed to be dealt with, as is always the case when preparing for a large event. Finally, all was ready and the *simgigyat, sigid'm hanaak,* other Indigenous dignitaries and community members, and *lixsgigyatimgyat* (non-Indigenous people) guests began to arrive. Each was announced formally by the speaker, Simogyat Wii Elast (Jim Angus), who called out his or her name and title. Guests were then escorted to their proper places in the hall.[4] The feast had begun.

Stepping into the Gitxsan Feast Hall to bear witness to stories – testimonies of loss and survival – standing and speaking truthfully to this history, and learning to follow the feasting protocols and ceremonies were all part of fulfilling my responsibility as one of the hosts. When everyone was seated, Simogyat Wii Elast spoke in Gitxsanimax to the *simgigyat, sigid'm hanaak,* and assembled guests, indicating what was to occur. Gitxsan were asked to explain the events to *lixsgigyatimgyat* as the feast progressed.[5] As a host, I then had to step forward to explain why certain feast protocols were not being followed and to apologize to the *simgigyat* and *sigid'm hanaak* for this breach. I will never forget this experience, which for me remains a personal benchmark in my own unsettling as a settler! I had not been forewarned that I would be speaking, but I had learned this protocol when we went to every Gitxsan community accompanied by hereditary chiefs, elders, and Matilda Daniels, the feast coordinator, to conduct the *tets* – the formal protocol for extending invitations to a feast. Therefore, I was able to conduct myself properly. I do remember that my knees were shaking as I stood before the assembled dignitaries and guests. I felt a great responsibility to make sure that I did not do or say anything that would bring further shame on Canada. To my great relief, no objections were made afterward to what I had said. Nevertheless, I found myself seeking reassurance from Daniels and others, throughout the afternoon and evening, about what we were to do and say. In so many ways, the feast was a powerful and humbling experience for me as I learned how much I did not understand about its complexities. It is one thing to read about the feast hall in a book: it is quite another to *be* in the feast hall.

As the time drew near for the Hazelton survivors to be formally returned to their nation, I thought about all they had been through to get to this moment and how much it meant to them to finally be given their rightful place in Gitxsan society. I thought about the times when our conversations had been excruciatingly difficult, as we went through the process of settling their claims. Yet here we all were on this day; the path we had travelled together to prepare for the feast had built a fragile trust between us. Such feelings do not translate easily onto the page, but to me this is the real work of reconciliation. It is forged in the hard places that our heads and hearts travel to as, each in our own way, we struggle to find a good way forward. One by one, the IRS survivors came forward as Simogyat Wii Elast called their names, striking his talking stick on the floor as he announced them to the assembled guests. Each survivor was met by *simgigyat* and *sigid'm hanaak* from their Houses and clans, who wrapped them in the commemorative button vests emblazoned with symbolic crests that were made especially for this occasion. They were welcomed home with traditional ceremonies and songs of lament and joy so poignant that, as the sound of voices soared upward and in the sacred silence that followed, the pain of deep loss and the evocative feeling of belonging – of coming home – hung tangibly in the air. The welcoming home ceremony was highly emotional for all present but most especially for the Gitxsan, both the survivors who came home after so many years and those who welcomed their return.

At times that evening, I felt overwhelmed by the damage that we, as settlers, have wrought upon Indigenous peoples. As I remembered the stories of each of the men and women who came forward to be welcomed home, I thought about the legacy of pain and loss that began for them when, as small children, they were taken from their homes to the residential school. Yet I also knew that their stories are powerful testaments to resilience, dignity, and quiet courage – the individual and collective strength of the Gitxsan people. As I fulfilled my responsibilities as a host – distributing feast soup, gifting, and offering *xgweekwx* (money) as payment to those who were witnesses – I was taught by Gitxsan men and women who guided me with an unfailing spirit of generosity and kindness.[6] They were at once IRS victims, survivors, and proud members of the Gitxsan Nation. I was at once a representative of a perpetrator nation, host, and willing learner.

This is the true pedagogical potential of reconciliation as encounter: victims are empowered, perpetrators are humbled. Reflecting back, I now have a fuller appreciation for the paradoxical richness of the feast hall. It is where we discover the full complexity of our multiple identities and our shared humanity. It is where, for a moment in time, oppressor and oppressed can break out of the binary roles that keep us stuck in a colonial relationship. Yet I am also mindful of one *simogyat*'s words as he formally responded to the apologies. He said that, although this feast was a good thing, it was only a beginning. Many more Gitxsan and other Native people are waiting for their truths to be heard, for moral justice to be done, before authentic reconciliation can begin between us.

Reconciliation as Encounter: Feast, Ceremony, Gifting
What can the Hazelton apology feast teach us, as settlers, about the importance of making decolonizing space for Indigenous diplomacy, law, and

peacemaking to guide truth-telling and reconciliation processes? How do we recognize and respect Indigenous ways of acknowledging wrongs, making restitution and apology, and commemorating the past – ways that are grounded in the stories, songs, ceremonies, and symbolic gifting that are performed in sacred spaces such as the Gitxsan Feast Hall? How do we conduct ourselves if we are invited into these spaces so that we honour the nationhood, the people, and the history of those who have given us this generous gift?

Here, I must set out a caveat. In describing the Hazelton feast, I am not proposing the development of a prescriptive model or template for truth-telling and reconciliation processes that would be based on the cultural practices of the Gitxsan. Although Indigenous peoples across North America share common political philosophies, each nation has its own unique ways of resolving conflict, righting wrongs, and making peace. To situate the Hazelton feast, I provide a brief contextual overview of the potlatch based on published literature. I explain the importance of ceremony and gifting but acknowledge my limited understanding of the many nuances of this complex system. Therefore, I do not attempt to offer an in-depth analysis or interpretation of Gitxsan law or feast protocols. To do so would be inappropriate and disrespectful to Gitxsan experts – the elders and hereditary chiefs. Rather, I write about my own participation in the feast, my own unsettling, as one of the settler hosts. I do so in the belief that, though my story is specific to my own experience, the challenges, questions, and issues that confronted me are by no means unique to me.

The teachings with which I was gifted in the feast hall contain more broadly applicable decolonizing principles that I have incorporated into an unsettling pedagogical strategy that can be replicated elsewhere. At first glance, these principles may seem deceptively simple. In actuality, they are extremely challenging to apply consistently when one is caught up in the exigencies of everyday work and the inevitable, often competing, political pressures that are part of most Indigenous-settler interactions. Whether one is a negotiator, policy maker, or community activist, taking the necessary time to critically reflect upon one's own decolonizing journey in ways that translate into action may seem to be an unaffordable luxury. Thus, in this chapter, I aim to provide a tangible example of how an unsettling pedagogy actually works in practice.

Gitxsan Diplomacy and Law: A Contemporary Example

The decision to hold the Hazelton feast constituted an act of moral imagination. That is, the Gitxsan connected the cultural loss experienced by IRS survivors to a powerful public reclaiming of history, culture, family, community, and nation in a way that also brought Canada and the United Church into the feast hall – as hosts with particular responsibilities to fulfill. With imagination and creativity, the Gitxsan risked taking the first tentative steps toward breaking the cycles of violence so deeply ingrained in Indigenous-settler relations and exemplified in the residential school experience.

A substantial body of literature deals with the importance of the potlatch, or feast system of the Northwest Coast nations, including the Gitxsan and Wet'suwet'en. The reader will recall that the Gitxsan and Wet'suwet'en have attempted to educate the courts and the Canadian public about the feast as the traditional medium for upholding the governance and legal systems that guide their internal and intergovernmental relations.[7] In his study of Indigenous law, John Borrows explains the importance of the feast for the Gitxsan and Wet'suwet'en:

> For millennia, their histories have recorded their organization into Houses and Clans in which the hereditary chiefs have been responsible for the allocation, administration and control of traditional lands. Within these Houses, chiefs pass on important histories, songs, crests, lands, ranks and property from one generation to the next. The transfer of these legal, political, social and economic entitlements is performed and witnessed through Feasts. Feasts substantiate the territories' relationships. A hosting House serves food, distributes gifts, announces the House's successors to the names of deceased chiefs, describes the territory, raises totem poles, and tells the oral history of the House. Chiefs from other Houses witness the actions of the Feast, and at the end of the proceedings they validate the decisions and declarations of the Host House. The Feast is thus an important institution through which the people governed themselves.[8]

Similarly, legal scholar Natalie Oman describes the feast hall as a place where international diplomatic relations are forged, legitimized, and recorded via the oral tradition of the nation: "By exposing witnesses to diverse perspectives on the same incidents, this telling is designed to inspire reflection on ... the multiplicity of their truths."[9] This is a dialogical process in which relational truths – narrative, social, and restorative truths – are exchanged in a way that encourages critical discussion and consensus building among participants.

The feast provides a legal and political mechanism for addressing acts of wrongdoing by making public restitution and apology before all those assembled. Writing about the potlatch, or *bah'lats*, of the Ned'u'ten people (also known as the Lake Babine Nation), close neighbours of the Gitxsan and Wet'suwet'en, Indigenous legal scholar June McCue describes the shaming and cleansing ceremonies in which Canada would be required to participate, according to her nation's law, in order to clear its name. She explains that "Canada's colonizing record would be heard ... Canada would acknowledge this wrongdoing, make apologies, and be prepared to compensate or retribute the Ned'u'ten for such conduct with gifts. It may take a series of bah'lats for Canada to bring respect to its name."[10] For McCue, the feast is the only legitimate venue for treaty making, a process that must begin by first addressing the wrongs of the past. In her view, the honour of the Crown can be restored only by making apologies, participating in the appropriate ceremonies, and gifting; all are necessary acts of restitution that provide material compensation and emotional comfort to those harmed and allow those who have committed wrongs to redeem themselves. In *Our Box Was Full*, anthropologist Richard Daly interviewed Gitxsan *sigid'm hanaak*, who explained the history of the feasting institution and the role that ceremony plays in peacemaking:

> Olive Ryan explained that peace settlements were arranged in a feast and ceremony called *gawagani* ... Some people say that gawagani originated in the course of ending a battle in which the Gitksan were involved. It is said that when the two sides drew apart after their hostilities, the down and feathers from a flock of white birds floated over the battlefield. That is why, once *mixk'aax* is "put out," there can be no further animosity and a peace settlement must be concluded. According to Ryan, "The spreading of eagle down is the chief's law." Kyologet, Mary McKenzie, and Pearl Trombley, Gwamoon, explained to me that, at the end of the *gawagani*, when it is done properly, the down should be floated over the protagonists. As it floats, suspended in the air, the speaker tells the chiefs from

both sides to think over the history of their people and to put the dispute and the bitter feelings behind them forever. While the feathery down settles around them, the speaker exhorts them. "Waa, simgiget! Walk softly on the breath of your ancestors."[11]

The *sigid'm hanaak* provide important insight into the symbolic meaning of the ceremonial aspects of the feast hall. As a settler who had only a brief exposure to the intricacies of the feasting system, I nevertheless came away from the Hazelton feast with a deeper appreciation for how such highly structured ritual performances provide a safe environment for participants to process difficult feelings while also attending to future relations by creating mutual and ongoing social obligations.

Daly observes that "the feast ... manages and sorts out a broad range of social relations through the reciprocal exchange of histories, emotions, goods, and services."[12] This is evident, for example, in the careful attention paid to seating protocol, which is determined according to chiefly rank and status. Any variations in this protocol must be carefully negotiated in advance, as was done for the Hazelton feast. To do otherwise would bring shame upon the hosts. Gifting protocol is a subtle form of diplomacy involving the acknowledgment and discharge of social debts while simultaneously accruing new obligations. The hosts offer gifts of food, blankets, and other items, which are distributed at the feast according to rank. Those who have worked or performed at the feast are paid. Payments are also made to witnesses who are expected to verify what has transpired. Chiefs, who had given the hosts small amounts of money at the *tets* to signal their acceptance of the invitation, are repaid with interest. To the ethnocentric Western eyes of nineteenth-century missionaries and government officials, who failed to understand the reciprocal nature of these elements of the feasting system, such practices were extravagant and wasteful.[13] Yet, to my admittedly untrained but more receptive eye, the system is an elegant combination of beauty and practicality – a living process by which the Gitxsan establish, maintain, and repair relationships on their own terms.

A living peacemaking process is capable of adapting old diplomatic and legal principles in new ways to accommodate changing circumstances. Taiaiake Alfred tells us that use of language, stories, ceremony, and ritual is essential to "the regeneration of authentic indigenous existences" and that these may be either "traditional or part of an innovative regenerated

Onkwehonwe culture."[14] In writing about the Hazelton feast, I do not want to imply that Gitxsan governance and legal systems have somehow remained intact or insulated from the ravages of colonialism. In describing the internal and external reconciliation issues that the Gitxsan are addressing, Val Napoleon points out that "many Gitxsan laws have been violated by both Gitxsan and non-Gitxsan, and this contributes to cultural paralysis, a kind of cultural cognitive dissonance. Reconciliation here would mean either an explicit acknowledgment of, and agreement to, the changes to Gitxsan law to fit contemporary circumstances, or application of Gitxsan laws to deal with transgressions ... It would be difficult to force participation by the transgressor, but nonetheless, the process of dealing with transgression through the Gitxsan system, even without the transgressing parties, would be healthy and constructive for the Gitxsan."[15]

The Hazelton feast is one example of how the Gitxsan are adapting their legal traditions – in this case, to repatriate IRS survivors and hold the transgressors, Canada and the United Church, to account by dealing with them within the Gitxsan system. In giving government and church responsibilities as hosts, the Gitxsan used their legal system to respond constructively to the legacy of residential schools. They sought a way to reintegrate into Gitxsan society those who had been lost. Employing innovation and creativity – the moral imagination advocated by John Paul Lederach – they broke down old ways of interacting so that everyone involved in the feast took on a multiplicity of roles that disrupted identities and old patterns of interaction between colonizer and colonized.

The Gitxsan involved us in the feast not as visitors who would fly in at the last moment but as hosts who were expected to learn about the feasting system, interacting with the community in the days and weeks leading up to the feast. For perpetrators, the government and church who had taken Gitxsan children, this meant returning them – making restitution and apology in the feast hall. In the process, the tables were turned. Now, settlers were in a diplomatic, political, and legal environment that was foreign to them, one where business was conducted in a language they did not understand and legitimized with unfamiliar storytelling, ceremonies, and rituals. There was a rich irony in the fact that the very institutions responsible for banning the potlatch had now come full circle to embrace it, making restitution and apology according to Gitxsan law. This in itself constituted a fitting symbolic act that reflected finely honed Gitxsan diplomatic skills. In all, these were humbling moments, rich with unsettling pedagogical possibilities.

From Western Law to Gitxsan Law

> Just as it is in the courthouse, there is also a protocol in the Feast Hall
> – everyone has their place and time to speak. Just as the judge has a
> gavel, we have a talking stick ... It is or would be a most favourable
> place to deal with whatever has happened ... There isn't anything
> saying that both systems cannot be partnered ... In the Feast Hall, the
> wrong would be addressed. People and family members are witness to
> the steps taken when payment has been made to the persons harmed,
> along with an apology ... In this form, it gives both parties opportunity
> to heal or at least [to] open the doors.
>
> – Matilda Daniels, pers. comm.

With these words, Hazelton feast coordinator Matilda Daniels (Gitxsan) explains how the feast hall is well suited to the pedagogical work of truth telling and reconciliation. She notes that both Western and Gitxsan legal systems have specific protocol and rituals but believes that, in the latter, restitution and apology are conducted in a way that also mends community rifts and rebuilds trust. This is consistent with relational forms of truth telling. Testimony is exchanged wherein wrongdoing is made right through embodied acts of truth telling, restitution, and apology that are performed.

My story begins after the first phase of the Hazelton ADR pilot project was completed. Here is what happened from my perspective. The project participants wanted to publicly commemorate the occasion in a way that would involve their families and the Gitxsan community. Thus, after settling their claims, they sought to have a potlatch where the Government of Canada and the United Church would apologize and make restitution according to Gitxsan law. Moreover, they wanted to be welcomed home by their Houses and clans, a symbolic act that speaks to cultural loss and the reclaiming of Gitxsan culture and identity. They wanted Canada and the United Church to host the feast, a privilege that had never before been granted to non-Indigenous people. At this time, my knowledge of the feasting system was not extensive, but I did know that, in entering the hall, we would move from Western law to Gitxsan law – from "settling claims" to truth telling, making restitution and apology according to Gitxsan criteria. I also understood that, as a host, I would take on certain serious responsibilities.

The planning group, under Gitxsan leadership, took steps to ensure that, as the feast preparations got under way, power and control shifted from Western hands to Gitxsan hands. The Gitxsan set the mandate for the feast, assigned responsibilities to everyone, and determined how it would unfold. If Canada and the United Church were to host the feast, the Gitxsan would have to be innovative because government and church had no legitimacy, no standing, in the potlatch system. For this reason, and because of the special nature of the occasion, some of the usual seating protocols could not be followed. Accordingly, the Gitxsan discussed among themselves whether or not such a feast could be held, and if so, how it would be conducted. As settlers, my colleagues and I were not privy to these discussions, but clearly the negotiations were successful. And so, it was done.

In the weeks before the feast, we worked as a team – survivors, the advisory group, elders, *simgigyat* and *sigid'm hanaak,* the feast coordinator, and government and church representatives. As the preparations unfolded, our roles became less defined by our cultural and institutional identities alone. By this, I mean that the Gitxsan saw government and church rep-resentatives not just as institutional bureaucrats but also as vulnerable human beings in need of their expert teaching and guidance. Non-Gitxsan learned about Gitxsan culture and the laws and complex protocols of the feast hall not by attending cross-cultural sensitivity training sessions but by learning to follow the direction of elders, *simgigyat,* and *sigid'm hanaak* as well as the feast coordinator to ensure that we would not bring further shame upon Canada and the United Church. Gradually, we began to see each other through new eyes, as an intercultural team with a combined responsibility to ensure that the feast was conducted properly – trans-forming ourselves, each other, and our relationship in the process.

As non-Gitxsan hosts, we were required to apologize in advance to the *simgigyat* and *sigid'm hanaak* for breaking some of the usual protocols and to ask permission to hold the feast. This was done two weeks prior to it, during the *tets,* the process whereby the hosts invite the chiefs of each House to a feast.[16] Over the course of two days, we travelled to each

Gitxsan community, accompanied by elders, chiefs, and the feast coordinator, all of whom guided us to ensure that we conducted ourselves properly. In each community, after the invitations had been extended and accepted, small payments were given to us. These would be returned with interest at the feast. We were invited to share food either at a community gathering or, in one instance, at someone's home. This generous hospitality was greatly appreciated and helped to ease my anxiety. In all the preparations leading up to the feast, and in the hall itself, I learned by listening, watching, and doing. At times this was challenging, scary, mystifying, and frustrating as I felt completely out of my depth – a humbling experience that I would now describe as deeply unsettling. I had to step outside my usual comfort zone, take off my cultural blinders, and surrender a need to control, placing my trust in the IRS survivors, elders, and chiefs with whom I worked in an environment and language that were foreign to me. But my experience was by no means a negative one; it was also exciting and rewarding to see the feast take shape.

As we navigated the labyrinth of sometimes conflicting requirements of Gitxsan, government, and church, maintaining good humour and the ability to laugh was essential. It helped to break the tension whenever discussions became too intense. At other times, our meetings were emotionally moving as, together, we shared our feelings, our fears, and our hopes for the day of the feast. In particular, I remember a meeting that encompassed all these characteristics, when one of the survivors asked us to speak about what conducting the *tets* was like. For me, this was an opportunity to risk sharing my experience and feelings honestly. There was much lively discussion, and I think that this meeting marked an important turning point for the group as we wrestled with and then accepted the full weight of responsibility that now rested upon our shoulders. In some ways, it is difficult for me to articulate all that I learned in this process – much of it is intangible. But the shift in our relationship was striking.

In contemplating what the feast taught me about working within an ethics of recognition and respect, I am reminded of Lederach's idea that, in our everyday work, we must focus less on learning specific techniques and skills and more on developing those "qualities of process and practice ... [that] support the complex challenge of authentic reconciliation."[17] Drawing on this, I summarize my understanding of the principles and practices that guided the Hazelton team as we prepared for the feast:

- · Building a relationship of trust: This entailed being consistent, transparent, and accountable, as well as keeping our commitments, communicating openly and quickly when problems arose, and working together to resolve them. It also demanded a willingness to "roll up our sleeves and pitch in" at the community level to perform a variety of tasks that required many hands.
- Authenticity: This was expressed in a genuine and deep commitment to the group and to the feast, as well as in a willingness to work and learn together with respect, caring, and good humour.
- Humility: For non-Gitxsan, this meant learning to listen, being open to new ways of doing things, and not assuming that we already knew the answers. Being honest with the group, sharing our feelings (fear, anxiety, sadness, joy, confusion, excitement), thinking creatively, reflecting on and learning from our experience, and staying flexible were also required.
- Engaging community: In moving from Western law to Gitxsan law, the larger community became involved as the circle expanded to include families, elders, hereditary chiefs, distinguished guests, and witnesses. Approximately 450-500 people attended the Hazelton feast.

Collective Testimony and Apology

The power of collective testimony – giving and receiving stories – goes far beyond a mere recitation of historical facts. Rather, it helps us to "work through post-traumatic symptoms in the present in a manner that opens up possible futures ... By bearing witness and giving testimony, narrative may help performatively to create openings ... that did not exist before."[18] This is fundamental to the restorying of colonial history. Historically, Indigenous peoples have always used an experientially based, embodied pedagogy that is rooted in storytelling, ceremony, and ritual to teach diverse peoples how to once again coexist peacefully after conflict has occurred. They understand, as some Western educators have now also discovered, that teaching/learning practices that connect head, heart, and spirit can sometimes transform people in powerful ways that may not be fully understood on a rational level alone. In the feast hall that day, many people spoke out in righteous anger about the injustices that had been done – to them, to their families, to their communities and their nation. This too is testimony. This truth telling spoke to me not just as a government representative but as a Canadian who must come to terms with my own identity and history as colonizer. As I stood in the feast hall to receive these living testimonies, etched in the human faces of a history that we Canadians have hidden so well from ourselves, denial was simply not possible.

Significantly, although the apologies offered by the government and church at the feast met many of the Western criteria for authentic apology as set out by Nicholas Tavuchis and Matt James, neither have been permanently recorded as written texts that are readily accessible to the Canadian public. Although this makes the apologies less authentic by Western standards, when measured against those of the Gitxsan, they hit closer to the mark. The apologies were conducted in conformity with Gitxsan principles of witnessing and evaluated according to their criteria for proper restitution and apology. Thus, the apologies became part of the oral history record, spoken in the feast hall, accepted or rejected by the chiefs assembled there, and duly witnessed by all in attendance. Although they were similar in substance and tone to the official apology delivered four years later by the prime minister, there were also important differences that had to do with place. In some respects, apologies delivered at the community level might be described as containing elements of both political and personal apology. By this, I do not mean that those who apologized did so because they were personally responsible for what happened to Gitxsan children who attended the schools. Rather, there is something about the very situatedness of standing in the feast hall before those with whom you have shared stories, ceremony, and food that brings an element of personal connection, which is simply not possible in a parliamentary setting.

Speaking on behalf of Canada, Shawn Tupper, then the director general of IRSRC, delivered an apology that said in part,

> I stand here today to offer, on behalf of the Government of Canada, a long awaited apology. We are truly sorry for what happened to you. The suffering you endured as a result of your experience at Edmonton Indian Residential School was wrong, it was our fault, it shall never happen again ... The shame is ours, not yours ... During our time together we have begun to understand the heavy burden you have carried because of the abuse you suffered ... We know this is a burden you no longer want to carry. You want to give that burden to Canada and we accept it. It is ours to bear ... We are deeply touched by the vivid image of little

children being put on the train alone, leaving behind on the platform, weeping mothers, fathers and grandparents. To the families who have lost their loved ones and who today have only cherished memories, we are sorry ... Today, we are shedding some of the burdens of our shared past. A past that is marked by policies which suppressed aboriginal culture and values ... A past that records, at times, events which have caused suffering and that are at odds with the commitment of Canadians to human justice. We wish these events had never happened. We wish that we could ignore or rewrite this history ... We cannot ... The settle-ment that has been reached ... is not merely an end to a process. It is a commitment by all parties to try and build a future that will be better; that brings to an end the racism, the hurt and pain, and the personal suffering that has been your experience ... In closing, for those of you who are able to find it within your hearts, either now or in the future, we ask your forgiveness.[19]

The United Church apology, delivered by former moderator Dr. Marion Best, said in part,

As we have heard these stories we have recognized the need for the United Church to understand its involvement in the colonization of aboriginal peoples and for its role in the residential schools system. On this and many other occasions yet to come we must accept responsibility for that involvement and that role ... On behalf of the United Church of Canada, I apologize for the pain and suffering our church's involvement in the Indian residential school system has caused. We are aware of some of the damage that this cruel and ill-conceived system of assimilation has perpetrated on Canada's First Nations peoples. For this we are truly and most humbly sorry. To those individuals who were physically, sexually and mentally abused ... I offer you our most sincere apology. You did nothing wrong. You were and are the victims of evil acts that cannot under any circumstances be justified or excused. To the Gitxsan nation I also offer words of apology. You have a rich culture that has existed since time immemorial. You have a language and a justice system. This culture, this language and the traditions of the feast hall were not re-spected by the newcomers to this land. The gifts which the Gitxsan nation had to offer were suppressed in the colonization of this land. The removal of children from families and communities, the punishment exacted for speaking Gitxsanimax in residential schools and the disruption of Gitxsan spirituality and tradition are wrongs which cannot be excused. For our role in this attack on the Gitxsan nation, we offer our profound apology. We also offer our commitment to seek new ways of walking with respect and honour for the Gitxsan language, spirituality and culture.[20]

From a diplomatic and political perspective, the fact that, at the time of the feast, neither the Gitxsan nor any other Indigenous people had yet received a formal apology delivered by the prime minister in Parliament was problematic for some. Such an apology would have set an important tone for the delivery of other apologies by lesser politicians or senior bureaucrats. Nevertheless, at Hazelton, the government accepted responsibility, acknowledged the harmful impacts of past assimilationist policies, and observed that the past cannot be remade but offered a commitment to work together to end racism. Finally, it asked for but did not demand forgiveness. Although the announcement issued by the Gitxsan chiefs emphasized that the apologies were to the nation as well as survivors, Canada's apology did not refer to nationhood or to the Gitxsan legal system as exemplified in the feast system, a subtle but important distinction that I suggest would not have gone unnoticed in Gitxsan territory.

In contrast, the United Church apology is more reflective in tone, identifying the need for the church to better understand its own role in implementing destructive assimilationist policy. The speaker made the connection between colonization and church actions. She did not specifically vow that these events would never happen again but was unequivocal in condemning church complicity. There was a strong recognition of Gitxsan nationhood, law, and culture. The residential schools were rightly described as an attack on the nation. The church acknowledged that the gift previously offered to newcomers by the Gitxsan had been spurned, and then committed to working together in new ways that honoured Gitxsan language, spirituality, and culture. Here, I note that, for many years prior to the feast and into the present, the United Church has been developing education strategies to encourage its congregations to address the IRS issue at the local level. It has also developed a vision statement with guiding principles for taking anti-racist, decolonizing actions within its own institutions and in its relationship with Native people.[21]

How were the apologies received by the Gitxsan? Writing in the *United Church Observer*, Keith Howard, who was one of the witnesses at the feast that day, explained that, after the church's apology (and his comments apply equally to that of Canada), "the survivors do not leap to their feet and say, 'Oh, it's alright. We know the church meant well and that you are good-intentioned people. We exempt you' ... Within the Gitanmaax feast hall there remains a sense of wait-and-see – for the church, Canada and the survivors. Maybe, if our lives reflect our words, forgiveness might be offered."[22] That is, our actions will speak louder than our words. Many of the *simgigyat* and *sigid'm hanaak* in the feast hall who responded formally to Canada and the church said as much as they stood up to either accept or reject the apologies.

Public Commemoration and Restorying History

In the feast hall that night, in an act of public commemoration, the names of all the Gitxsan children – those still living and those now lost to their families and nation – who had attended the Edmonton Indian Residential School were read out in order to remember and honour them. It was a long list, marked solemnly by a drum beat after the reading of each name, and many people wept openly as they listened carefully for the name of their loved one. The ceremony stood as stark testament to how many lives were changed irrevocably by those who, in their cultural arrogance, thought that their ways were better. Performative acts such as this serve a critical function in truth-telling and reconciliation processes. They constitute an embodied representation of Indigenous counter-narrative, essentially restorying history. In doing so, they speak back to settler history, challenging settler historical consciousness on intellectual and emotional levels.[23]

In announcing the Hazelton feast, the Gitxsan chiefs stated that, as a commemoration of the Gitxsan residential school experience, the event would be filmed with a view to distributing it within their own region and more widely. They signalled their intention that the feast would become a permanent legacy to survivors that would also serve as a public teaching tool beyond their own communities. Although the film has educative potential, it is clear that such efforts face considerable practical challenges. It remains to be seen whether the Gitxsan and other Indigenous nations across the country will succeed in restorying the history and legacy of Indian residential schools in Canada, on their own terms and in their own voices. I understand that, to date, the Gitxsan have been unable to secure the necessary funding to complete editing and production of the film. Nevertheless, they are pursuing various ways to continue researching and documenting their own IRS history in a manner consistent with their own oral history, legal traditions, and reconciliation (peacemaking) practices.

The Teachings of the Feast Hall

> The lessons learned came when both the church and government recognized that we do have a system and that it is ours to use and has worked wonders for one's wellness, especially those who had survived residential school ... It would take 'generations' before the wrong done to the people could be restored. We can't just put a bandage on it and hope that it would go away. We have to work together to take responsibility for everyone's well being – to take that step to put closure to such an ordeal and to open another door to a nation's wellness. Acknowledgment; acceptance; responsibility; harmony.
>
> – MATILDA DANIELS, PERS. COMM.

Reflecting on what we might learn from the Hazelton feast, Matilda Daniels identifies how recognition and respect are crucial to the work of truth telling and reconciliation. On 20 March 2004, the Gitxsan Feast Hall was a place of reconciliation – an intercultural encounter where there is no token use of ceremony; rather, it is embedded in, and integral to, the practice of Gitxsan legal traditions. The feast taught me important lessons, compelling me to rethink my cultural assumptions about the meanings of history, truth, justice, and reconciliation. I learned that history resides not in dusty books but lives in the stories we carry in our hearts, minds, and spirits as we struggle to understand, acknowledge, and transform the past that is still present. I learned that truth is not only about facts but about the harsh realities of a shared colonial experience that is rooted in human relationships. I learned that justice is found not only in case law and courtrooms but in the exquisite beauty of sacred dances, symbols, and songs, in the strong words of elders, *simgigyat, sigid'm hanaak,* and families, and in the healing ceremonies and rituals of the feast hall that express the laws of the Gitxsan Nation. I learned that reconciliation is not a goal but a place of transformative encounter where all participants gather the courage to face our troubled history without minimizing the damage that has been done, even as we learn new decolonizing ways of working together that shift power and perceptions. I learned that Indigenous sacred places are powerful. They make space for us to connect with each other, exchanging testimony, making restitution and apology in ways that speak to our highest values as human beings.

This story is one of many that mark the first small steps in a long journey that Native and non-Native people must take together to restore right relations between us. Ultimately, the teachings of the feast hall enriched and deepened my thinking about why it is so crucial to unsettle the settler within, decolonizing a history of violence and trauma that is located in both the personal and the political aspects of Indigenous-settler relations. The Hazelton feast hall in Gitxsan territory is a long way from the urban office towers where we can safely feel distanced from the victims of our benevolent peacemaking. Shifting from denial to recognition requires engaging history authentically, listening respectfully to testimonies. The Gitxsan Feast Hall is one of many places of public memory where Indigenous diplomacy, law, and peacemaking have been enacted since time immemorial. For all its complexity, the work of truth telling and reconciliation is paradoxically simple. The making of space for Indigenous knowledge systems and pedagogy thus acts as a fulcrum point, decolonizing and rebalancing our relationship.

Indigenous peoples know much about how to achieve moral justice and repair broken relationships in sacred spaces that reveal our shared humanity while respecting our differences. The challenge for settlers is to listen attentively, reflectively, and with humility when we are invited into these spaces. Our responsibility to "those who arrive facing us; who ... draw near, demanding – not just apology, memorialization and reparation but something of our time, energy, and thought – thought that includes the difficult challenge of rethinking itself," demands nothing less of us.[24] This is the pedagogical work of unsettling the settler within. Being in the Gitxsan Feast Hall, in this space of "not knowing," of unsettling, working through my own discomfort, opened up to me the possibility of transformative learning that engages our whole being, our heads, our hearts, our spirits. As Matilda Daniels tells us, the teachings of the Gitxsan Feast Hall might open a door to a nation's well-being. And so, the story of the Hazelton feast and the teachings it holds for us both ends and begins here.

8

Peace Warriors and Settler Allies

REFLECTIONS

On 11 June 2009, the first anniversary of Canada's apology to IRS survivors, I witnessed a public dialogue convened in Ottawa to mark the occasion.[1] "Day of Hope: Roundtable on Reconciliation" brought together Canada's governor general Michaëlle Jean, then AFN national chief Phil Fontaine, Chief Robert Joseph, and John Ralston Saul. In her opening remarks, the governor general asked Canadians to "embrace the luminous promise of the truth rather than push this chapter [of Canada's history] from our minds because if the present doesn't recognize the wrongs of the past, the future takes its revenge."[2] In various ways, each speaker touched upon the themes I have explored in *Unsettling the Settler Within:* the importance of truth telling and bearing ethical witness, the decolonizing potential and power of Indigenous ceremonies, the need to recognize and respect Indigenous history and presence on these lands we now share, and the ongoing quest for justice and dignity that brought IRS survivors to the House of Commons a year ago to the day.

Thus, I come full circle in this book, reflecting on my thoughts and feelings on that day of commemoration. Despite all that has happened and not happened over the past year, I maintain critical hope – not because Canadians have yet breathed substantive life into the apology but because the governor general asked the audience what may seem a simple question: "How do we go from words to actions?"[3] In doing so, she invited ordinary Canadians to embrace difficult truths as a reconciliatory bridge to restoring trust and establishing positive relations. Yet I know from experience that moving from words to action is not an easy task. Then I remember the survivors who set me on this pathway with powerful testimonies that challenged my thinking, gripped my heart, and touched my soul. I remember other settlers I have met along the way, some who turned away in denial and others who courageously stepped forward, faltered, and yet spoke up. I remember these things and I choose once again to struggle to live in truth and to act. Will you?

On Living in Truth, Reconciliation as Resistance, and Critical Hope

On one level, this book is a pedagogical strategy for designing decolonizing truth-telling and reconciliation processes. On a deeper level, it is also about learning to live in truth, envisioning reconciliation as a liberatory form of non-violent resistance. Reframed as the lifeblood of a socio-political movement, struggle can then be understood as the transformative bridge between truth telling and reconciliation. For this to happen, the TRC must spark our collective imagination, inspiring change even as it hears our worst stories about ourselves and our country.

In *The Unconquerable World*, American peace scholar Jonathan Schell explores the global history of non-violent revolutions that have triggered socio-political change. He examines the writings of Gandhi, Václav Havel, and others who have led grassroots social movements that were based on a philosophical belief in the inherent "logic of peace – a cycle of non-violence" that has truth as its prerequisite.[4] Tapping into a groundswell of social discontent, such leaders become role models for ordinary citizens who then empower themselves to make peaceful and significant change in the world. Thus, a key connection is made between the importance of living with ethical intent in one's everyday life and transformation of the broader socio-political environment. Schell states that

> Havel's explanation [of living in truth] constitutes one of the few attempts ... to address the peculiarly ineffable question of what the inspiration of positive, constructive non-violent action is. By living within the lie – that is, conforming to the system's demands – Havel says, "individuals confirm the system, fulfill the system, make the system, *are* the system." A "line of conflict" is then drawn through each person, who is invited in the countless decisions of daily life to choose between living in truth and living in the lie. Living in truth – directly doing in your immediate surroundings what you think needs doing, saying what you think is true and needs saying, acting the way you think people should act – is a form

of protest, Havel admits, against living in the lie, and so those who try to live in truth are indeed in opposition. But that is neither all they are nor the main thing they are. Before living in truth is a protest, it is an affirmation.[5]

Schell makes the compelling point that, although living in truth as an act of resistance is most commonly understood as oppositional, for Havel (and others like him) it is foremost an act of critical hope. Thus, resistance is a continuous learning of how to act with integrity in one's own life and in the larger world. Although Havel's insights emerged as a counter to totalitarianism, they are also relevant for citizens living in settler societies where decolonization has yet to occur. Real socio-political change will not come from hegemonic institutional and bureaucratic structures within these societies. If it is to happen, it will come from those people who are willing to take up, again and again, the struggle of living in truth.

Drawing on this neglected aspect of resistance theory and practice in the works of Ghandi, Frantz Fanon, Edward Said, Desmond Tutu, and others who advocated strategies of resistance as a force of socio-political change, post-colonial critical studies scholar David Jefferess expands on this theme. He argues that, if societies and people are to transcend the thinking that keeps them trapped in the roles of colonizer and colonized, resistance must be understood not only as subversive or oppositional, though it is both of these, but as transformational in its ability to alter world views, structures, systems, and cultures of power.[6] In a study of the South African Truth and Reconciliation Commission within the context of the anti-apartheid struggle, Jefferess reframes the process of reconciliation itself as resistance:

The idea of reconciliation ... serves as both an ideal of liberation and a praxis of resistance ... National reconciliation, as it is defined in the TRC report ... has a much broader mandate than revealing 'truths' or instilling confidence in the institutions of the state; indeed, reconciliation may challenge the status of such institutions ... As an attempt to permanently end the cycle of violence of oppression/opposition, reconciliation constitutes an interrelated process of material and cultural transformation and not just interpersonal reconciliation between the perpetrators and victims of human rights abuses ... Reconciliation requires the deconstruction of the binary framework of the apartheid experience; yet, as a politics of social change, reconciliation challenges the politics of identity ... in order to transform relationships. As a mode of resistance, the object of reconciliation is not the oppressor/oppression but the antagonistic material and discursive relationship of colonialism ... Reconciliation resists, by seeking to transform, the antagonistic binary framework of apartheid.[7]

In the Canadian context, I have criticized reconciliation discourse, as manifested in the ADRP, as simply a regifting of old colonial attitudes masquerading as an enlightened approach to the goal of reconciliation between Indigenous people and the state. However, to dismiss Canada's Truth and Reconciliation Commission out of hand as merely another manifestation of this is to miss an opportunity to tap into its decolonizing and ultimately liberatory potential as a site and praxis of resistance and change.

Incorporating an unsettling pedagogical approach into truth-telling and reconciliation processes introduces the concepts of struggle and hope as necessary not only to decolonization but to the development of ethical reconciliation practices. Public education strategies for civic engagement will be more effective if they are able to increase knowledge about the residential school system in ways that empower the public to act. Sociologist Henry Giroux tells us that hope is the transformative force that connects education to struggle in ways that are constructively subversive: "Hope makes the leap for us between *critical education,* which tells us what must be changed; *political agency,* which gives us the means to make change; and the *concrete struggles* through which change happens. Hope, in short, gives substance to the recognition that every present is incomplete ... Hope is anticipatory rather than messianic, mobilizing rather than therapeutic ... Educated hope is a subversive force when it pluralizes politics by opening up space for dissent, making authority accountable, and becoming an activating presence in promoting social transformation."[8]

On 20-21 February 2009, I attended a think tank on civic engagement and reconciliation convened by the Aboriginal Healing Foundation (AHF). The meeting brought together people from survivor organizations, governments, universities, non-profit groups, and the media with expertise in residential school issues, health and community well-being, information campaigns, community outreach, and public engagement. Participants discussed many of the issues I have explored in greater depth in this book. In its subsequent report, the AHF identified five key themes that emerged from the meeting: engagement and reconciliation, education and knowledge sharing, emotional issues and historical trauma, sensitive messages, and framing truth-and-reconciliation-strengths-based messaging.[9] Participants noted that other TRCs, including those in East Timor, Guatemala, and Argentina, have left a legacy of "ongoing activities to reform and engage in civil society and human rights issues on a national scale long after the close of their truth commissions." They urged Canada's TRC to take a similar approach as part of a broader social movement of reconciliation – "a long-term effort that can be built from some initial short-term actions."[10] This choice would enable the commission to make a significant contribution to changing Canada's reconciliation discourse from empty rhetoric into a practice of peaceful resistance that is rooted in critical hope.

Whether one is an educator, a policy maker, a negotiator, a church layperson, a professional or blue-collar worker, or an ordinary citizen committed to social justice, reconciliation as resistance involves accepting personal and political responsibility for shifting colonial attitudes and actions that do not serve us well in our relationships with Indigenous peoples. It is helpful to recall Taiaiake Alfred's thoughts on personal decolonization as the place to begin the work of social and political transformation. Taking the risk of confronting our fear and turning aside our post-modern cynicism to undertake acts of critical hope can seem futile in the face of seemingly overwhelming challenges. We need therefore to understand and remember the link between personal change and political action. Alfred reminds us that "all of the world's big problems are in reality very small and local problems. They are brought into force as realities only in the choices made every day and in many ways by people who are enticed by certain incentives and disciplined by their fears. So, confronting huge forces like colonialism is a personal and, in some ways, a mundane process."[11]

So we must begin from where we are, not from where we want to be, remembering that decolonization is a lifelong struggle filled with uncertainty and risk taking. As we have seen, confronting this reality can lead to paralysis fuelled by the settler guilt and denial that breed frustration, cynicism, or apathy. Breaking free from this paralysis requires us to be mindful of the cumulative effect of all those small everyday actions that can ultimately build a powerful momentum for just and peaceful change. Living in truth is about making a lifelong commitment to creating the conditions in which mutual respect and responsibility can flourish. Reconciliation as resistance is about finding new ways to incorporate decolonizing principles and practices into our daily lives and working in ways that shift binary colonizer/colonized identities. This demands that we challenge ourselves and others to *think* and *feel* and *act* with fierce courage and humble tenacity in the struggle to right our relationship. John Paul Lederach reminds us that "to be gauged authentic ... change can neither be ahistorical nor superficially utopian."[12] Settlers avoid these traps by engaging directly with Indigenous people in unsettling encounters that keep us living in truth.

On Peace Warriors and Paradox

In *The Missing Peace,* American historians James C. Juhnke and Carol M. Hunter call for a new pedagogy that teaches people about the little-known history of peace in North America. Whereas the history of war has been well documented, this counter-narrative of peace remains virtually invisible to most Americans. Like Saul, who writes in the Canadian context, they trace the genesis of a unique North American peace philosophy, ethics, and peacemaking back to Indigenous roots. Noting that American history books tend to focus on Indigenous warriors rather than on peacemakers, they argue that

> there is a missing peace to the Native American story. The challenge is to recover it, to make it real, and to integrate it eventfully with the broader narrative of American history. Each of the five hundred Native American tribes or nations had its own distinctive peace tradition. The relentless white invasion challenged and subverted that traditional peace heritage. External assault on any community tends to elicit counterviolence. Even so, there are many hidden and inspiring stories of Indians meeting violent threats with peaceable restraint. For an honest and true

understanding of Indian-White encounter in North America, we must learn about the Indian peacemakers and peace traditions. And we must confront the question of which Indians contributed most to the survival of Native American culture and identity in the face of their holocaust. Was it the Indian warriors who ensured ongoing life for their people? Or was it their peacemakers and peace prophets?[13]

Although I agree with Juhnke and Hunter that such a restorying of North American history, a making of space for an Indigenous counter-narrative, is essential, their argument is framed problematically. In juxtaposing the warrior and the peacemaker, they reinforce an oppositional binary that reflects the confusion about warrior identity that currently prevails among many people in both Canada and the US. The answer to their question is that both warriors and peacemakers ensured the cultural, spiritual, and economic survival of their people. Paradoxically, within the long history of Indigenous diplomacy, law, and peacemaking, warriors are also peacemakers.

Chippewa scholar Gail Guthrie Valaskakis states that the public image and identity of the violent Mohawk warrior has deep colonial roots that existed long before the 1990 Oka crisis, a dispute over sacred burial grounds in which masked warriors were pitted against the Canadian army and provincial police. Yet, as we have seen in Chapter 5, this stereotype ingrained in North American consciousness stems in part from ignorance about the complexities of Indigenous philosophies of peace. In an empirical study on warrior societies produced for the Ipperwash Inquiry, Taiaiake Alfred and Lana Lowe point out that "contrary to the militaristic and soldierly associations of the term in European languages – and in common usage – the words translated from indigenous languages as 'warrior' generally have deep and spiritual meaning ... which literally means, 'carrying the burden of peace.'"[14] However, as Valaskakis observes, the media play a key role in perpetuating the violent warrior stereotype, feeding public confusion and contributing to the growing factionalism and ideological differences in many Native communities about what it means to be a warrior. Moreover, she suggests that the warrior identity has been appropriated in problematic ways by youth gangs and those involved in illegal activities.[15] Valaskakis highlights the various ways in which the warrior identity as sacred protector is invoked along a strategic continuum of violent and non-violent responses to perceived and actual threats to community well-being:

> Warriors have long been an important social force – and a contradictory presence – in Mohawk culture. Historically, warriors were peacekeepers, the men drawn from separate nations cemented in matrilineal clans and common experience, allied in the Iroquois Confederacy to protect against threats to "the Great Peace" ... In these arenas of cultural persistence, Mohawk warriors represent those who support peace and those who incite war and their contradictory conduct is confusing to both Indians and outsiders. While some Mohawk built barricades in the 1990s, others supported the approach of the Ogichidaw warriors of the Waswagon Treaty Association in Wisconsin, who stood in the controlled silence of six spring spearing seasons in the 1980s, absorbing the racism and rock-throwing of hundreds of non-Indians who protested their legal right to spear the spawning fish. The Chippewa won this struggle over the exercise of treaty rights through peaceable cultural practice at the boat landings and combat in the courts, where they obtained an injunction against the harassment that ended the protest.[16]

At the heart of both strategies is the warrior's sacred responsibility to protect the people and the lands. In the latter case, the cultural practices described are grounded in a philosophy of peace that effectively defuses violent acts. Speaking truth to power in peaceful ways is increasingly important if the world's citizens are to step back from the abyss of spiraling global violence and ethnic conflict in a post-9/11 world.

Here, it is important to note that Native peoples in Canada have always overwhelmingly preferred to resolve conflicts through peaceful means and have never condoned or practised terrorist-like activities against the settler population. In an analysis of case studies in which violence erupted, Alfred and Lowe found that, "in every instance where conflict has arisen between warrior societies and Canadian authorities, the violent interaction was instigated by police or other government authorities, or by local non-indigenous interests opposed to indigenous people."[17] In the Ipperwash Inquiry report, Commissioner Sidney B. Linden cited various witnesses whose testimony provides further insight into the spiritual and ceremonial aspects of warrior culture as protector and peacemaker:

> Within a month of the occupation [of Ipperwash Park], a sacred fire had been lit. It burned from May until the end of October, twenty-four hours a day, seven days a week ... People gathered at the fire to share stories, knowledge, documents, and memories about the area and the occupation. The Stoney Point people planted a peace tree in the army camp. A ceremony was held to "bury the hatchet." The ceremony signified that no weapons would be used in the reclaiming of the land and that it would be peaceful ... To its participants, the ceremony represented a sacred commitment to pursue the return of the lands in a peaceful way ... Consistent with the obligations of a warrior, the group had meetings to discuss the community's needs, collected firewood and had a wood-cutting bee, organized birthday parties, conducted patrols so they would be present as witnesses to anything that might happen, assisted the Elders with winterization, and helped with fundraising for their leadership (Glenn George and Maynard T. George) so that they could travel. The group was not militant ... They understood their role as one consistent with that of a warrior or peacekeeper.[18]

An in-depth analysis of warrior identity and the history of Native occupations as a non-violent strategy lies beyond the scope of this book, but I raise the issue to make the point that IRS survivors are also peace warriors in their own right whose activism is situated within the context of Indigenous rights and self-determination movements.

The residential school survivor movement, which emerged as a loosely organized grassroots response to the IRS experience, understandably draws heavily on the discourse of victimization and historical intergenerational trauma. It incorporates a healing metaphor as a necessary strategy for addressing the harms inflicted on students as well as the intergenerational and community impacts of the residential schools. Sociologist Thomas E. DeGloma Jr. identifies the common characteristics of various survivor social movements, stating that they all "cohere around the narratives of individual survivors and the collective process of overcoming or living through a past experience they collectively work to (re)define as atrocious and harmful in particular ways."[19] IRS survivors have come together in events ranging from community-based gatherings to international conferences and various other public forums concerning residential school issues.[20] They have established advocacy groups to lobby formally and informally for the rights and interests of survivors.[21]

DeGloma infers that survivor movements create safe spaces in which remembering the past is a form of resistance that serves as a basis for challenging dominant-culture historical narratives, demanding justice, and advocating for socio-political change.[22] He explains that "the concept of safe space ... accurately captures the survivor movement emphasis on protection and consciousness-raising ... The socio-cognitive transformations around which survivor movements cohere thus take the form of a 'discovery' or uncovering of 'truth' as a function of protection."[23] Given this, IRS survivor gatherings constitute safe spaces for truth telling. Equally importantly, DeGloma points out that these spaces also serve as a catalyst for bringing a historical counter-narrative into the public realm: "Survivor movements continually proclaim the past in public venues ... Such public proclamations of the past propel the survivor movement's reframed version of the past into the social consciousness. The public proclamation of the past, the public telling of the survivor's story, becomes symbolic of a collective moral victory. The survivor narrative thus becomes available 'at large,' functioning as an invitation to social consciousness-raising, an open form of the consciousness-raising that goes on behind closed doors in the safe space of therapy sessions and political meetings."[24] Thus, residential school survivors, much like the warriors at Ipperwash, aim to protect the people – in this instance, not only those who have suffered directly but also the generations that followed. Although the IRS survivor movement is generally one of healing, it is also integral to the global Indigenous rights movement, with particular linkages to reparations politics and international human rights discourse.

Survivors have used various non-violent strategies including individual and class-action litigation and political advocacy to pursue justice and reparations. They sought compensation for the sexual, physical, and emotional abuses they themselves suffered as well as those that have fallen upon their children and grandchildren. These harms are attributable to the assimilation policy and pedagogical practices in the schools that resulted in loss of language and culture as well as disconnection from families, communities, and traditional lands. In addition, survivors sought non-monetary forms of restitution including a truth and reconciliation commission, commemoration, and a formal public apology from Canada. Although many legal and political factors were involved in obtaining both the settlement agreement and the government apology, neither would have been accomplished without the courageous actions of survivors who played a significant role in pushing the boundaries of reparations politics in Canada.

Sociologist John Torpey distinguishes between what he describes as "commemorative/symbolic and anti-systemic/economic reparations claims" to argue that, for those seeking the former, symbolic acts such as apology may be sufficient, whereas those pursuing the latter in the form of financial compensation or return of lands or property "are more likely to be connected to broader movements for egalitarian social change."[25] He notes that, in the case of Australia, the impetus for reparations has focused primarily on "assaults on aboriginal culture rather than land claims" and concludes that "the situation in Canada with regard to residential schools for aboriginal children is quite similar."[26] Conversely, I have suggested that the struggle to obtain reparations, restitution, and apology for residential school injustices is one component of a much wider political struggle for self-determination as fundamental to the human rights and dignity of Indigenous peoples. In a similar vein, Andrew Woolford argues that the policies and practices that dispossessed Indigenous peoples of their lands and resources, and that attacked their traditional systems of governance, must be placed in conjunction with the restrictions imposed by the Indian Act and the cultural impacts of residential schools. As he observes, "it is worth noting that these actions remain a source of great bitterness in the collective memory of the First Nations of British Columbia and, combined with the anger of the long denial of Aboriginal title, produce a sense of injustice in the modern Aboriginal consciousness that cannot be easily placated."[27]

At a 28 January 2009 public forum hosted by the Law Society of British Columbia, Tl'azt'en grand chief Edward John, who is political executive for the First Nations Summit (FNS), gave a speech in which he connected Canada's IRS apology to the broader socio-political environment of problematic treaty negotiations, ongoing Aboriginal title and rights litigation and land claims, and Canada's failure to endorse the United Nations Declaration on the Rights of Indigenous Peoples:

> The FNS acknowledges Prime Minister Harper's 11 June 2008 apology for Canada's involvement in the Indian Residential Schools system. Now it is time to move from apology to action. As a member of the HRC [Human Rights Council], Canada must adhere to the highest standards of human rights. At a minimum, Canada must endorse and implement the *Declaration*. Canada's position regarding Aboriginal title, rights and treaty negotiations consistently impedes efforts by First Nations to exercise their right to self-determination and to improve the socioeconomic conditions of their communities. Canada's denial of First Nations' land rights falls well short of the minimum standards affirmed by the *Declaration* and demonstrates a clear failure by Canada to implement its human rights obligations. Prime Minister Harper's apology to survivors of Indian residential schools and to their families ... acknowledged that such a policy of assimilation was wrong and has created great harm and has no place in our country. It is no accident that First Nations find themselves largely in the margins of Canada's social and economic well-being. Given this history, the pattern of conduct of Indigenous Peoples has been one of perseverance, persistence, and patience. Canada's policy of denying Aboriginal title and rights is premised on the very same attitudes that Prime Minister Harper referred to in his residential school apology. It is time for these attitudes and any policies flowing from them to be cast aside.[28]

In urging Canadians to move from apology to action, Grand Chief John placed Canada's apology squarely within a discourse of Indigenous self-determination and human rights that is both national and international in scope. In the context of reparations politics, he linked the symbolic function of the apology to the structural and systemic realities of land dispossession and socio-economic disadvantage, all of which found their genesis in the assimilation policies and colonial attitudes of the settler majority.

Survivors themselves use the language of human rights and self-determination in describing what is required to overcome the injustices perpetrated in the IRS system. They emphasize the importance of restoring human dignity by revitalizing Indigenous governance and knowledge systems, languages, and cultural and ceremonial practices that are rooted literally in the landscapes of traditional territories. In a pilot research project with Nuu-chah-nulth survivors living in British Columbia, Indigenous scholars Jeff Corntassel, Chaw-win-is, and T'lakwadzi explore the connections between Indigenous storytelling, community-based truth telling, and approaches to reconciliation processes. They remark that "Indigenous storytelling is connected to our homelands and is crucial to the cultural and political resurgence of Indigenous nations."[29] The authors observe that, in Western forms of reparative justice, "the issue of land is treated as a separate issue from that of the residential school, ignoring the fact that the issues survivors contend with from the residential school era are rooted in the forced removal of entire families and communities from their homelands."[30] In a discussion of storytelling within a human rights discourse, gender studies scholars Kay Schaffer and Sidonie Smith identify the ways in which the testimonies of some Stolen Generations survivors interweave both the language of human rights, which describes "separation, institutionalization, destruction of culture and heritage, the loss of language, limited educational opportunities, restrictions on freedom, segregation, physical and sexual abuse, mental and physical cruelty, unjust detention, coercive practices, and the intergenerational effects of separation on families and communities," and the language of self-determination, which "exceeds these parameters to acknowledge entitlements to land, law, culture and language as a culturally distinct people."[31] Both studies are consistent with my argument that, with their non-violent socio-political focus, survivor movements incorporate healing metaphors and cultural practices in ways that also speak to Indigenous self-determination and human rights.

On Peace Warriors' Visions: Imagination and Restorying History

Stories operate in the world and get results. Stories shape our understandings of the past, tell us who we are, and provide a vision for the future. Because they define our communities, they provide a rationale for collective action. Stories have "narrative potency" ... Peace building may require voicing or re-imagining our stories. However, our stories, voices and imagination, and power are constrained. Stories operate within a context of ideological, economic, and power constraints. Peace building requires facilitating social spaces where people can voice their experience, develop shared understandings, and build trusting relationships. Throughout history, storytellers have served as community leaders, memory-keepers, cross-cultural ambassadors, consciousness-raisers, and mediators ... [They use] stories in numerous creative ways towards goals of promoting personal and social change.[32]

– JESSICA SENEHI, "CONSTRUCTIVE STORYTELLING IN INTERCOMMUNAL CONFLICTS: BUILDING COMMUNITY, BUILDING PEACE"

George Manuel (1921-89), whose Indian residential school experience was described briefly in Chapter 4, was a Secwepemc (Shuswap) chief from the interior region of British Columbia and former president of two Indigenous political organizations – the National Indian Brotherhood and the Union of BC Indian Chiefs. As a leader in the Canadian Native rights movement, and founder of the World Council of Indigenous Peoples (1975-81), he was a peace warrior – an activist and political visionary whose work spanned the globe.[33] One of the great ironies of the IRS system in British Columbia and elsewhere is that, because it brought children from various cultural groups into the isolation of the schools, it inadvertently planted the seeds of a pan-Indigenous political movement that ultimately worked to "promote a new and wider Indian awareness and identity."[34] George Manuel was one of these future leaders. In writing his autobiography *The Fourth World*, he observed that

when we come to a new fork in an old road we continue to follow the route with which we are familiar, even though wholly different, even better avenues might open up before us. The failure to heed [the] plea for a new approach to Indian-European relations is a failure of imagination. The greatest barrier to recognition of aboriginal rights does not lie with the courts, the law, or even the present administration. Such recognition necessitates the re-evaluation of assumptions, both about Canada and its history and about Indian people and our culture ... Real recognition of our presence and humanity would require a genuine

reconsideration of so many people's role in North American society that
it would amount to a genuine leap of imagination.[35]

Manuel penned these words in 1974. Thirty-six years later, most ordinary
Canadians have yet to take this genuine leap of imagination to question
our assumptions – our myths – about Canada's past or to understand how
these influence our relationship with Indigenous people in connection
with unresolved historical conflicts. Manuel spent his life resisting the
systemic political, economic, and social injustices faced by Indigenous
people everywhere. I have focused particularly on the cultural, psychological, and relational aspects of colonialism that he identified as significant
obstacles to decolonization. He saw the source of the problem in Canada
– our persistence in clinging to old colonial myths that perpetuate denial,
fear, and guilt. These myths inhibit our ability to imagine something different. But he also saw a way forward – a transformative pathway that
would lead to a more just and peaceful coexistence – a pathway that, should
we choose it, requires us to think more deeply about what it would mean
to *fully* recognize and respect the *presence and humanity* of the people
whose lands we now share.

Speaking in 1972, Manuel challenged the settler majority to think about
their role and responsibility in decolonization: "The question now is for
non-Indian North Americans to decide how they want to relate to this
struggle. We will steer our own canoe, but we will invite others to help
with the paddling."[36] He was a rare combination of visionary and grassroots
pragmatist who saw that the work of decolonization cannot rest on the
backs of Indigenous people alone. He knew that settlers have a different,
yet critical role to play on this front – one that we must find for ourselves.
Restorying the history of Indian residential schools and of Indigenous-
settler relations more broadly entails using our imaginations in the way
that Manuel advocates. In essence, he cuts to the heart of the matter. Both
Indigenous people and settlers must take action that is radically different
if we are to change our relationship. He points the way for settlers who
want to take up the challenge, but we are responsible for finding our own
pathways.

In previous chapters, I underlined the urgent need to find new ways to
break through cycles of colonial violence. I have argued that, in this regard,
we have much to learn from Indigenous peoples, who have a long history

of resolving conflicts and restoring peaceful relations. I described how the Gitxsan adapted their law, as enacted through the traditional feasting system, to fit new circumstances as they involved non-Indigenous people in the ceremonies and protocols related to apology, restitution, and repatriation of Gitxsan IRS survivors. This form of non-violent intervention momentarily broke existing patterns of violence, temporarily shifting the identities of colonized victim and colonizer-perpetrator. The Gitxsan showed vision, leadership, courage, tenacity, strength, and creativity, all of which exemplify the warrior spirit. As warriors of peace, they offer us principled teachings that can be applied to the Truth and Reconciliation Commission of Canada as it undertakes its work. Other Indigenous nations across Turtle Island may do likewise, utilizing their own culturally specific histories of diplomacy, law, and peacemaking.

Against all odds, and in the face of social dysfunction, lateral violence, health problems, and the poverty that is endemic in their communities today, Indigenous peoples remember who they are and where they come from. A rich, culturally diverse history is embedded in the stories, ceremonial practices such as gifting, smoking the sacred pipe, condolence rituals, and feasting that are still practised across Turtle Island. I have outlined the ways in which this history is at odds with the settler peacemaker myth. Yet, should Indigenous people choose to share it, this counternarrative has much to teach all of us about how to establish reciprocal trust, nurture mutual respect, and sustain peaceful relationships.[37] Having laid out a rationale for why survivors who have been victimized by the residential school system are in fact peace warriors, I now consider how they, along with those settler allies who also choose to live in truth, might participate in the TRC as an act of transformative liberatory resistance that is infused with critical hope.

Peace Warriors, Settler Allies, and the TRC

In thinking about how Native and non-Native people might engage in a testimonial encounter during and beyond the life of the TRC, what qualities and values might assist both groups in reframing the entrenched identities that act as barriers to living in truth and socio-political change? In an essay entitled "When Survivors Become Warriors," Rupert Ross contemplates what might happen if, as survivors come forward to speak their truths to the TRC, skilled listeners were able to ask questions that might shift the storytellers' self-understanding in ways that shed new light on their life stories. This might encourage survivors to focus not solely on the many ways they think they have failed themselves, their families, and communities because of the damage left in the wake of their residential school experiences. For example, a grandmother might gain new self-awareness, thereby empowering herself with the realization that "far from being a failure, she had accomplished a near-miracle in retaining her core human and aboriginal validity, despite the onslaught." Ross asks a compelling question: "What if she came before the Commission as a survivor and walked out a warrior?"[38]

What would it mean to walk out a warrior? As Ross points out, for many former students this would involve seeing, perhaps for the first time, that surviving the pain of their darkest traumatic moments and somehow carrying on with their lives has taken tremendous courage, tenacity, and strength. Perhaps this survivor-grandmother also works in her community to improve living conditions and family well-being. On a collective level, as increasing numbers of survivors come forward with stories not only of abuse but of resistance and renewal, there is potential for the Canadian public to begin to recognize the vision and leadership that survivors have shown to the world as human beings with dignity who have chosen to live in truth. These qualities exemplify the peace warrior spirit. Contemporary peace warriors use righteous words and non-violent actions to confront the colonizer on a number of fronts.

I now pose a related question to settlers. What if a settler came before the commission as a colonizer and walked out an Indigenous ally? What if skilled listeners asked former IRS staff and church and government officials a different set of questions that might also shift their self-understanding in ways that shed new light on their life stories? What if the public discourse that emerges from the TRC educates ordinary Canadians not only about the devastating impact of residential schools as a significant human rights infringement but also teaches them about the strength of the human spirit and the profound sacredness of human dignity as exemplified by survivors? Although allies are not warriors, we too can choose to live in truth. To do so, we must come to the TRC both as testifiers and as ethical witnesses who listen to Indigenous testimonies with a decolonizing ear. We bear witness, and in doing so, we accept responsibility for making change in the world. Rather than adopting the stance of the colonizer-perpetrator who listens to survivor testimonies with the empathy of a spectator, thereby simply reinscribing colonial relations, we must attend to our unsettling responses to testimonies as important clues to our own decolonization.

As allies, we learn to listen with humility and vulnerability to the history of dispossession, racism, and oppression that is still alive. We critically reflect upon these stories as a catalyst for action. We take full responsibility for the IRS system. We can then walk out of the Truth and Reconciliation Commission proceedings with a sense of critical hope that prompts action. In solving the settler problem, we would educate ourselves about the history of Indigenous-settler relations not only as it relates to residential schools but to the whole colonial project. We would learn about how the broken treaties, unresolved land claims, and conflicts over traditional lands and resource rights have a detrimental impact today. We would work in solidarity with Indigenous people to restory the IRS history and legacy through ethical testimonial exchange and in public history and commemoration projects as part of national truth telling. We would commit ourselves to the ongoing struggle of reconciliation as liberatory resistance.

Restorying Possibilities: Future Research

Restorying history takes place on many levels in truth and reconciliation processes. Many Indigenous communities across the country are convening gatherings of survivors, former IRS staff, church and government representatives, and local residents to participate in dialogue circles and ceremonial practices of remembering and commemoration.[39] National initiatives such as "1000 Conversations" are creating space for public dialogue about the IRS issue. Conferences bring together Indigenous and non-Indigenous academics, policy makers, and practitioners. Public history exhibits such as the Legacy of Hope's "Where Are the Children? Healing the Legacy of Residential Schools" and "We Were So Far Away: The Inuit Experience of Residential Schools" are travelling across Canada and are also available on-line.[40] Such exhibits have the potential to educate in unexpected yet powerful ways at the community level, bringing together survivors, their families, and communities as well as non-Native people. Curators and archivists at local museums can play a significant role in bringing this difficult history home, a commitment that is sometimes sparked by their own disquieting responses to these exhibits.[41] Commemorative exhibits encourage people to share their own residential school stories, memories, photographs, and memorabilia. This may facilitate local dialogue and generate Indigenous community histories about the IRS system, including its greater implications for Indigenous-settler relations, thus restorying history at the community level.

It is clear that, if settler Canadians are to truly come to grips with our responsibility for the IRS system, we must learn more about two interrelated aspects of our history. First, what are the stories of earlier generations of Indigenous allies? In *With Good Intentions,* co-editors Celia Haig-Brown and David Nock present a collection of essays, a decolonizing project, that explores the complex and contradictory motivations of educators, lawyers, missionaries, and social justice activists who worked with and on behalf of Native peoples in the past.[42] We need to know more of these stories. Second, we need to learn from the stories of former IRS staff. In "Truth and Reconciliation," British Canadian writer Natalie A. Chambers identifies the challenges involved in assembling the stories of IRS teachers and administrators. Reflecting on research interviews she conducted, she touches on themes that I have also identified in my own work. She too describes the complexity of her position, her emotional turmoil, and the ethical issues she confronted:

> Talking to former staff and hearing their stories of working in the schools was an extremely challenging process for me emotionally. I had started the project with the hope that through the process of participating in the interviews and receiving feedback on their interviews from the First Nations participants (communicated through me) would create possibilities for former staff to question their commonsensical beliefs and ideas about the cultural superiority of non-Indigenous peoples. I had hoped that the sharing of stories would help to "forge a common story that could serve as a basis for a different kind of reconstructed memory ... [an] exceptionally difficult" challenge. These hopes were only partially realized. Only Christine, a former teacher, seemed deeply

emotionally invested in the process of examining the values and beliefs
that had led her to work in the schools, as well as her actions during her
period of employment ... I am still not entirely sure what we may learn
from talking with and listening to former staff and other colonial actors.
Christine's emotional journey seemed to suggest that further textual
dialogues between First Nations Survivors and former staff may contribute to a shift in colonial consciousness in the larger society. However,
as the interviewer responsible for facilitating the process, it was difficult
to consider the emotional turmoil that Christine, as a compassionate
and self-critical human being, may have experienced as a result of her
participation.[43]

Here, I want to make two points. First, even if an individual's understanding of his or her life experience remains static, we can learn much by
undertaking a larger sampling of these stories and analyzing them with a
view to uncovering patterns of settler denial, complicity, or resistance
within the residential school system. Second, Chambers ultimately concludes (based on an admittedly small sampling) that dialogue between
Indigenous people and settlers may indeed create a shift in historical consciousness. This is an intriguing possibility, congruent with my own hypothesis about the decolonizing pedagogical potential of truth-telling and
reconciliation processes. Although, in many instances, former staff may
prefer to be interviewed by themselves, group dialogues with other staff
members or, where appropriate, directly with IRS survivors may increase
the likelihood of gaining new insight into the complexities of student-staff
relationships in the schools. Moreover, when conducted in a safe environment, such interactions provide space for healing and transformation for
both colonizer and colonized.

Further study might reveal whether dialogue forums do in fact engender a collective moral responsibility that may otherwise be absent. My own
experience reveals that the public linking of personal experience to wider
responsibility through testimonial, ceremonial, and commemorative
practices is key to shifting historical consciousness and restorying the past.
To further complicate the situation, what of Indigenous people who
themselves worked in the IRS system? What new truths can we learn from
these untold parts of the storyline? How might an unsettling pedagogical

strategy be applied and extended in these research contexts? Documenting the Truth and Reconciliation Commission's own process in conjunction with community-based research initiatives may generate new insights into the efficacy of dialogue circles, testimonial encounter, and ceremonial commemorative practices to decolonize and transform Indigenous-settler relations.

Indigenous Allies: Strategies of History and Hope

> I believe it is possible to move beyond this ugly and often violent history, to be a society that is founded not on mere "tolerance," but on respect, a society that lives up to its word. But I know we can't move forward until we look the past in the eye, until we understand our-selves more deeply, acknowledging and exploring even the darker aspects of our history – not to damn our forebears, but with hope for a more humane world.
>
> — VICTORIA FREEMAN, *DISTANT RELATIONS:*
> *HOW MY ANCESTORS COLONIZED NORTH AMERICA*

In *Unsettling the Settler Within,* I have used my own stories to explore a pedagogy for restorying a shared but conflicting colonial history. A process of relational truth telling – a constructive critical dialogue with Indigen-ous people about Indian residential schools – might precipitate a much broader re-examination of Indigenous-settler relations. Those settlers who think that no reconciliation is necessary or that a cheap reconciliation is enough may never aspire to change the socio-political relationships, structures, and institutions of colonialism. Taiaiake Alfred reminds us that, "from the perspective of the Onkwehonwe struggle, the enemy is not the white man in racial terms, it is a certain way of thinking with an im-perialist's mind."[44] Thus, it is possible and necessary for those settlers who would be Indigenous allies to reject the imperialist's mind in favour of living in truth, accepting that we will struggle and be discomforted and unsettled.

· In Chapter 7, I set out the decolonizing principles that guided the Hazelton feast-planning group. These are not intended to be a prescriptive to-do list that, once completed, can be forgotten. Rather, they are meant to be touchstones that guide us as we travel along routes of change. They are applicable within the context of the TRC but also more generally in a variety of settings: classrooms, negotiating tables, policy forums, community halls, and public history and commemorative spaces. Adopting an unsettling pedagogy enables us to gain a better understanding of why myth and history matter in the work that we do, the classes we teach, the law and policy we make, and the history that we have hitherto denied. In this way, reflection and action are linked to a vision of justice and peace that infuses our everyday lives and work with critical hope. As Lederach suggests, we must develop "qualities of practice" whereby those of us who are involved in transforming deep-rooted conflict and transcending cycles of violence can work more effectively within "the actual messiness of ideas, processes, and change."[45] This work is not prescriptive; it involves a genuine spirit of inquiry that is respectful of the dignity and humanity of others. Lederach advises us to "focus on people and their experience. Seek a genuine and committed relationship rather than results ... Be leery of quick fixes. Respect complexity but do not be paralyzed by it. Think comprehensively about the voices you hear that seem contradictory, both within a person, between people, and across a whole community ... No matter how small, create spaces of connection between them. Never assume you know better or more than those you are with that are struggling with the process. You don't. Do not fear the feeling of being lost ... Give it time."[46] These qualities of practice seem counterintuitive because they are the antithesis of the way in which people are encouraged to conduct their work. Yet taking the necessary time to reflect on a process even as we are immersed within it yields rich insights and moments of inspiration – the leap of imagination that is so vital to making change in the world.

On Unsettling Possibilities

Imagine how you as writers from the dominant society might turn over some of the rocks in your own garden for examination. Imagine ... courageously questioning and examining the values that allow the de-humanizing of peoples through domination ... Imagine writing in honesty, free from the romantic bias about the courageous 'pioneering spirit' of colonialist practise and imperialist process. Imagine interpreting for us your own people's thinking towards us, instead of interpreting for us, our thinking, our lives, our stories.

– Jeanette Armstrong, "The Disempowerment
of First North American Native Peoples and
Empowerment through Their Writings"

Okanagan author and activist Jeanette Armstrong asks the non-Indigenous to cast a critical eye on the imperial garden we have cultivated with our colonial tools, on the lands and in the lives of Indigenous peoples. She asks us to turn over the rocks and face whatever ugly creatures slither out, examining them honestly and unflinchingly. To challenge the romantic myths we believe about ourselves and to focus our energies on questioning our own identity, values, and experience as colonizers. To share honestly with Native people what we learn about ourselves in the process, and more importantly, how we will change our attitudes and actions.

In this book, I have turned over some of these rocks to unearth one colonial creature that still inhabits our garden – the benevolent peacemaker. In doing so, I challenge a popular Canadian historical myth. The story of our identity as neutral arbiters of law and justice is solidified in nineteenth-century treaty making and Indian policy, rooted in a racist mindset of cultural superiority. I argue that various forms of settler violence against Indigenous peoples can be traced from these origins through to the flawed reconciliation discourse that now dominates Indigenous-settler relations.

This is Canada's *true* story. It is our colonizer identity that we want most to deny. Without a truth telling in which we confront our own history and identity, and make visible how these colonial practices continue today, there can be no ethical or just reconciliation with Indigenous peoples. Much like our ancestors, who merely went through the motions of gift exchange during treaty making, we will achieve nothing but a re-assertion of the colonial status quo if our promise of reconciliation entails no more than a well-intentioned regifting. The violent nature of our relationship is revealed most starkly in the history and legacy of Indian residential schools, where perpetrator/victim patterns of behaviour and attitudes are entrenched. The public controversy over Canada's Alternative Dispute Resolution Program, which was designed to resolve IRS claims, demonstrates the authenticity gap that exists between the rhetoric of reconciliation and the reality on the ground. We see conflicting visions of reconciliation, as the parliamentary committee meetings revealed an ADR model that privileges neutrality over engagement – legal certainty over moral justice. This regifted reconciliation was destined to fail.

Historically and to the present, we remain obsessed with solving the Indian problem, even as we deflect attention from the settler problem. In doing so, we ignore our complicity in maintaining the colonial status quo. The question now is whether we will remain colonizer-perpetrators or strive to become more ethical allies in solidarity with Indigenous people. As a settler ally, I must continuously confront the colonizer-perpetrator in myself, interrogating my own position as a beneficiary of colonial injustice. Exploring the epistemological tensions of working between these two identities means embracing persistent uncertainty and vulnerability. If we have not explored the myths upon which our identity is based, or fully plumbed the depths of our repressed history, we lack a foundation for living in truth. What we have instead is a foundation of untruths, upon which we have built a discourse of reconciliation that promises to release Indigenous-settler relations from the shackles of colonialism but will actually achieve just the opposite.

Writing about the necessity of creating a culture of peace, educator Anne Goodman asks those with whom she works a key question, one designed to provoke both critical reflection and action that is based in a larger vision: "How are you working towards a culture of peace?"[47] As settler allies, we might ask ourselves additional questions as we go about our everyday work. Does the action I am about to take, or the words I am about to speak or write, come from the head, heart, and hands of a colonizer-perpetrator or a settler ally? How am I working in decolonizing ways? What am I doing on a daily basis within myself and in my relationships with my family, my community, my school, or my workplace that keeps me living in truth? Are my actions leading toward more just and peaceful relations with Indigenous people? It is my critical hope that, in answering these questions, we will be deeply unsettled in our minds, our hearts, and our spirits, and know that this is a good thing. The transformative pathways in our garden are rich and fertile but need our time, attention, love, and energy to flourish. This is the work of the settler ally.

I'm convinced that, unless we who are non-Indigenous undertake to turn over the rocks that remain in our colonial garden, we will never achieve what we claim to want so badly – to transform and reconcile our relationship with Indigenous people. Rather, we will remain benevolent peacemakers, colonizer-perpetrators bearing the false gift of a cheap and meaningless reconciliation that costs us so little and Indigenous people so much. But what if we were to offer the gift of humility as we come to the work of truth telling and reconciliation? Bearing this gift would entail working through our own discomfort and vulnerability, opening ourselves to the kind of experiential learning that engages our whole being – our heads, our hearts, our spirits. Reconciliation is then a teaching/learning place of encounter where acts of resistance and freedom occur. This involves nothing less than a paradigm shift that moves us from a culture of denial toward an ethics of recognition.

I ask non-Indigenous readers to resist denying, dismissing, or rationalizing my words. I invite you instead to question the myth, to name the violence, to face the history – to turn over the rocks in your own garden, which has been cultivated with such care. Connecting head, heart, and spirit in ways that value vulnerability and humility enables us to accept harsh truths and to use our moral imagination in order to reclaim our own humanity. Social activist and author Anne Bishop reminds us that, as we struggle with forces much larger than ourselves – globalization, global warming, ethnic conflict, poverty, and injustice – we must envision the kind of world we want to live in. We must take heart in knowing that "there are small, courageous experiments happening everywhere, based in and on local conditions, but aware of the whole world ... Our recovery of hope – full-colour, three-dimensional, hard working, clearly thinking, wildly radical, living hope – is our key to liberation."[48] Unsettling the settler within necessarily involves critical self-reflection and action in our lives – a difficult learning that is part of the struggle we must undertake. At the same time, we must also work in respectful and humble partnership with Indigenous people to generate critical hope – vision that is neither cynical nor utopian but rooted in truth as an ethical quality in the struggle for human dignity and freedom. We can then understand turning over the rocks in our garden as an act of wildly radical, living hope.

Notes

Foreword

1 Taiaiake Alfred, *Wasáse: Indigenous Pathways of Action and Freedom* (Peterborough, ON: Broadview Press, 2005).

Introduction: A Settler's Call to Action

1 Harper's formal apology for Indian residential schools was delivered in Parliament on 11 June 2008. For the full text, see "Prime Minister Harper Offers Full Apology on Behalf of Canadians for the Indian Residential Schools System," Office of the Prime Minister, http://www.pm.gc.ca/eng/media.asp?category=2&id=2149.

2 The Indian problem was defined by Duncan Campbell Scott, deputy superintendent of Indian Affairs from 1913 to 1932, as that of how to assimilate Indigenous people into mainstream Canadian society. The education of children was a key element in the broader assimilation project. In 1920, Scott introduced amendments to the Indian Act that made residential school attendance mandatory. In recommending such measures, Scott explained, "I want to get rid of the Indian problem. I do not think as a matter of fact, that the country ought to continuously protect a class of people who are able to stand alone ... Our objective is to continue until there is not a single Indian in Canada that has not been absorbed into the body politic and there is no Indian question, and no Indian Department, that is the whole object of this Bill." Duncan Campbell Scott, deputy superintendent general of Indian Affairs, testimony before the Special Committee of the House of Commons examining Indian Act amendments of 1920, Library and Archives Canada, Ottawa, RG 10, vol. 6810, file 470-2-3, pt. 7, 55 (L-3) and 63 (N-3), quoted in E. Brian Titley, *A Narrow Vision: Duncan Campbell Scott and the Administration of Indian Affairs in Canada* (Vancouver: UBC Press, 1986), 50. See also John S. Milloy, *A National Crime: The Canadian Government and the Residential School System, 1879 to 1986*, 3rd ed. (Winnipeg: University of Manitoba Press, 2001), 3, 7. In his response in the House of Commons to Canada's apology, former Assembly of First Nations (AFN) national chief Phil Fontaine said that "never again will

this House [the House of Commons] consider us to be the Indian problem just for being who we are." Phil Fontaine, video and transcript, Indian Residential Schools Statement of Apology, 11 June 2008, http://www.ainc-inac.gc.ca/ai/rqpi/apo/pfafn-eng.asp.

3 Under the IRS Settlement Agreement, there were no federally recognized residential schools in Newfoundland and Labrador, Prince Edward Island, or New Brunswick. Of note, five residential schools operated in Newfoundland and Labrador, and a class-action lawsuit alleging abuse was certified in the Supreme Court of that province on 8 June 2010. CBC News Online, "N.L. Residential School Lawsuit Can Proceed," 8 June 2010, http://www.cbc.ca/canada/newfoundland-labrador/story/2010/06/08/nl-residential-schools-608.html. For an account of the problems associated with the architecture, design, building, and maintenance of the schools with regard to detrimental effects on the health and well-being of students, see Milloy, *A National Crime*, chaps. 4 and 5.

4 Variations on this phrase have been used. Canada's apology states that "the treatment of children in residential schools is a sad chapter in our history." The Statement of Reconciliation issued by Ottawa in 1998 expresses Canada's "profound regret for past actions of the federal government which have contributed to these difficult pages in the history of our relationship together." See "Notes for an Address by the Honourable Jane Stewart Minister of Indian Affairs and Northern Development on the Occasion of the Unveiling of *Gathering Strength – Canada's Aboriginal Action Plan*," Indian and Northern Affairs Canada, http://www.ainc-inac.gc.ca/ai/rqpi/apo/js_spea-eng.asp. In his response to Canada's apology, Phil Fontaine refers to this "dreadful chapter in our shared history." Fontaine, Video and transcript, Indian Residential Schools Statement of Apology, 11 June 2008. His comment on the first anniversary of Canada's apology emphasizes the importance of "facing the dark moments of the country's history with the original residents of the land." Fontaine, quoted in Jorge Barrera, "Procession Marks First Anniversary of Residential Schools Apology," *Vancouver Sun*, 11 June 2009, http://www.vancouversun.com/news/.

5 Here, it is important to define what I mean by "making space." Colonization involves the taking of space: geographic, historical, narrative, cultural, political, legal, intellectual, and pedagogical. Decolonization requires settlers to make space through substantive acts of apology and various forms of restitution, even as Indigenous people are reclaiming and renaming such space through acts of resistance and renewal. I thank Dr. Leslie Brown for pointing out this concept of making and retaking space as a decolonizing act. Pers. comm., 16 September 2004. I also thank Dr. Maggie Hodgson for her insights from an Indigenous perspective on how this concept is useful within the context of Indian residential schools. Pers. comm., 20 November 2005.

6 *Indian Residential Schools Settlement Agreement*, 2006, http://www.residentialschool settlement.ca/settlement.html.

7 For biographies of Sinclair, Littlechild, and Wilson, see "Meet the Commissioners," Truth and Reconciliation Commission of Canada, n.d., http://www.trc-cvr.ca/commissioners.html.

8 Schedule N: Mandate for the Truth and Reconciliation Commission, *Indian Residential Schools Settlement Agreement,* 2006, http://www.residentialschoolsettlement.ca/settlement.html.

9 Helen Cobban, *Amnesty after Atrocity? Healing Nations after Genocide and War Crimes* (Boulder, CO: Paradigm, 2007), see especially Chapter 2, "South Africa: Amnesties, Truth-Seeking – and Reconciliation?" 80-135.

10 Andrea Smith, *Indigenous Peoples and Boarding Schools: A Comparative Study,* Report prepared for the Secretariat of the United Nations Permanent Forum on Indigenous Issues, n.d., 9, http://www.un.org/esa/socdev/unpfii/documents/IPS_Boarding_Schools.pdf. See also Aboriginal Healing Foundation, *The Healing Has Begun: An Operational Update from the Aboriginal Healing Foundation* (Ottawa: Aboriginal Healing Foundation, 2002), 8.

11 Robert I. Rotberg, "Truth Commissions and the Provision of Truth, Justice and Reconciliation," in *Truth v. Justice: The Morality of Truth Commissions,* eds. Robert I. Rotberg and Dennis Thompson (Princeton: Princeton University Press, 2000), 16-17.

12 Madeline Dion Stout and Rick Harp, *Lump Sum Compensation Payments Research Project: The Circle Rechecks Itself* (Ottawa: Aboriginal Healing Foundation, 2007), http://www.ahf.ca/publications/research-series.

13 For an overview of the Oka crisis, see, for example, Linda Pertusati, *In Defense of Mohawk Land: Ethnopolitical Conflict in Native North America* (Albany: State University of New York, 1997); Gerald R. Alfred, *Heeding the Voices of Our Ancestors: Kahnawake Mohawk Politics and the Rise of Native Nationalism* (Toronto: Oxford University Press, 1995); Geoffrey York and S. Pindera, *Peoples of the Pines: The Warriors and Legacy of Oka* (Toronto: Little Brown, 1991). On Gustafsen Lake, see Sandra Lambertus, *Wartime Images, Peacetime Wounds: The Media and the Gustafsen Lake Stand-Off* (Toronto: University of Toronto Press, 2004). On Burnt Church, see Ken S. Coates, *The Marshall Decision and Native Rights* (Montreal and Kingston: McGill-Queen's University Press, 2000). On Ipperwash Park, see Ontario, Ipperwash Inquiry, *Report of the Ipperwash Inquiry,* 6 vols. (Toronto: Ministry of the Attorney General, 2007), http://www.ipperwashinquiry.ca.

14 Within Canada's multicultural context, Western European philosophy, political systems, law, and values still define dominant Canadian culture. The term "settler," as I use it in this book, therefore refers not only to Euro-Canadians whose ancestors came to Canada during the colonial period but also to more recent immigrants from a variety of ethnic and cultural backgrounds who are part of contemporary settler society. Throughout the text, I use the terms "Indigenous people" and "Native" interchangeably and "Indian" and "Aboriginal" only where the context warrants it, to reflect the vernacular commonly used in historical and public policy documents, published literature, and popular media coverage.

15 Roger Epp, "We Are All Treaty People: History, Reconciliation and the 'Settler Problem,'" in *Dilemmas of Reconciliation: Cases and Concepts,* eds. Carol A.L. Prager and Trudy Govier (Waterloo: Wilfrid Laurier University Press, 2003), 228.

16 Elizabeth A. Cole and Karen Murphy, "Research Brief: History Education Reform, Transitional Justice and the Transformation of Identities," New York, International Center for Transitional Justice, October 2009, http://www.ictj.org/en/research/projects/research6/thematic-studies/3201.html.

17 Catherine Bell and David Kahane, eds., *Intercultural Dispute Resolution in Aboriginal Contexts* (Vancouver: UBC Press, 2004).

18 Nor do the opinions expressed herein represent the views of any federal government department that has been involved in the IRS claims settlement process.

19 Critical researchers use historical-comparative analysis to reinterpret data in ways that challenge old explanations and develop new concepts and theory. William Neuman, for example, says that historically comparative research "combines a sensitivity to specific historical or cultural contexts with theoretical considerations." William Lawrence Neuman, *Social Research Methods: Qualitative and Quantitative Approaches,* 3rd ed. (Boston: Allyn and Bacon, 1997), 388. He notes that critical social science research is particularly associated with conflict theory because "it focuses on change and conflict, especially paradoxes or conflicts that are inherent in the very organization of social relations. Such paradoxes or inner conflicts reveal much about the true nature of social reality." W. Lawrence Neuman, *Social Research Methods: Qualitative and Quantitative Approaches,* 2nd ed. (Boston: Allyn and Bacon, 1994), 67.

20 Gabriel, quoted in Jeff Heinrich, "A Struggle for a Cause Turns Nasty," *Montreal Gazette,* 7 March 2004, 3, quoted in Gail Guthrie Valaskakis, *Indian Country: Essays on Contemporary Native Culture* (Waterloo: Wilfrid Laurier University Press, 2005), 64.

21 On remembrance as an ethical obligation, see Roger Simon and Claudia Eppert, "Remembering Obligation: Witnessing Testimonies of Historical Trauma," in Roger Simon, *The Touch of the Past: Remembrance, Learning and Ethics* (New York: Palgrave Macmillan, 2005), 51. Here, I draw on the metaphor of polishing the Iroquois covenant chain. The Iroquois treaty alliances made during the Encounter era, known as the covenant chain, were constantly renewed, or polished: "a chain of friendship ... too strong to ever be broken, and polished and brightened so pure as never to rust." Mohawk speaker, quoted in Robert A. Williams Jr., *Linking Arms Together: American Indian Treaty Visions of Law and Peace, 1600-1800* (Oxford: Oxford University Press, 1997), 121.

Chapter 1: An Unsettling Pedagogy

1 See, for example, Kay Pranis, Barry Stuart, and Mark Wedge, *Peacemaking Circles: From Crime to Community* (St. Paul, MN: Living Justice Press, 2003), 7, 9.

2 I acknowledge Brenda Ireland's substantive contribution to the development of this workshop and thank her for providing feedback on my reflections. She is an educator, trainer, and intercultural facilitator whose research focuses on integrating

Indigenous knowledge and pedagogy into educational systems as critical to authentic reconciliation. See Brenda Ireland, *Moving from the Head to the Heart: Addressing the "Indian's Canada Problem" in Reclaiming the Learning Spirit: Aboriginal Learners in Education* (Ottawa: Canadian Council on Learning, 2010), http://www.ccl-cca.ca/pdfs/ablkc/AboriginalLearnersEdu_en.pdf.

3 Henry Giroux, *Schooling and the Struggle for Public Life: Critical Pedagogy in the Modern Age* (Minneapolis: University of Minnesota Press, 1988), cited in Egon G. Guba and Yvonna S. Lincoln, "Competing Paradigms in Qualitative Research," in *The Landscape of Qualitative Research: Theories and Issues,* eds. Norman K. Denzin and Yvonna S. Lincoln (Thousand Oaks: Sage, 1998), 206.

4 Susan Strega, "The View from the Poststructuralist Margins: Epistemology and Methodology Reconsidered," in *Research as Resistance: Critical, Indigenous, and Anti-Oppressive Approaches,* eds. Leslie Brown and Susan Strega (Toronto: Canadian Scholars Press/Women's Press, 2005), 208.

5 Paulo Freire, *Pedagogy of Hope: Reliving Pedagogy of the Oppressed* (New York: Continuum, 1995), 8, 9.

6 Daniel Schugurensky, "Transformative Learning and Transformative Politics: The Pedagogical Dimension of Participatory Democracy and Social Action," in *Expanding the Boundaries of Transformative Learning: Essays on Theory and Praxis,* eds. Edmund V. O'Sullivan, Amish Morrell, and Mary Ann O'Connor (New York: Palgrave, 2002), 62, 63.

7 bell hooks, *Teaching Community: A Pedagogy of Hope* (New York: Routledge, 2003), xiv. Although, as a feminist, hooks critiques the sexism in Freire's work, she nevertheless concludes that his liberatory theory and pedagogical philosophy speak powerfully to decolonization and anti-racism. For an account of Freire's influence on hooks' theory and practice, see bell hooks, *Teaching to Transgress: Education as the Practice of Freedom* (New York: Routledge, 1994), 45-58.

8 hooks, *Teaching Community,* 61.

9 Paulo Freire, *Pedagogy of the Oppressed* (New York: Continuum, 1970), 31, 34.

10 Sandy Grande, *Red Pedagogy: Native American Social and Political Thought* (Lanham, MD: Rowman and Littlefield, 2004), 151. In critiquing white mainstream feminism, Grande is careful to note that anti-racist and critical feminists do address issues related to race, class, and gender. See ibid., chap. 5.

11 Emma LaRocque, "Métis and Feminist: Ethical Reflections on Feminism, Human Rights and Decolonization," in *Making Space for Indigenous Feminism,* ed. Joyce Green (Black Point, NS: Fernwood, 2007), 67, 68.

12 Andrea Smith, "Native American Feminism, Sovereignty and Social Change," in Green, *Making Space for Indigenous Feminism,* 94-95 (emphasis in original).

13 Makere Stewart-Harawira, "Practising Indigenous Feminism: Resistance to Imperialism," in Green, *Making Space for Indigenous Feminism,* 127.

14 Ibid., 134.

15 Ibid., 127-28.

16 Mehmoona Moosa-Mitha, "Situating Anti-Oppressive Theories within Critical and Difference-Centred Perspectives," in Brown and Strega, *Research as Resistance*, 66-67.

17 Alison Jones, with Kuni Jenkins, "Rethinking Collaboration: Working the Indigene-Colonizer Hyphen," in *Handbook of Critical and Indigenous Methodologies*, eds. Norman K. Denzin, Yvonna S. Lincoln, and Linda Tuhiwai Smith (Thousand Oaks: Sage, 2008), 473.

18 Wanda D. McCaslin and Denise C. Breton, "Justice as Healing: Going Outside the Colonizer's Cage," in Denzin, Lincoln, and Smith, *Handbook of Critical and Indigenous Methodologies*, 513.

19 Jones and Jenkins, "Rethinking Collaboration," 471.

20 McCaslin and Breton, "Justice as Healing," 519.

21 Robin Jarvis Brownlie, "First Nations Perspectives and Historical Thinking in Canada," in *First Nations, First Thoughts: The Impact of Indigenous Thought in Canada,* ed. Annis May Timpson (Vancouver: UBC Press, 2009), 35-36.

22 Mary Jo Maynes, Jennifer L. Pierce, and Barbara Laslett, *Telling Stories: The Use of Personal Narratives in the Social Sciences and History* (Ithaca: Cornell University Press, 2008), 94. For Indigenous approaches to personal narrative and storytelling methodology, see Jo-ann Archibald (Q'um Q'um Xiiem), *Indigenous Storywork: Educating the Heart, Mind, Body, and Spirit* (Vancouver: UBC Press, 2008); Qwul'sih'yah'maht (Robina Anne Thomas), "Honouring the Oral Traditions of My Ancestors through Storytelling," in Brown and Strega, *Research as Resistance*, 237-54. See also D. Jean Clandinin and F. Michael Connelly, *Narrative Inquiry: Experience and Story in Qualitative Research* (San Francisco: Jossey-Bass, 2000); D. Jean Clandinin and F. Michael Connelly, "Personal Experience Methods," in *Collecting and Interpreting Qualitative Materials*, eds. Norman K. Denzin and Yvonna S. Lincoln (Thousand Oaks: Sage, 1998), 150-78; and Sally A. Kimpson, "Stepping Off the Road: A Narrative (of) Inquiry," in Brown and Strega, *Research as Resistance*, 73-96.

23 "Introduction: Emergent Methods in Social Research within and across Disciplines," in *Emergent Methods in Social Research*, eds. Sharlene Nagy Hesse-Biber and Patricia Leavy (Thousand Oaks: Sage, 2006), xxii.

24 Tony Penikett, *Reconciliation: First Nations Treaty Making in British Columbia* (Vancouver: Douglas and McIntyre, 2006); John Ciaccia, *The Oka Crisis: A Mirror of the Soul* (Dorval: Maren, 2000).

25 Ciaccia, *The Oka Crisis*, 17-18.

26 Jessica Senehi, "Constructive Storytelling in Intercommunal Conflicts: Building Community, Building Peace," in *Reconcilable Differences: Turning Points in Ethnopolitical Conflict*, eds. Sean Byrne and Cynthia L. Irvin (West Hartford, CT: Kumarian Press, 2000), 96-97.

27 Here, I note that I consulted with Matilda Daniels, the Gitxsan Hazelton feast coordinator, to gauge support for recounting my own perceptions of the feast as

one aspect of my doctoral dissertation research project. After consulting with the Hazelton feast advisory group, she told me that it supported the project in principle but did not see a need to be involved directly. The Gitxsan had undertaken their own initiative to document the Hazelton feast as a way to educate the public. To this end, they recorded the entire feast as a public event that was subsequently reported by the media, who were invited to attend. Daniels also provided me with extensive feedback on a research paper regarding the feast that I had produced for the Law Commission of Canada. She and I co-presented the paper at the Canadian Association of Law Teachers (CALT) annual conference held at the University of British Columbia, Vancouver, BC, 22-24 June 2005. The paper was subsequently published as Paulette Regan, "An Apology Feast in Hazelton: Indian Residential Schools, Reconciliation, and Making Space for Indigenous Legal Traditions," in *Indigenous Legal Traditions*, ed. Law Commission of Canada, Legal Dimensions Series (Vancouver: UBC Press, 2007), 40-76. I also received feedback from various other individuals including my co-hosts at the feast, Deanna Sitter, resolution manager at Indian Residential Schools Resolution Canada (IRSRC), and Brian Thorpe, who was then senior advisor for the United Church of Canada's Residential Schools Steering Committee. In addition, Dr. Maggie Hodgson, Carrier elder, special advisor to IRSRC, and former CEO of the Nechi Institute in Edmonton, who attended the Hazelton feast, provided me with further insights. Niis Noolh (Raymond Jones), Gitxsan member of the Indigenous Governance Council, Indigenous Governance Program at the University of Victoria, kindly participated in the formal evaluation of my dissertation, and he subsequently received two copies of it to be shared appropriately for the benefit and use of the Gitxsan. None of those named are responsible for the final product. Finally, I note that, in order to respect survivors' confidentiality and privacy concerns, I do not describe the negotiations involved in resolving their individual IRS claims.

28   Archibald, *Indigenous Storywork*, 2-3.

29   Norman K. Denzin, "Emancipatory Discourses and the Ethics and Politics of Interpretation," in Denzin and Lincoln, *Collecting and Interpreting Qualitative Materials*, 439.

30   Stacy Holman Jones, "Autoethnography: Making the Personal Political," in Denzin and Lincoln, *Collecting and Interpreting Qualitative Materials*, 206.

31   Denzin, "Emancipatory Discourses," 454-55.

32   Roger Simon and Claudia Eppert, "Remembering Obligation: Witnessing Testimonies of Historical Trauma," in Roger Simon, *The Touch of the Past: Remembrance, Learning and Ethics* (New York: Palgrave Macmillan, 2005), 62.

33   Linda Tuhiwai Smith, *Decolonizing Methodologies: Research and Indigenous Peoples* (London: Zed Books, 1999).

34   This literature is now extensive, but in addition to Smith, ibid., it includes, for example, Devon A. Mihesuah, ed., *Natives and Academics: Researching and Writing about American Indians* (Lincoln: University of Nebraska Press, 1998); Devon Abbott

Mihesuah and Angela Cavender Wilson, eds., *Indigenizing the Academy: Transforming Scholarship and Empowering Communities* (Lincoln: University of Nebraska Press, 2004); Grande, *Red Pedagogy*; and Kathy Absolon and Cam Willett, "Putting Ourselves Forward: Location in Aboriginal Research," in Brown and Strega, *Research as Resistance*, 97-126.

35 Patricia Monture-Angus, "Citizens Plus: Sensitivities versus Solutions," in *Bridging the Divide between Aboriginal Peoples and the Canadian State*, Research Paper (Montreal: Centre for Research and Information on Canada, 2001), 8-9.

36 More recently, other scholars have advocated a similar approach in research, education, and teaching contexts. See, for example, Jones and Jenkins, "Rethinking Collaboration," 482; and Margaret Kovach, "Being Indigenous in the Academy: Creating Space for Indigenous Scholars," in Timpson, *First Nations, First Thoughts*, 64-65.

37 Val Napoleon, "Who Gets to Say What Happened? Reconciliation Issues for the Gitxsan," in *Intercultural Dispute Resolution in Aboriginal Contexts*, eds. Catherine Bell and David Kahane (Vancouver: UBC Press, 2004), 183.

38 Roger Epp, "We Are All Treaty People: History, Reconciliation and the 'Settler Problem,'" in *Dilemmas of Reconciliation: Cases and Concepts*, eds. Carol A.L. Prager and Trudy Govier (Waterloo: Wilfrid Laurier University Press, 2003), 228.

39 Elazar Barkan, *The Guilt of Nations: Restitution and Negotiating Historical Injustice* (Baltimore: Johns Hopkins University Press, 2000), 328.

40 Trudy Govier, "What Is Acknowledgement and Why Is It Important?" in Prager and Govier, *Dilemmas of Reconciliation*, 78-79.

41 Stanley Cohen, *States of Denial: Knowing about Atrocities and Suffering* (Cambridge: Polity Press, 2001), 66-67. See also Bernhard Giesen, "The Trauma of Perpetrators: The Holocaust as the Traumatic Reference of German National Identity," in Jeffrey C. Alexander et al., *Cultural Trauma and Collective Identity* (Berkeley: University of California Press, 2004), 120.

42 Cohen, *States of Denial*, 113.

43 Ibid., 114. See also Dean Neu and Richard Therrien, *Accounting for Genocide: Canada's Bureaucratic Assault on Aboriginal People* (Black Point, NS: Fernwood, 2003).

44 David E. Lorey and William H. Beezley, "Introduction," in David E. Lorey and William H. Beezley, eds., *Genocide, Collective Violence, and Popular Memory: The Politics of Remembrance in the Twentieth Century* (Wilmington, DE: Scholarly Resources, 2002), xv.

45 Giesen, "The Trauma of Perpetrators," 121-22.

46 Cohen, *States of Denial*, 106.

47 John Torpey, "Introduction: Politics and the Past," in *Politics and the Past: On Repairing Historical Injustices*, ed. John Torpey (Lanham, MD: Rowman and Littlefield, 2003), 5-7.

48 Mahmood Mamdani, "A Diminished Truth," in *After the TRC: Reflections on Truth and Reconciliation in South Africa*, eds. Wilmot James and Linda van de Vijver (Athens:

Ohio University Press, 2001), 59, quoted in Torpey, "Introduction: Politics and the Past," 10 (emphasis added).

49 Peter Harrison, "Dispelling Ignorance of Residential Schools," in *Response, Responsibility and Renewal: Canada's Truth and Reconciliation Journey,* eds. Gregory Younging, Jonathan Dewar, and Mike DeGagné (Ottawa: Aboriginal Healing Foundation, 2009), 151, 153.

50 See, for example, John S. Milloy, *A National Crime: The Canadian Government and the Residential School System, 1879 to 1986,* 3rd ed. (Winnipeg: University of Manitoba Press, 2001); Elizabeth Furniss, *Victims of Benevolence: The Dark Legacy of the Williams Lake Residential School* (Vancouver: Arsenal Pulp Press, 1992); Celia Haig-Brown, *Resistance and Renewal: Surviving the Indian Residential School,* 6th ed. (Vancouver: Tillacum Library, Arsenal Pulp Press, 1993); Suzanne Fournier and Ernie Crey, *Stolen from Our Embrace: The Abduction of First Nations Children and Restoration of Aboriginal Communities* (Vancouver: Douglas and McIntyre, 1997); Terry Glavin and Former Students of St. Mary's, *Amongst God's Own: The Enduring Legacy of St. Mary's Mission* (Mission, BC: Longhouse, 2002); Canada, *Report of the Royal Commission on Aboriginal Peoples,* vol. 1, *Looking Forward, Looking Back* (Ottawa: Minister of Supply and Services Canada, 1996), pt. 2, chap. 10, "Residential Schools"; J.R. Miller, *Shingwauk's Vision: A History of Native Residential Schools* (Toronto: University of Toronto Press, 1996); and Law Commission of Canada, ed., *Restoring Dignity: Responding to Child Abuse in Canadian Institutions* (Ottawa: Minister of Public Works and Government Services, 2000).

51 For a fuller discussion on genocide, see Roland Chrisjohn and Sherri Young, *The Circle Game: Shadows and Substance in the Indian Residential School Experience in Canada* (Penticton, BC: Theytus Books, 1997). The authors urge Canadians to look more closely at the definition of genocide as it relates to the residential school system.

Article 2 of the United Nations Convention on the Prevention and Punishment of the Crime of Genocide, adopted in 1948, defines genocide as follows:

In the present Convention, genocide means any of the following acts committed with intent to destroy, in whole or in part, a national, ethnical, racial or religious group, as such:

(a) Killing members of the group;

(b) Causing serious bodily or mental harm to members of the group;

(c) Deliberately inflicting on the group conditions of life calculated to bring about its physical destruction in whole or in part;

(d) Imposing measures intended to prevent births within the group;

(e) Forcibly transferring children of the group to another group.

52 Neu and Therrien, *Accounting for Genocide,* 25.

53 Milloy, *A National Crime.*

54 Andrew Woolford, *Between Justice and Certainty: Treaty Making in British Columbia,* edited by W. Wesley Pue, Law and Society Series (Vancouver: UBC Press, 2005), 118.

55 Ibid., 36-38.

56 Kevin Avruch, "Introduction: Culture and Conflict Resolution," in *Conflict Resolution: Cross-Cultural Perspectives,* eds. Kevin Avruch, Peter W. Black, and Joseph A. Scimecca (Westport, CT: Greenwood Press, 1991), 7.

57 Cohen, *States of Denial,* 58-59.

58 Ibid., 62.

59 Woolford, *Between Justice and Certainty,* 130.

60 John Forester, *The Deliberative Practitioner: Encouraging Participatory Planning Processes* (Cambridge, MA: MIT Press, 1999), chap. 7.

61 Michelle LeBaron, "Learning New Dances: Finding Effective Ways to Address Intercultural Disputes," in Bell and Kahane, *Intercultural Dispute Resolution,* 15.

62 David Kahane, "What Is Culture? Generalizing about Aboriginal and Newcomer Perspectives," in Bell and Kahane, *Intercultural Dispute Resolution,* 29-30.

63 Environics Research Group, "National Benchmark Survey" (prepared for Indian Residential Schools Resolution Canada and the Truth and Reconciliation Commission, Ottawa, May 2008), 7, http://epe.lac-bac.gc.ca/100/200/301/pwgsc-tpsgc/por-ef/indian_residential_schools/2008/414-07-e/summary.doc.

64 Ibid., 16.

65 Ibid., 14.

66 Susan Crean, "Both Sides Now: Designing White Men and the Other Side of History," in Younging, Dewar, and DeGagné, *Response, Responsibility and Renewal,* 62-63.

67 See, for example, Milloy, *A National Crime,* xviii.

68 W. Barnett Pearce and Stephen W. Littlejohn, *Moral Conflict: When Social Worlds Collide* (Thousand Oaks: Sage, 1997), 157-67.

69 E. Franklin Dukes, *Resolving Public Conflict: Transforming Community and Governance* (Manchester: Manchester University Press, 1996), 138.

70 I thank Dr. Jeff Corntassel for pointing out the importance of making this distinction. Pers. comm., 18 June 2005.

71 Janna Thompson, *Taking Responsibility for the Past: Reparation and Historical Injustice* (Cambridge: Polity Press, 2002), vii-xxi, ix.

72 Ibid., 130-36.

73 Govier, "What Is Acknowledgment and Why Is It Important?" 78.

74 David Spurr, *The Rhetoric of Empire: Colonial Discourse in Journalism, Travel Writing and Imperial Administration* (Durham: Duke University Press, 1993), 20, quoted in Keith D. Smith, *Liberalism, Surveillance, and Resistance: Indigenous Communities in Western Canada, 1887-1927* (Edmonton: Athabasca University Press, 2009), 18.

75 Roger Simon, "Worrying Together: The Problematics of Listening and the Educative Responsibilities of the IRSTRC" (paper presented at "Breaking the Silence: Inter-

national Conference on the Indian Residential Schools Commission of Canada," University of Montreal, 19 September 2008), 2.

76   Ibid., 5.

77   Ravi de Costa, "Reconciliation and Neoliberalism" (paper presented at the Canadian Political Science Association annual conference, Carleton University, Ottawa, 2009), 5, 7, http://www.cpsa-acsp.ca/papers-2009/deCosta.pdf.

78   Ibid., 6.

79   Ibid., 12.

80   Sue Campbell, "Challenges to Memory in Political Contexts: Recognizing Disrespectful Challenge" (paper prepared for the Indian Residential Schools Truth and Reconciliation Commission, 2008), 4.

81   Ibid., 3.

82   Simon, "Worrying Together," 4.

83   Megan Boler, *Feeling Power: Emotions and Education* (New York: Routledge, 1999), 2.

84   Ibid., 6.

85   Ibid., 21.

86   Ibid., 164, 166.

87   Roger Simon, "The Pedagogy of Remembrance," in Simon, *The Touch of the Past*, 18-19.

88   Ibid., 23.

89   Conversely, sociologist Jeffrey C. Alexander notes that, throughout the Western world and beyond, it has become commonplace to speak of being traumatized by various events ranging from acts of violence to more benign occurrences associated with social change. Talk of trauma is so much the norm that thinking of it as exceptional has become increasingly difficult. Alexander says that "the trick is to gain reflexivity, to move from the sense of something commonly experienced to the sense of strangeness that allows us to think sociologically. For trauma is not something naturally existing; it is something constructed by society ... In this task of making trauma strange, its embeddedness in everyday life and language ... now presents itself as a challenge to be overcome." Jeffrey C. Alexander, "Toward a Theory of Cultural Trauma," in Alexander et al., *Cultural Trauma*, 2.

90   Dominick LaCapra, *History in Transit: Experience, Identity, Critical Theory* (Ithaca: Cornell University Press, 2004), 135, 137.

91   Boler, *Feeling Power,* 164.

92   Jones and Jenkins, "Rethinking Collaboration," 480.

93   Daniel R. Wildcat, "Understanding the Crisis in American Education," in Vine Deloria Jr. and Daniel R. Wildcat, *Power and Place: Indian Education in America* (Golden, CO: Fulcrum Resources, 2001), 36.

94   Elmer Ghostkeeper, "Weche Teachings: Aboriginal Wisdom and Dispute Resolution," in Bell and Kahane, *Intercultural Dispute Resolution,* 165.

95 Taiaiake Alfred, *Wasáse: Indigenous Pathways of Action and Freedom* (Peterborough, ON: Broadview Press, 2005), 149.

96 Edmund O'Sullivan, "The Project and Vision of Transformative Education: Integral Transformative Learning," in O'Sullivan, Morrell, and O'Connor, *Expanding the Boundaries*, 11.

97 Megan Boler and Michalinos Zembylas, "Discomforting Truths: The Emotional Terrain of Understanding Difference," in *Pedagogies of Difference: Rethinking Education for Social Change*, ed. Peter Pericles Trifonas (New York: RoutledgeFalmer, 2003), 111. See also Shoshana Felman, "Education and Crisis, or the Vicissitudes of Teaching," in Shoshana Felman and Dori Laub, *Testimony: Crises of Witnessing in Literature, Psychoanalysis, and History* (New York: Routledge, Chapman and Hall, 1992), 1-56; Rachel N. Baum, "What I Have Learned to Feel: The Pedagogical Emotions of Holocaust Education," *College Literature* 23,3 (1996): 44-57.

98 Forester, *The Deliberative Practitioner*, 130.

99 Ibid., 211.

Chapter 2: Rethinking Reconciliation

1 I thank Chief Robert Joseph for permission to describe his guest lecture.

2 See, for example, David A. Crocker, "Reckoning with Past Wrongs: A Normative Framework," in *Dilemmas of Reconciliation: Cases and Concepts*, eds. Carol A.L. Prager and Trudy Govier (Waterloo: Wilfrid Laurier University Press, 2003), 39-40; Elazar Barkan, *The Guilt of Nations: Restitution and Negotiating Historical Injustice* (Baltimore: Johns Hopkins University Press, 2000), especially chaps. 7-12; John Torpey, "Introduction: Politics and the Past," in *Politics and the Past: On Repairing Historical Injustices*, ed. John Torpey (Lanham, MD: Rowman and Littlefield, 2003), 1-34.

3 Barkan, *The Guilt of Nations*, xix.

4 Duncan Ivison, Paul Patton, and Will Sanders, eds., *Political Theory and the Rights of Indigenous Peoples* (Cambridge: Cambridge University Press, 2000), 3.

5 James Tully, "The Struggles of Indigenous Peoples for and of Freedom," in Ivison, Patton, and Sanders, *Political Theory and the Rights of Indigenous Peoples*, 36-50 (Cambridge: Cambridge University Press, 2000).

6 Barkan, *The Guilt of Nations*, 345.

7 See, for example, Gail Guthrie Valaskakis, "Right and Warriors: Media Memories and Oka," in Gail Guthrie Valaskakis, *Indian Country: Essays on Contemporary Native Culture* (Waterloo: Wilfrid Laurier University Press, 2005), 35-65; Ontario, Ipperwash Inquiry, *Report of the Ipperwash Inquiry* (Toronto: Ministry of the Attorney General, 2007), vol. 1, http://www.attorneygeneral.jus.gov.on.ca/inquiries/ipperwash/report/vol_1/pdf/E_Vol_1_Full.pdf.

8 Dr. Graham Hingangaroa Smith, pers. comm., 6 April 2006.

9 William Bradford, "'With a Very Great Blame on Our Hearts': Reparations, Reconciliation, and an American Indian Plea for Peace with Justice," *American Indian Law Review* 27,1 (2002-03): 133.

10 Ibid., 153.

11 Eric K. Yamamoto, *Interracial Justice: Conflict and Reconciliation in Post-Civil Rights America*, edited by Richard Delgado and Jean Stefancic, Critical America Series (New York: New York University Press, 1999), 11.

12 For a comprehensive comparative overview of the policies of the United States, Canada, New Zealand, and Australia, with regard to official apologies, see Melissa Nobles, *The Politics of Official Apologies* (Cambridge: Cambridge University Press, 2008).

13 Human Rights and Equal Opportunity Commission, *Bringing Them Home: Report of the National Inquiry into the Separation of Aboriginal and Torres Strait Islander Children from Their Families* (Sydney: Australian Human Rights Commission, 1997), http://www.humanrights.gov.au/Social_Justice/bth_report/report/index.html.

14 For the council's tool kits, see "Toolkit for Local Reconciliation Groups," n.d., http://www.austlii.edu.au/au/other/IndigLRes/car/2000/17/; and "Learning Circle Kit," n.d., http://www.austlii.edu.au/au/other/IndigLRes/car/pubs.html#resource.

15 For a full description of Reconciliation Australia's mandate, goals, and initiatives, see Reconciliation Australia, http://www.reconciliation.org.au/.

16 For background on the Sorry Books, see Australian Institute of Aboriginal and Torres Strait Islander Studies, http://www1.aiatsis.gov.au/exhibitions/sorrybooks/sorrybooks_backgrnd.htm.

17 Nobles, *The Politics of Official Apologies*, 123-28.

18 Kevin Rudd, "Apology to Australia's Indigenous Peoples" (speech, House of Representatives, Parliament House, Canberra, 13 February 2008), http://www.pm.gov.au/node/5952.

19 Tom Calma, "Let the Healing Begin: Response to Government to the National Apology to the Stolen Generations" (Members' Hall, Parliament House, Canberra, 13 February 2008), http://www.humanrights.gov.au/pdf/social_justice/speech/let_the_healing_begin.pdf.

20 Barbara McMahon, "Snatched from Home for a Racist Ideal: Now a Nation Says Sorry," *Manchester Guardian*, 11 February 2008, http://www.guardian.co.uk/world/2008/feb/11/australia/print.

21 "Stolen Generations Lawsuits Could Top Compensation Bid," *Melbourne Herald Sun*, 8 January 2008, http://www.news.com.au/heraldsun/.

22 *Healing Happens* (Edmonton: National Day of Healing and Reconciliation, 2009), http://www.ndhr.ca/images/ndhr_booklet_web.pdf.

23 Environics Research Group, "National Benchmark Survey" (prepared for Indian Residential Schools Resolution Canada and the Truth and Reconciliation Commission, Ottawa, May 2008), 29 (emphasis in original), http://epe.lac-bac.gc.ca/100/200/301/pwgsc-tpsgc/por-ef/indian_residential_schools/2008/414-07-e/index.html.

24 Ibid., 32-33.

25 See Andrew Woolford, *Between Justice and Certainty: Treaty Making in British Columbia*, edited by W. Wesley Pue, Law and Society Series (Vancouver: UBC Press, 2005); Tony Penikett, *Reconciliation: First Nations Treatymaking in British Columbia* (Vancouver: Douglas and McIntyre, 2006); and Val Napoleon, "Who Gets to Say What Happened? Reconciliation Issues for the Gitxsan," in *Intercultural Dispute Resolution in Aboriginal Contexts*, eds. Catherine Bell and David Kahane (Vancouver: UBC Press, 2004), 176-95.

26 Taiaiake Alfred, *Wasáse: Indigenous Pathways of Action and Freedom* (Peterborough, ON: Broadview Press, 2005), 151.

27 Ibid., 152.

28 Taiaiake Alfred and Jeff Corntassel, "Being Indigenous: Resurgences against Contemporary Colonialism," *Government and Opposition* 40,4 (2005): 597-98, 601-2, http://www.corntassel.net/being_indigenous.pdf.

29 Alfred, *Wasáse*, 35.

30 Ibid., 21. For Onkwehonwe, a Kanien'kehaka word, see ibid., 288.

31 Jeff Corntassel and Cindy Holder, "Who's Sorry Now? Government Apologies, Truth Commissions, and Indigenous Self-Determination in Australia, Canada, Guatemala, and Peru," *Human Rights Review* 9,4 (December 2008): 465-89, http://www.corntassel.net/CorntasselHolder.pdf.

32 Simon Fisher et al., *Working with Conflict: Skills and Strategies for Action* (London: Zed Books, 2000), 133.

33 Jennifer J. Llewellyn, "Bridging the Gap between Truth and Reconciliation: Restorative Justice and the Indian Residential Schools Truth and Reconciliation Commission," in *From Truth to Reconciliation: Transforming the Legacy of Residential Schools*, eds. Marlene Brant Castellano, Linda Archibald, and Mike DeGagné (Ottawa: Aboriginal Healing Foundation, 2008), 191.

34 Ibid., 188-89.

35 Waziyatawin, *What Does Justice Look Like? The Struggle for Liberation in Dakota Homeland* (St. Paul: Living Justice Press, 2008), 71-72.

36 Ibid., 77-78.

37 Sandy Grande, *Red Pedagogy: Native American Social and Political Thought* (Lanham, MD: Rowman and Littlefield, 2004), 2-3 (emphasis added).

38 Ibid., 8.

39 Ibid., 175.

40 Edward W. Said, *Culture and Imperialism* (New York: Vintage Books, 1994), xii-xiii, xxi-xxii.

41 Stanley Cohen, *States of Denial: Knowing about Atrocities and Suffering* (Cambridge: Polity Press, 2001), 249 (emphasis added).

42 Barkan, *The Guilt of Nations*, x.

43 Ibid., xvii-xviii.

44 Brian Rice and Anna Snyder, "Reconciliation in the Context of a Settler Society: Healing the Legacy of Colonialism in Canada," in Castellano, Archibald, and DeGagné, *From Truth to Reconciliation*, 54.

45 Richard Slotkin, *The Fatal Environment: The Myth of the Frontier in the Age of Industrialization, 1800-1890* (New York: Atheneum, 1985), 19.

46 David I. Kertzer, *Ritual, Politics, and Power* (New Haven: Yale University Press, 1988), 12-13.

47 Ibid., 12.

48 Michelle LeBaron, *Bridging Cultural Conflicts: A New Approach for a Changing World* (San Francisco: Jossey-Bass, 2003), 280-81. See also Yamamoto, *Interracial Justice*, 184.

49 Robert A. Williams Jr., *Linking Arms Together: American Indian Treaty Visions of Law and Peace, 1600-1800* (Oxford: Oxford University Press, 1997), 17.

50 Jeff Corntassel and Richard Witmer advance this argument in a study of American policy makers, but their point applies equally to Canada. Jeff Corntassel and Richard C. Witmer, *Forced Federalism: Contemporary Challenges to Indigenous Nationhood* (Norman: University of Oklahoma Press, 2008), 8-16; see also Elizabeth Furniss, *The Burden of History: Colonialism and the Frontier Myth in a Rural Canadian Community* (Vancouver: UBC Press, 1999), 53-60; Valaskakis, *Indian Country*, 41.

51 Paige Raibmon, *Authentic Indians: Episodes of Encounter from the Late-Nineteenth Century Northwest Coast* (Durham: Duke University Press, 2005), 3; Julie Cruikshank, *The Social Life of Stories: Narrative and Knowledge in the Yukon Territory* (Vancouver: UBC Press, 1998), 60.

52 John Sutton Lutz, "Introduction: Myth Understandings; or First Contact, Over and Over Again," in *Myth and Memory: Stories of Indigenous-European Contact*, ed. John Sutton Lutz (Vancouver: UBC Press, 2007), 1.

53 Ibid., 4, 5.

54 J. Edward Chamberlin, "Close Encounters of the First Kind," in Lutz, *Myth and Memory*, 27.

55 Celia Haig-Brown and David A. Nock, "Introduction," in *With Good Intentions: Euro-Canadian and Aboriginal Relations in Colonial Canada*, eds. Celia Haig-Brown and David A. Nock (Vancouver: UBC Press, 2006), 4.

56 Susan Strega, "The View from the Poststructuralist Margins: Epistemology and Methodology Reconsidered," in *Research as Resistance: Critical, Indigenous, and Anti-Oppressive Approaches*, eds. Leslie Brown and Susan Strega (Toronto: Canadian Scholars Press/Women's Press, 2005), 63.

57 J.R. Miller, *Reflections on Native-Newcomer Relations: Selected Essays* (Toronto: University of Toronto Press, 2004), 13-36.

58 J.L. Granatstein, *Who Killed Canadian History?* rev. ed. (Toronto: Harper Collins, 2007), xii.

59 See also Russel Lawrence Barsh, "Aboriginal Peoples and Canada's Conscience," in *Hidden in Plain Sight: Contributions of Aboriginal Peoples to Canadian Identity*

and Culture, eds. David R. Newhouse, Cora J. Voyageur, and Dan Beavon (Toronto: University of Toronto Press, 2005), 270.

60 Granatstein, *Who Killed Canadian History?* 107.

61 Ibid., 110.

62 On the power of apology, see, for example, Nicholas Tavuchis, *Mea Culpa: A Sociology of Apology and Reconciliation* (Stanford: Stanford University Press, 1991).

63 Eva Mackey, *The House of Difference: Cultural Politics and National Identity in Canada* (Toronto: University of Toronto Press, 2002), 26.

64 John Ralston Saul, *A Fair Country: Telling Truths about Canada* (Toronto: Viking Canada, 2008), 21.

65 Ibid., 69 (emphasis in original).

66 Ibid., 94.

67 John Borrows, *Recovering Canada: The Resurgence of Indigenous Law* (Toronto: University of Toronto Press, 2002), xi-xii.

68 Saul, *A Fair Country,* 4.

69 Michael Ignatieff, "Limiting the Range of Permissible Lies: The Importance of the Record" (keynote address at "Truth Commission: Sharing the Truth about Residential Schools – A Conference on Truth and Reconciliation as Restorative Justice," University of Calgary, Calgary, 14-17 June 2007).

70 Linda Tuhiwai Smith, *Decolonizing Methodologies: Research and Indigenous Peoples* (London: Zed Books, 1999), 34.

71 John Paul Lederach, *The Moral Imagination: The Art and Soul of Building Peace* (New York: Oxford University Press, 2005), 58-59.

72 Vern Neufeld Redekop, *From Violence to Blessing: How an Understanding of Deep-Rooted Conflict Can Open Paths to Reconciliation* (Toronto: Novalis, 2002), 161, 164.

73 Alfred, *Wasáse,* 77.

74 Eric Foner, *Who Owns History? Rethinking the Past in a Changing World* (New York: Hill and Wang, 2002), xv-xvi.

75 Ibid., xiv.

76 Bain Attwood, *Telling the Truth about Aboriginal History* (Crows Nest, NSW: Allen and Unwin, 2005), 19-20.

77 Ibid., 29, 31.

78 Arthur J. Ray, "History Wars and Treaty Rights in Canada: A Canadian Case Study," in *The Power of Promises: Rethinking Indian Treaties in the Pacific Northwest,* ed. Alexandra Harmon (Seattle: University of Washington Press, 2008), 283.

79 Margaret MacMillan, *The Uses and Abuses of History* (Toronto: Viking Canada, 2008), 30.

80 Michel-Rolph Trouillot, *Silencing the Past: Power and the Production of History* (Boston: Beacon Press, 1995), 149.

81 Dian Lynn Million, "Telling Secrets: Sex, Power and Narrative in the Rearticulation of Canadian Residential School Histories" (PhD diss., University of California, Berkeley, 2004), 140-41.

82   Trouillot, *Silencing the Past*, 152.

83   Ibid., 150-51.

84   Roger Simon, "The Pedagogical Insistence of Public Memory," in *Theorizing Historical Consciousness*, ed. Peter Seixas (Toronto: University of Toronto Press, 2004), 189.

85   Timothy J. Stanley, "Why I Killed Canadian History: Conditions for an Anti-Racist History in Canada," *Histoire sociale/Social History* 33,65 (2000): 79-103.

86   Megan Boler, *Feeling Power: Emotions and Education* (New York: Routledge, 1999), 176.

87   International Center for Transitional Justice, "Memory, Memorials and Museums," Program description, New York, ICTJ, November 2009, http://www.ictj.org/en/tj/785.html.

88   John Bodnar, *Remaking America: Public Memory, Commemoration, and Patriotism in the Twentieth Century* (Princeton: Princeton University Press, 1992), 15.

89   Sue Campbell, "Remembering for the Future as a Lens on the Indian Residential Schools Truth and Reconciliation Commission" (paper prepared for the Truth and Reconciliation Commission, 2008), 3.

90   In a case study of the controversy over the Vietnam Veterans Memorial in the United States, John Bodnar identifies a similar tension. See Bodnar, *Remaking America*, 3-9.

91   Paul Connerton, *How Societies Remember*, 10th ed. (Cambridge: Cambridge University Press, 2003), 14-15.

92   J.K. Olick, "Genre Memories and Memory Genres," *American Sociological Review* 64 (June 1999): 381, quoted in Barbara A. Misztal, *Theories of Social Remembering* (Maidenhead, UK: Open University Press, 2003), 126.

93   Jennifer J. Nelson, *Razing Africville: A Geography of Racism* (Toronto: University of Toronto Press, 2008), 145-46.

94   Ibid., 24 (emphasis in original).

95   Ibid., 149.

96   Waziyatawin (Angela Wilson), "Manipi Hena Owas'in Wicunkiksuyapi (We Remember All Those Who Walked)," in *In the Footsteps of Our Ancestors: The Dakota Commemorative Marches of the 21st Century*, ed. Waziyatawin Angela Wilson (St. Paul: Living Justice Press, 2006), 1-2. For more details concerning Dakota experience in Canada, see, for example, "Doris Pratt, Dakota, Manitoba," in Agnes Grant, *Finding My Talk: How Fourteen Native Women Reclaimed Their Lives after Residential School* (Calgary: Fifth House, 2004), 112-16.

97   Waziyatawin (Angela Wilson), "A Journey of Healing and Awakening," in Wilson, *In the Footsteps of Our Ancestors*, 116.

98   Waziyatawin (Angela Wilson), "Voices of the Marchers from 2004," in Wilson, *In the Footsteps of Our Ancestors*, 263.

99   Ibid., 270-86.

100   Pilar Riaño-Alcalá, *Dwellers of Memory: Youth and Violence in Medellín, Colombia* (New Brunswick, NJ: Transaction, 2006), 16, 17, 18.

Chapter 3: Deconstructing Canada's Peacemaker Myth

1 Jill St. Germain, *Indian Treaty-Making Policy in the United States and Canada 1867-1877* (Lincoln: University of Nebraska Press, 2001), xvii-xxii.

2 Northrop Frye coined the term "the peaceable kingdom" to describe the defining characteristics of Canadian national identity in Christian pastoral terms. See Philip Kokotailo, "Creating the Peaceable Kingdom: Edward Hicks, Northrop Frye, and Joe Clark," in *Creating the Peaceable Kingdom: And Other Essays on Canada*, ed. Victor Howard (East Lansing: Michigan State University Press, 1998), 3-10; Brian E. Titley, *A Narrow Vision: Duncan Campbell Scott and the Administration of Indian Affairs in Canada* (Vancouver: UBC Press, 1986); Arthur J. Ray, Jim Miller, and Frank Tough, *Bounty and Benevolence: A History of Saskatchewan Treaties* (Montreal and Kingston: McGill-Queen's University Press, 2000).

3 Ray, Miller, and Tough, *Bounty and Benevolence*, xvii.

4 *Delgamuukw v. British Columbia*, [1997] 3 S.C.R. 1010.

5 Richard Day, "Who Is This We That Gives the Gift? Native American Political Theory and the Western Tradition," *Critical Horizons* 2,2 (2001): 173-201. Day argues that, in the contemporary context, the "gift" is one of granting (or bestowing) recognition of minority populations via liberal multiculturalism theory.

6 James Tully, "The Struggles of Indigenous Peoples for and of Freedom," in *Political Theory and the Rights of Indigenous Peoples*, eds. Duncan Ivison, Paul Patton, and Will Sanders (Cambridge: Cambridge University Press, 2000), 36-59.

7 Wayne Warry, *Unfinished Dreams: Community Healing and the Reality of Aboriginal Self-Government* (Toronto: University of Toronto Press, 1998).

8 Ray, Miller, and Tough, *Bounty and Benevolence*, 205.

9 See also Sarah Carter, *Aboriginal People and Colonizers of Western Canada to 1900* (Toronto: University of Toronto Press, 2003), 103.

10 Alexander Morris, *The Hudson's Bay and Pacific Territories* (Montreal, 1859), 13, quoted in ibid., 41.

11 See, for example, Sarah Carter, *Lost Harvests: Prairie Indian Reserve Farmers and Government Policy* (Montreal and Kingston: McGill-Queen's University Press, 1990).

12 Doug Owram, *Promise of Eden: The Canadian Expansionist Movement and the Idea of the West, 1856-1900* (Toronto: University of Toronto Press, 1980), 131. See also Graham Parker, "Canadian Legal Culture," in *Law and Justice in a New Land: Essays in Western Canadian History*, ed. Louis A. Knafla (Toronto: Carswell, 1986), 12.

13 See, for example, Louis A. Knafla and Jonathan Swainger, eds., *Laws and Societies in the Canadian Prairie West, 1670-1940*, Law and Society Series (Vancouver: UBC Press, 2005); Hamar Foster, Benjamin L. Berger, and A.R. Buck, eds., *The Grand Experiment: Law and Legal Culture in British Settler Societies*, Law and Society Series (Vancouver: UBC Press, 2008); Sherene H. Razack, ed., *Race, Space, and the Law: Unmapping a White Settler Society*, 2nd ed. (Toronto: Between the Lines, 2005).

14 David Kahane, "What Is Culture? Generalizing about Aboriginal and Newcomer Perspectives," in *Intercultural Dispute Resolution in Aboriginal Contexts*, eds. Catherine Bell and David Kahane (Vancouver: UBC Press, 2004), 29-30.

15 Carl Berger, *The Writing of Canadian History: Aspects of English-Canadian Historical Writing, 1900-1970* (Toronto: Oxford University Press, 1976), 175.

16 Robin Fisher, *Contact and Conflict: Indian-European Relations in British Columbia, 1774-1890*, 2nd ed. (Vancouver: UBC Press, 1992), xxvi.

17 Brian W. Dippie, "One West, One Myth: Transborder Continuity in Western Art," in *One West, Two Myths II: Essays on Comparison*, eds. C.L. Higham and Robert Thacker (Calgary: University of Calgary Press, 2006), 33. See, for example, Warren Elofson, *Cowboys, Gentlemen and Cattle Thieves: Ranching on the Western Frontier* (Montreal and Kingston: McGill-Queen's University Press, 2000); and Warren Elofson, "Law and Disorder on the Ranching Frontiers of Montana and Alberta/Assiniboia," *Journal of the West* 42 (Winter 2003): 40-51.

18 Louis A. Knafla, "Introduction: Laws and Societies in the Anglo-Canadian North-West Frontier and Prairie Provinces, 1670-1940," in Knafla and Swainger, *Laws and Societies*, 1-5.

19 Ibid., 3.

20 Keith D. Smith, *Liberalism, Surveillance, and Resistance: Indigenous Communities in Western Canada, 1887-1927* (Edmonton: Athabasca University Press, 2009), 2.

21 Roger L. Nichols, "Myths and Realities in American-Canadian Studies: Challenges to Comparing Native Peoples' Experiences," in Higham and Thacker, *One West, Two Myths II*, 116.

22 Sidney L. Harring, "'There Seemed to Be No Recognized Law': Canadian Law and the Prairie First Nations," in Knafla and Swainger, *Laws and Societies*, 94.

23 Ibid.

24 Ibid., 110, 111.

25 Carter, *Aboriginal People and Colonizers*, 142-44, 147-49. With regard to Cree starvation policy, see also Gerald Friesen, *The Canadian Prairies: A History* (Toronto: University of Toronto Press, 2004), 150.

26 Carter, *Aboriginal People and Colonizers*, 133-34.

27 Knafla, "Introduction: Laws and Societies," 6-7.

28 Carter, *Aboriginal People and Colonizers*, 119-20.

29 Ray, Miller, and Tough, *Bounty and Benevolence*, 204-5.

30 David Laird, "Memorandum," in *British Columbia, Papers Connected with the Indian Land Question, 1850-75* (Victoria: R. Wolfenden, 1874), 151.

31 See, for example, Fisher, *Contact and Conflict*; Paul Tennant, *Aboriginal Peoples and Politics: The Indian Land Question in British Columbia, 1849-1989* (Vancouver: UBC Press, 1990); Cole Harris, *Making Native Space* (Vancouver: UBC Press, 2003).

32 Laird, "Memorandum," 154.

33 Ibid., 155.

34 George A. Walkem, "Report of the Government of British Columbia on the Subject of Indian Reserves," in *British Columbia, Papers Connected with the Indian Land Question,* 223.

35 Titley, *A Narrow Vision,* 201.

36 Dean Neu and Richard Therrien, *Accounting for Genocide: Canada's Bureaucratic Assault on Aboriginal People* (Black Point, NS: Fernwood, 2003), 88-89.

37 Titley, *A Narrow Vision,* 24; for an overview of Scott's career, see chap. 2.

38 Ibid., 154-55.

39 Ibid., 161.

40 Duncan Campbell Scott, quoted in Daniel Francis, *The Imaginary Indian: The Image of the Indian in Canadian Culture,* 7th ed. (Vancouver: Arsenal Pulp Press, 1992), 199. Originally published in the December 1906 *Scribner's Magazine,* Scott's "The Last of the Indian Treaties" was reprinted in Duncan Campbell Scott, *The Circle of Affection* (Toronto: McClelland and Stewart, 1947), 109-22.

41 Neu and Therrien, *Accounting for Genocide,* 89.

42 J.R. Miller, *Lethal Legacy: Current Native Controversies in Canada* (Toronto: McClelland and Stewart, 2004), 31-37. See also Carter, *Aboriginal People and Colonizers,* 115-18.

43 John S. Milloy, *A National Crime: The Canadian Government and the Residential School System, 1879 to 1986,* 3rd ed. (Winnipeg: University of Manitoba Press, 2001), 54.

44 Alexander Morris, *The Treaties of Canada with the Indians* (Saskatoon: Fifth House, 1991; first published 1880), 314, quoted in Miller, *Lethal Legacy,* 243.

45 Ibid., 244.

46 Ibid.

47 Milloy, *A National Crime,* 31. He refers here to the Department of Indian Affairs.

48 Inspector J.A. Macrae to the Superintendent General of Indian Affairs, 7 December 1900, Library and Archives Canada, Ottawa, RG 10, vol. 3947, file 123764, MR C 10166, quoted in Milloy, *A National Crime,* 32.

49 Canada, *Report of the Royal Commission on Aboriginal Peoples,* vol. 1, *Looking Forward, Looking Back* (Ottawa: Minister of Supply and Services Canada, 1996), pt. 2, "False Assumptions and a Failed Relationship," chap. 10, "Residential Schools," Indian and Northern Affairs Canada, http://www.collectionscanada.gc.ca/webarchives/20071211055821/http://www.ainc-inac.gc.ca/ch/rcap/sg/sg31_e.html.

50 Milloy, *A National Crime,* 157-58; for an overview, see chaps. 4-8.

51 Miller, *Lethal Legacy,* 240.

52 David A. Nock, "Aboriginals and Their Influence on E.F. Wilson's Paradigm Revolution," in *With Good Intentions: Euro-Canadian and Aboriginal Relations in Colonial Canada,* eds. Celia Haig-Brown and David A. Nock (Vancouver: UBC Press, 2006), 158.

53 David A. Nock and Celia Haig-Brown, "Introduction," in Haig-Brown and Nock, *With Good Intentions,* 2.

54 C.L. Higham, *Noble, Wretched, and Redeemable: Protestant Missionaries to the Indians in Canada and the United States, 1820-1900* (Albuquerque: University of New Mexico, 2000), 3-4.

55 Keith Walden, *Visions of Order* (Toronto: Butterworth Canada, 1982).

56 Arthur J. Ray, *I Have Lived Here since the World Began: An Illustrated History of Canada's Native People* (Toronto: Lester, 1996), 5-20, 209-14; Robert A. Williams Jr., *Linking Arms Together: American Indian Treaty Visions of Law and Peace, 1600-1800* (Oxford: Oxford University Press, 1997), 75-82.

57 Neu and Therrien, *Accounting for Genocide*, 72.

58 For an overview on fur trade diplomacy, see Ray, Miller, and Tough, *Bounty and Benevolence*, chap. 1.

59 Titley, *A Narrow Vision;* see especially chap. 9.

60 Richard Slotkin, *Regeneration through Violence: The Mythology of the American Frontier, 1600-1860* (Middletown: Wesleyan University Press, 1973), 5.

61 Elizabeth Furniss, *The Burden of History: Colonialism and the Frontier Myth in a Rural Canadian Community* (Vancouver: UBC Press, 1999), 63.

62 Francis, *The Imaginary Indian*, 61; see especially chaps. 4 and 9.

63 William Katerberg, "A Northern Vision: Frontier and the West in the Canadian and American Imagination," in *One West, Two Myths II: Essays on Comparison*, eds. C.L. Higham and Robert Thacker (Calgary: University of Calgary Press, 2006), 66.

64 Ibid.

65 Canadian Broadcasting Corporation, "Pioneers Head West: Can Ottawa Settle the Frontier without Bloodshed?" Canada: A People's History, http://www.cbc.ca/history/SECTIONSE1EP10CH3LE.html.

66 Canadian Broadcasting Corporation, "Treaties Signal End: Natives Sign Over Land and Watch a Way of Life Slip Away," http://www.cbc.ca/history/EPISCONTENTSE1EP10CH2PA3LE.html; and "Mounties Saddle Up: A Legendary Police Force Is Born on the Western Frontier," Canada: A People's History, http://www.cbc.ca/history/EPISCONTENTSE1EP10CH3PA1LE.html.

67 Lyle Dick, "A History for the New Millennium: Canada: A People's History," *Canadian Historical Review* 85,1 (2004): 95.

68 Ibid., 102.

69 Ibid., 98.

70 Richard Slotkin, *The Fatal Environment: The Myth of the Frontier in the Age of Industrialization, 1800-1890* (New York: Atheneum, 1985), 19.

71 John Paul Lederach, *The Moral Imagination: The Art and Soul of Building Peace* (New York: Oxford University Press, 2005), 28-29.

72 See, for example, Tom Flanagan, *First Nations? Second Thoughts* (Montreal and Kingston: McGill-Queen's University Press, 2000); and Melvin H. Smith, *Our Home or Native Land? What Government's Aboriginal Policy Is Doing to Canada* (Victoria: Crown Western, 1995).

73 Furniss, *The Burden of History,* 12.

74 Francis, *The Imaginary Indian,* 223.

75 J.L. Granatstein, *Whose War Is It? How Canada Can Survive in the Post-9/11 World* (Toronto: HarperCollins, 2007), 25.

76 Canada, *Report of the Royal Commission on Aboriginal Peoples,* vol. 2, *Restructuring the Relationship* (Ottawa: Minister of Supply and Services Canada, 1996), chap. 2, "Treaties," http://www.collectionscanada.gc.ca/webarchives/20071211054912/http:// www.ainc-inac.gc.ca/ch/rcap/sg/sh3_e.html.

77 Allan Gotlieb, "Romanticism and Realism in Canada's Foreign Policy" (Benefactors Lecture, C.D. Howe Institute, Toronto, 3 November 2004), http://www.cdhowe.org/ pdf/benefactors_lecture_2004.pdf.

78 Richard Sanders, "Dismantling the Myth of 'Canada the Peacemaker,'" *Press for Conversion!* 40 (April 2000), http://www.peace.ca/dismantlingmyth.htm.

79 Michael Campbell, "Canadians Are Sold on Empty Moralizing," *Vancouver Sun,* 21 April 2005, D3.

80 Anne Goodman, "Transformative Learning and Cultures of Peace," in *Expanding the Boundaries of Transformative Learning: Essays on Theory and Praxis,* eds. Edmund V. O'Sullivan, Amish Morrell, and Mary Ann O'Connor (New York: Palgrave, 2002), 195.

81 Neu and Therrien, *Accounting for Genocide,* 6.

82 Rodolfo Stavenhagen, *Report of the Special Rapporteur on the Situation of Human Rights and Fundamental Freedoms of Indigenous People. Addendum. Mission to Canada* (New York: United Nations Economic and Social Council, Commission on Human Rights, 2004), 10, http://daccess-dds-ny.un.org/doc/UNDOC/GEN/G05/100/26/PDF/ G0510026.pdf?OpenElement.

83 Canada, Department of Canadian Heritage, *A Canada for All: Canada's Action Plan against Racism* (Ottawa: Department of Canadian Heritage, 2005), 9, http://www. racialequitytools.org/resourcefiles/departmentofcanadianheritage.pdf.

84 Centre for Research and Information on Canada, *Facing the Future: Relations between Aboriginal and Non-Aboriginal Canadians,* CRIC Paper 14 (Ottawa: Centre for Research and Information on Canada, 2004), 17, http://www.library.carleton.ca/ ssdata/surveys/documents/cric-poc-03-not2_000.pdf.

85 Edward John et al., "As the Barriers Come Down, Education for Native Children Is Improving," *Vancouver Sun,* 29 September 2005, A21.

Chapter 4: The Alternative Dispute Resolution Program

1 A federal government department established in 2001, Indian Residential Schools Resolution Canada was intended to deal exclusively with IRS claims. In 2008, it became part of the Department of Indian and Northern Affairs Canada.

2 "Residential Schools Legacy: Is Reconciliation Possible?" University of Calgary, Calgary, 12-14 March 2004. Quotes in the following discussion are from the author's notes. For an overview of the conference and subsequent events, see Assembly of

First Nations, *Report on Canada's Dispute Resolution Plan to Compensate for Abuses in Indian Residential Schools* (Ottawa: Assembly of First Nations, 2004), 9-10, http://www.afn.ca/residentialschools/resources.html (AFN, *Report on Canada's Dispute Resolution*).

3 *Blackwater v. Plint* concerned alleged sexual abuse at the Alberni Residential School in Port Alberni, BC. The defendant was convicted in criminal court, but issues of liability and damages were dealt with at the BC Supreme Court in 2001. The court ruled, among other things, that Canada was 75 percent liable for vicarious trauma and associated damages, and that the church apportionment was 25 percent. *Blackwater v. Plint*, 2001 BCSC 997, http://www.courts.gov.bc.ca/jdb-txt/sc/01/09/2001bcsc0997.htm.

  The decision was subsequently appealed to the BC Court of Appeal, which ruled in 2003 that the federal government was 100 percent liable for damages. *Blackwater v. Plint*, 2003 BCCA 671, http://www.courts.gov.bc.ca/Jdb-txt/CA/03/06/2003BCCA0671.htm. Canada appealed to the Supreme Court of Canada; in 2005, it reversed the Court of Appeal decision regarding vicarious liability and damages in favour of the BC Supreme Court finding. *Blackwater v. Plint*, 2005 SCC 58, [2005] 3 S.C.R. 3, http://csc.lexum.umontreal.ca/en/2005/2005scc58/2005scc58.html.

4 John S. Milloy, *A National Crime: The Canadian Government and the Residential School System, 1879 to 1986,* 3rd ed. (Winnipeg: University of Manitoba Press, 2001), xviii (emphasis in original).

5 Dr. Roland Chrisjohn made this point during a June 2005 public lecture in Vancouver, BC. See also Roland Chrisjohn and Sherri Young, *The Circle Game: Shadows and Substance in the Indian Residential School Experience in Canada* (Penticton, BC: Theytus Books, 1997).

6 Stan McKay, "Expanding the Dialogue on Truth and Reconciliation – In a Good Way," in *From Truth to Reconciliation: Transforming the Legacy of Residential Schools,* eds. Marlene Brant Castellano, Linda Archibald, and Mike DeGagné (Ottawa: Aboriginal Healing Foundation, 2008), 107.

7 Roger Fisher and William Ury, *Getting to Yes: Negotiating Agreement without Giving In,* 2nd ed. (New York: Penguin Books, 1991).

8 Sara Cobb and Janet Rifkin, "Practice and Paradox: Deconstructing Narrative in Mediation," *Law and Social Inquiry* 16 (1991): 50-51.

9 Ibid., 58-60.

10 See, for example, Sara Cobb, "A Narrative Perspective on Mediation: Towards the Materialization of the 'Storytelling' Metaphor," in *New Directions in Mediation: Communication Research and Perspectives,* eds. Joseph P. Folger and Tricia S. Jones (Thousand Oaks: Sage, 1994), 48-63; John Winslade and Gerald Monk, *Narrative Mediation: A New Approach to Conflict Resolution* (San Francisco: Jossey-Bass, 2000); D.M. Kolb and L.L. Putnam, "Through the Looking Glass: Negotiation Theory Refracted through the Lens of Gender," in *Workplace Dispute Resolution: Directions*

for the Twenty-First Century, ed. Sandra E. Gleason (East Lansing: Michigan State University Press, 1997); and Kevin Avruch, Peter W. Black, and Joseph A. Scimecca, eds., *Conflict Resolution: Cross-Cultural Perspectives* (Westport, CT: Greenwood Press, 1991).

11 David Dyck, "The Mediator as Nonviolent Advocate: Revisiting the Question of Mediator Neutrality," *Mediation Quarterly* 18,2 (2000): 131.

12 Ibid., 131-32.

13 Ibid., 138.

14 Robert A. Bush and J. Folger, *The Promise of Mediation: Responding to Conflict through Empowerment and Recognition* (San Francisco: Jossey-Bass, 1994). See also David Kahane, "What Is Culture? Generalizing about Aboriginal and Newcomer Perspectives," in *Intercultural Dispute Resolution in Aboriginal Contexts,* eds. Catherine Bell and David Kahane (Vancouver: UBC Press, 2004), 29.

15 Bernard S. Mayer, *Beyond Neutrality: Confronting the Crisis in Conflict Resolution* (San Francisco: Jossey-Bass, 2004), 149-50.

16 Christopher Mitchell, "Beyond Resolution: What Does Conflict Transformation Actually Transform?" *Peace and Conflict Studies* 9,1 (2002): 20.

17 The Statement of Reconciliation was issued in conjunction with Canada's formal response to the royal commission. See *Gathering Strength: Canada's Aboriginal Action Plan* (Ottawa: Minister of Indian Affairs and Northern Development, 1998). For the text of the Statement of Reconciliation, see http://www.ainc-inac.gc.ca/ai/rqpi/apo/js_spea-eng.asp.

18 Indian Affairs and Northern Development, *Reconciliation and Healing: Alternative Resolution Strategies for Dealing with Residential School Claims* (Ottawa: Indian Affairs and Northern Development, 2000), 107-16.

19 Ibid., 111, 112.

20 Kaufman, Thomas and Associates, "Review of Indian Residential Schools Dispute Resolution Projects: Final Report" (report prepared for the Office of Indian Residential Schools Resolution, October 2002), 1:2-3, http://www.ainc-inac.gc.ca/ai/rqpi/info/nwz/pdf/20081027_fro1_eng.pdf.

21 Ibid., 12.

22 Law Commission of Canada, ed., *Restoring Dignity: Responding to Child Abuse in Canadian Institutions* (Ottawa: Minister of Public Works and Government Services, 2000). In 1997, then minister of justice Anne McLellan requested that the law commission research and prepare the report. Part 1C examines Indian residential schools.

23 Ibid., 157-60.

24 Ibid., 303-4.

25 Andrew Pirie, legal scholar and ADR expert, defines adjudication as "any dispute resolution process in which a neutral third party hears each party's evidence and arguments and renders a decision that is binding on them. This decision is usually based on objective standards. The term adjudication includes arbitration and

litigation." Restorative justice, he says, "would emphasize reconciliation for both the perpetrators and victims of crime. Healing would be added to the pre-existing goal of rehabilitation within the criminal justice system. Restorative justice can be related to ideas of reconciliation and can be thought to have some genesis in Aboriginal justice systems or the values of various faith communities." Andrew Pirie, *Alternative Dispute Resolution: Skills, Science, and the Law* (Toronto: Irwin Law, 2000), 47, 51. For a critique of ADR models in the residential school context, see Jennifer Llewellyn, "Dealing with the Legacy of Native Residential School Abuse in Canada: Litigation, ADR, and Restorative Justice," *University of Toronto Law Journal* 52 (2002): 253-300.

26 Llewellyn, "Dealing with the Legacy," 270-72.

27 Department of Canadian Heritage, "Minister Copps Announces the Creation of an Aboriginal Languages and Cultures Centre," news release, 19 December 2002.

28 AFN, *Report on Canada's Dispute Resolution.*

29 *Cloud v. Canada (Attorney General)* (2004), 247 D.L.R. (4th) 667 at para. 73.

30 Ibid., para. 92.

31 For a detailed analysis of all aspects of the ADRP, see AFN, *Report on Canada's Dispute Resolution;* and Canadian Bar Association, *The Logical Next Step: Reconciliation Payments for All Indian Residential School Survivors* (Ottawa: Canadian Bar Association, 2005), http://www.cba.org/CBA/Sections/pdf/residential.pdf.

32 AFN, *Report on Canada's Dispute Resolution,* 14.

33 Ibid., 1-3, 20.

34 Canadian Bar Association, *The Logical Next Step,* 16.

35 Ibid., 20.

36 Canada, *House of Commons Debates* (9 February 2005), 1915 (Jim Prentice, MP), http://www2.parl.gc.ca/.

37 For information on the Commission of Inquiry into Sponsorship Program and Advertising Activities, see Susan Munroe, "Gomery Inquiry," About.com: Canada Online, http://canadaonline.about.com/od/governmentspending/p/gomeryinquiry.htm.

38 House of Commons Standing Committee on Aboriginal Affairs and Northern Development, "Study on the Effectiveness of the Government ADR Process for the Resolution of IRS Claims," Evidence (15 February 2005), http://www2.parl.gc.ca/ (Standing Committee, "Study," Evidence). The Indian Residential School Survivors Society is a grassroots non-profit organization that provides counselling support for IRS survivors, public education, and outreach on residential school issues. For more information, see the society's website: http://www.irsss.ca/.

39 Standing Committee, "Study," Evidence (17 February 2005).

40 Ibid.

41 Ibid.

42 Ibid. Lunn refers to Jon Faulds, who also appeared as a witness, representing the National Consortium of Residential School Survivors' Counsel.

43 Ibid. (22 February 2005).

44   Ibid.

45   Bill Curry, "McLellan under Attack over Native-School Redress," *Toronto Globe and Mail,* 23 February 2005, A11. See also James Travers, "Indian Abuse Claims Turning into Fiasco," *Toronto Star,* 17 February 2005, A25; Paul Samyn, "School Abuse Delays Lashed, Aboriginals Suffering, Fontaine Tells MPs," *Winnipeg Free Press,* 23 February 2005, A3; Cristin Schmitz, "Government Takes Heat for Inaction over Abuse Claims," *Toronto National Post,* 23 February 2005.

46   James Travers, "Martin's Chance to Atone for Native Abuse," *Toronto Star,* 31 March 2005, A27. See also Cristin Schmitz, "Opposition Unites on Residential School Vote," *Victoria Times Colonist,* 24 March 2005.

47   House of Commons Standing Committee on Aboriginal Affairs and Northern Development, "Fourth Report: Study on the Effectiveness of the Government Alternative Dispute Resolution Process for the Resolution of Indian Residential School Claims," http://www2.parl.gc.ca/ (Standing Committee, "Fourth Report").

48   Standing Committee, "Study," Evidence (24 March 2005).

49   Standing Committee, "Fourth Report."

50   Ibid.

51   Assembly of First Nations, "Assembly of First Nations National Chief Supports Supreme Court Decision on Cloud Class Action Case," news release, 13 May 2005, http://www.afn.ca/article.asp?id=1100.

52   Cristin Schmitz, "$1B Payout Expected in Native Cases," *Toronto National Post,* 14 May 2005, A4.

53   Paul Samyn, "Ottawa Ready to Sign New Accord with First Nations," *Vancouver Sun,* 27 May 2005, A8.

54   "Assembly of First Nations National Chief Signs Historic Political Accord to Resolve the Legacy of Residential Schools," news release, 30 May 2005, http://www.afn.ca/article.asp?id=1185. See also Political Agreement, 30 May 2005, http://www.afn.ca/cmslib/general/IRS-Accord.pdf.

55   Indian and Northern Affairs Canada, "Government of Canada Announces Landmark Agreement toward a Lasting Resolution of the Legacy of Indian Residential Schools and Appoints Representative to Lead Discussions," news release, 30 May 2005, http://www.iacobucci.gc.ca/doc-eng.asp?action=20050530nr.

56   Assembly of First Nations, "Assembly of First Nations National Chief Signs Historic Political Accord"; National Consortium of Residential School Survivors' Counsel, "National Consortium Negotiations with the Honourable Mr. Justice Iacobucci Will Be Focused on Reaching a Viable Settlement of All Residential School Claims," news release, 18 July 2005.

57   Indian Residential School Survivors Society and National Residential School Survivors' Society, "Advocates Disappointed with Delay in Resolving Residential School Claims – Move to Expedite Federal Mediator's Mandate," news release, 2 June 2005, http://www.irsss.ca/media_page.html.

58   Cristin Schmitz, "Billions for Natives: Talks to Compensate Residential School Students Start at $4-Billion," *Toronto National Post*, 31 May 2005, A1, A6.

59   Don Martin, "A How-to on Getting Liberal Money," *Toronto National Post*, 31 May 2005, A1, A6.

60   Jeffrey Simpson, "Pay, Pay, Pay: Will the Residential Schools Mess Go Away?" *Toronto Globe and Mail*, 3 June 2005.

61   For a comprehensive overview of all aspects of the settlement agreement, see the official court website: http://www.residentialschoolsettlement.ca/English.html.

Chapter 5: Indigenous Diplomats

1   John Ralston Saul, *A Fair Country: Telling Truths about Canada* (Toronto: Viking Canada, 2008), 93.

2   Ibid., 99.

3   Ibid., 97.

4   McLeod is quoting Alexander Morris, *The Treaties of Canada with the Indians of Manitoba and the North-West Territories, Including the Negotiations on Which They Were Based* (1880; reprint Saskatoon: Fifth House, 1991), 191.

5   Note the different spelling of Gitxsan and Wet'suwet'en being used in 1994, the year in which *Eagle Down Is Our Law* was published.

6   Taiaiake Alfred, *Peace, Power, Righteousness: An Indigenous Manifesto* (Don Mills: Oxford University Press, 1999), xvi. See also Robert A. Williams Jr., *Linking Arms Together: American Indian Treaty Visions of Law and Peace, 1600-1800* (Oxford: Oxford University Press, 1997), 127-28.

7   Schedule N: Mandate for the Truth and Reconciliation Commission, *Indian Residential Schools Settlement Agreement*, 2006, s. 1(d), http://www.residentialschoolsettlement. ca/settlement.html.

8   Ibid., s. 4(d).

9   Paulette Regan, "An Apology Feast in Hazelton: Indian Residential Schools, Reconciliation, and Making Space for Indigenous Legal Traditions," in *Indigenous Legal Traditions*, ed. Law Commission of Canada, Legal Dimensions Series (Vancouver: UBC Press, 2007), 43.

10   Arthur J. Ray, "History Wars and Treaty Rights in Canada: A Canadian Case Study," in *The Power of Promises: Rethinking Indian Treaties in the Pacific Northwest*, ed. Alexandra Harmon (Seattle: University of Washington Press, 2008), 285.

11   Williams, *Linking Arms Together*, 10-11. See also Vine Deloria Jr. and Raymond J. DeMallie, *Documents of American Indian Diplomacy: Treaties, Agreements and Conventions, 1775-1979* (Norman: University of Oklahoma Press, 1999), 6-8.

12   Ravi de Costa, "History, Democracy, and Treaty Negotiations in British Columbia," in Harmon, *The Power of Promises*, 313. Interestingly, former treaty negotiator Tony Penikett also argues that the complex legalistic language of modern-day treaty making is problematic but recommends that treaties be "written in plain language as

principled agreements, and constitutional documents, with the details attached in appendices." See Tony Penikett, *Reconciliation: First Nations Treatymaking in British Columbia* (Vancouver: Douglas and McIntyre, 2006), 272.

13 De Costa, "History, Democracy, and Treaty Negotiations," 312-13.

14 Ibid., 314.

15 Perry Shawana, "Legal Processes, Pluralism in Canadian Jurisprudence, and the Governance of Carrier Medicine Knowledge," in Law Commission of Canada, *Indigenous Legal Traditions*, 117.

16 De Costa, "History, Democracy, and Treaty Negotiations," 312.

17 Ibid., 315. De Costa quotes Michael Asch, "Self-Determination and Treaty-Making: Consent and the Resolution of Political Relations between First Nations and Canada" (paper presented at the Consortium on Democratic Constitutionalism: Consent as the Foundation for Political Community, University of Victoria, Victoria, BC, 1-3 October 2004).

18 Alexandra Harmon, "Introduction," in Harmon, *The Power of Promises*, 11.

19 Renisa Mawani, *Colonial Proximities: Crossracial Encounters and Juridical Truths in British Columbia, 1871-1921* (Vancouver: UBC Press, 2009), 23-24.

20 For an overview, see Arthur J. Ray, Jim Miller, and Frank Tough, *Bounty and Benevolence: A History of Saskatchewan Treaties* (Montreal and Kingston: McGill-Queen's University Press, 2000), 204-8.

21 For an overview of this early historical writing in the Canadian context, see Bruce Trigger, *Natives and Newcomers: Canada's Heroic Age Reconsidered* (Montreal and Kingston: McGill-Queen's University Press, 1985), chap. 1.

22 Richard White, *The Middle Ground: Indians, Empires and Republics in the Great Lakes Region, 1650-1815* (New York: Cambridge University Press, 1991), x.

23 Richard White, "The Fictions of Patriarchy: Indians and Whites in the Early Republic," in *Native Americans and the Early Republic*, eds. Frederick E. Hoxie, Ronald Hoffman, and Peter J. Albert (Charlottesville: University of Virginia Press, 1999), 66.

24 Williams, *Linking Arms Together*, 10-11. See also J. Edward Chamberlin, "Culture and Anarchy in Indian Country," in *Aboriginal and Treaty Rights in Canada: Essays on Law, Equity and Respect for Difference*, ed. Michael Asch (Vancouver: UBC Press, 1997); Anthony J. Hall, *The American Empire and the Fourth World* (Montreal and Kingston: McGill-Queen's University Press, 2003), especially chap. 5.

25 Francis Jennings, "Introduction," in Francis Jennings et al., eds., *The History and Culture of Iroquois Diplomacy: An Interdisciplinary Guide to the Treaties of the Six Nations and Their League* (Syracuse: Syracuse University Press, 1985), xiv-xv.

26 William Fenton, "Structure, Continuity and Change in the Process of Iroquois Treaty Making," in Jennings et al., *The History and Culture*, 4.

27 Williams, *Linking Arms Together*, 4.

28 Michael K. Foster, "Another Look at the Function of Wampum in Iroquois-White Councils," in Jennings et al., *The History and Culture*, 101.

29   Ibid., 110.

30   Daniel K. Richter, "Ordeals of the Longhouse: The Five Nations in Early American History," in *Beyond the Covenant Chain: The Iroquois and Their Neighbors in Indian North America, 1600-1800,* eds. Daniel K. Richter and James Merrell (Syracuse: Syracuse University Press, 1987), 22.

31   Mary Druke, "Linking Arms: The Structure of Iroquois Intertribal Diplomacy," in Richter and Merrell, *Beyond the Covenant Chain,* 29-39.

32   Williams, *Linking Arms Together,* 60.

33   Matthew Dennis, *Cultivating a Landscape of Peace: Iroquois-European Encounters in Seventeenth Century America* (Ithaca: Cornell University Press, 1993), 6.

34   Ibid., 268 (emphasis in original).

35   Alfred, *Peace, Power, Righteousness,* xii.

36   Ibid., xix.

37   John Borrows, "Wampum at Niagara: The Royal Proclamation, Canadian Legal History and Self-Government," in Asch, *Aboriginal and Treaty Rights,* 165.

38   Dennis, *Cultivating a Landscape,* 125.

39   John Borrows, *Recovering Canada: The Resurgence of Indigenous Law* (Toronto: University of Toronto Press, 2002), 13.

40   Sarah Carter, *Aboriginal People and Colonizers of Western Canada to 1900* (Toronto: University of Toronto Press, 1999), 131-32.

41   Williams, *Linking Arms Together,* 81-82.

42   Hamar Foster and Benjamin L. Berger, "From Humble Prayers to Legal Demands: The Cowichan Petition of 1909 and the British Columbia Indian Land Question," in *The Grand Experiment: Law and Legal Culture in British Settler Societies,* eds. Hamar Foster, Benjamin L. Berger, and A.R. Buck, Law and Society Series (Vancouver: UBC Press, 2008), 243.

43   Treaty 7 Tribal Council, Walter Hildebrandt, Sarah Carter, and Dorothy First Rider, *The True Spirit and Intent of Treaty 7* (Montreal and Kingston: McGill-Queen's University Press, 1996), 7, 115.

44   Betty Bastien, *Blackfoot Ways of Knowing: The Worldview of the Siksikaitsitapi* (Calgary: University of Calgary Press, 2004), 31-32.

45   Neal McLeod, *Cree Narrative Memory: From Treaties to Contemporary Times* (Saskatoon: Purich, 2007), 18.

46   Ibid., 58.

47   Joseph Campbell and Bill Moyers, *The Power of Myth* (New York: Anchor Books, 1991), 39. See also David I. Kertzer, *Ritual, Politics, and Power* (New Haven: Yale University Press, 1988), 12.

48   Lisa Schirch, *Ritual and Symbol in Peacebuilding* (Bloomfield: Kumarian Press, 2005).

49   Campbell and Moyers, *The Power of Myth,* xii-xiii.

50   Arthur Ray, "Native History on Trial: Confessions of an Expert Witness," *Canadian Historical Review* 84,2 (2003): 56.

51 The literature on *Delgamuukw* is extensive, but see Robin Fisher, "Judging History: Reflections on the Reasons for Judgment in *Delgamuukw v. B.C.*," in "Anthropology and History in the Courts," special issue, *BC Studies* 95 (Autumn 1992): 43-54; Dora Wilson-Kenni, "Time of Trial: The Gitksan and Wet'suwet'en in Court," in "Anthropology and History in the Courts," special issue, *BC Studies* 95 (Autumn 1992): 7-11; Dara Culhane, *The Pleasure of the Crown: Anthropology, Law and First Nations* (Burnaby: Talon Books, 1998); Medig'm Gyamk (Neil Sterritt), "It Doesn't Matter What the Judge Said," in *Aboriginal Title in British Columbia: Delgamuukw v. The Queen*, ed. Frank Cassidy (Lantzville, BC: Oolichan Books Institute for Research on Public Policy, 1992), 303-7; and Yagalahl (Dora Wilson), "It Will Always Be the Truth," in Cassidy, *Aboriginal Title*, 199-205.

52 Skanu'u (Ardythe Wilson), "Preface," in Don Monet and Skanu'u (Ardythe Wilson), *Colonialism on Trial: Indigenous Land Rights and the Gitksan and Wet'suwet'en Sovereignty Case* (Gabriola Island, BC: New Society, 1992), vii.

53 Quoted in Monet and Skanu'u, *Colonialism on Trial*, 22.

54 Quoted in ibid., 42.

55 Quoted in ibid., 187, 188, 189.

56 Adele Perry, "Colonialism and the Politics of History in *Delgamuukw v. British Columbia*" (paper presented at the International Committee of Historical Sciences conference, Sydney, Australia, 2005), n.p.

57 Culhane, *The Pleasure of the Crown*, 366.

58 See, for example, the collection of essays in "Anthropology and History in the Courts," special issue, *BC Studies* 95 (Autumn 1992). In "Judging History," 47, historian Robin Fisher defines ethnohistory as "the technique now used to write native history. Recognizing that no single source provides the key to unlock the past, ethnohistorians use oral tradition, ethnography, and archaeology as well as the written record ... All of these sources must be critically evaluated, for each one has its own particular power as well as its deficiencies."

59 *R. v. Van der Peet*, [1996] 2 S.C.R. 507; *Delgamuukw v. British Columbia*, [1997] 3 S.C.R. 1010.

60 *Delgamuukw* at para. 87.

61 For a discussion of the methodological issues related to expert evidence in Aboriginal litigation, see Drew Mildon, "A Bad Connection: First Nations Oral Histories in the Canadian Courts," in *Aboriginal Oral Traditions: Theory, Practice, Ethics*, eds. Renee Hulan and Renate Eigenbrod (Halifax: Fernwood, 2008), 79-97.

62 *Victor Buffalo v. Regina*, [2006] 1 C.N.L.R. 100 at para. 453.

63 McLeod, *Cree Narrative Memory*, 16.

64 Arthur J. Ray, "Ethnohistorical Evidence and First Nations, Metis, and Tribal Claims in North America: A Review of Past and Present Experiences with an Eye to the Future" (paper presented at the Continuing Legal Education Society of British Columbia, Aboriginal Law Conference, Vancouver, BC, June 2006), 2.3.20.

65 *Victor Buffalo v. Regina* at para. 457.

66 Ardith Alison Walkem, "Bringing Water to the Land: Re-cognize-ing Indigenous Oral Traditions and the Laws Embodied within Them" (LLM thesis, University of British Columbia, Vancouver, BC, 2005), 94; see especially chap. 4.

67 David Kahane, "What Is Culture? Generalizing about Aboriginal and Newcomer Perspectives," in *Intercultural Dispute Resolution in Aboriginal Contexts,* eds. Catherine Bell and David Kahane (Vancouver: UBC Press, 2004), 30.

68 *Tsilhqot'in Nation v. British Columbia,* 2007 BCSC 1700 at para. 132.

69 Ibid., para. 1356.

70 Ibid., para. 1350.

71 Ibid., para. 20.

72 William Bradford, "'With a Very Great Blame on Our Hearts': Reparations, Reconciliation, and an American Indian Plea for Peace with Justice," *American Indian Law Review* 27,1 (2002-03): 75, 164.

73 Marie Battiste and James (Sa'ke'j) Youngblood Henderson, *Protecting Indigenous Knowledge and Heritage: A Global Challenge* (Saskatoon: Purich, 2000), 213.

74 See, for example, Task Force on Aboriginal Languages and Cultures, *Towards a New Beginning: A Foundational Report for a Strategy to Revitalize First Nation, Inuit and Metis Languages and Cultures* (Ottawa: Department of Canadian Heritage, 2005).

75 Wayne Warry, *Unfinished Dreams: Community Healing and the Reality of Aboriginal Self-Government* (Toronto: University of Toronto Press, 1998), 221-22.

76 Val Napoleon, "Who Gets to Say What Happened? Reconciliation Issues for the Gitxsan," in Bell and Kahane, *Intercultural Dispute Resolution,* 188.

77 Taiaiake Alfred, *Wasáse: Indigenous Pathways of Action and Freedom* (Peterborough, ON: Broadview Press, 2005), 250.

78 Ibid.

79 See, for example, Dale Turner, *This Is Not a Peace Pipe: Towards a Critical Indigenous Philosophy* (Toronto: University of Toronto Press, 2006).

80 Linda Tuhiwai Smith, *Decolonizing Methodologies: Research and Indigenous Peoples* (London: Zed Books, 1999), 91-92.

81 Alfred, *Wasáse,* 250.

Chapter 6: The Power of Apology and Testimony

1 Eric Brahm, "Trauma Healing," *Beyond Intractability,* eds. Guy Burgess and Heidi Burgess, Conflict Research Consortium, University of Colorado, Boulder, 2004, n.p., http://www.beyondintractability.org/essay/trauma_healing/.

2 Rhoda E. Howard-Hassmann and Mark Gibney, "Introduction: Apologies and the West," in *The Age of Apology: Facing Up to the Past,* eds. Mark Gibney et al. (Philadelphia: University of Pennsylvania Press, 2008), 3, 4.

3 Ibid., 7.

4 Megan Boler, *Feeling Power: Emotions and Education* (New York: Routledge, 1999), 168.

5 Priscilla Hayner, *Unspeakable Truths: Facing the Challenge of Truth Commissions* (New York: Routledge, 2002), 25.

6 Neil J. Smelser, "Psychological Trauma and Cultural Trauma," in Jeffrey C. Alexander et al., *Cultural Trauma and Collective Identity* (Berkeley: University of California Press, 2004), 36-37.

7 Martha Minow, *Between Vengeance and Forgiveness: Facing History after Genocide and Mass Violence* (Boston: Beacon Press, 1998), 74.

8 Stanley Cohen, *States of Denial: Knowing about Atrocities and Suffering* (Cambridge: Polity Press, 2001), 255-59.

9 Melissa Nobles, *The Politics of Official Apologies* (Cambridge: Cambridge University Press, 2008), 71-72.

10 Angus Reid, "Canadians Divided on Australia-Style Apology to Aboriginal Population," 5 March 2008, http://www.angus-reid.com/uppdf/2008.03.05_Aboriginal.pdf.

11 Angus Reid, "Reconciliation with Aboriginals Possible for Two-in-Five Canadians," 8 May 2008, http://www.angus-reid.com/uppdf/2008.05.07_TRC.pdf.

12 Angus Reid, "Canadians Agree with Prime Minister's Apology to Aboriginal Community," 11 August 2008, http://www.angus-reid.com/uppdf/2008.08.11_Aboriginal.pdf.

13 Nicholas Tavuchis, *Mea Culpa: A Sociology of Apology and Reconciliation* (Stanford: Stanford University Press, 1991), 8.

14 Ibid., 19 (emphasis in original).

15 Ibid., 13, 18.

16 Ibid., 23.

17 Ibid., 102.

18 Nobles, *The Politics of Official Apologies*, 42.

19 Matt James, "Wrestling with the Past: Apologies, Quasi-Apologies, and Non-Apologies in Canada," in Gibney et al., *The Age of Apology*, 139.

20 Ibid., 141.

21 Ibid., 140, 141.

22 Andrew Coyne, "Natives as Nations," *Time Canada,* n.d., http://andrewcoyne.com/essays/Magazines/Time%20Canada/Time_Natives.rtfd/TXT.html.

23 Tavuchis, *Mea Culpa,* 100-1.

24 Annalise Acorn, *Compulsory Compassion: A Critique of Restorative Justice* (Vancouver: UBC Press, 2004), 17. Others argue the opposite – that restorative justice as Indigenous justice is highly effective in achieving these goals. See, for example, Kay Pranis, Barry Stuart, and Mark Wedge, *Peacemaking Circles: From Crime to Community* (St. Paul: Living Justice Press, 2003).

25 Ibid., 59.

26   Val Napoleon, "Who Gets to Say What Happened? Reconciliation Issues for the Gitxsan," in *Intercultural Dispute Resolution in Aboriginal Contexts*, eds. Catherine Bell and David Kahane (Vancouver: UBC Press, 2004), 176.

27   Ibid., 184.

28   Michelle LeBaron, "Learning New Dances: Finding Effective Ways to Address Intercultural Disputes," in Bell and Kahane, *Intercultural Dispute Resolution*, 16-21.

29   David Kahane, "What Is Culture? Generalizing about Aboriginal and Newcomer Perspectives," in Bell and Kahane, *Intercultural Dispute Resolution*, 46.

30   Julie McFarlane, "Commentary: When Cultures Collide," in Bell and Kahane, *Intercultural Dispute Resolution*, 95.

31   On ADR as an ideology, see Andrew Pirie, "Commentary: Intercultural Dispute Resolution Initiatives across Canada," in Bell and Kahane, *Intercultural Dispute Resolution*, 334-36.

32   John Borrows, "A Separate Peace: Strengthening Shared Justice," in Bell and Kahane, *Intercultural Dispute Resolution*, 344.

33   Ibid., 350-53.

34   Patricia A. Monture, "Community Governance and Nation (Re)Building: Centering Indigenous Learning and Research" (First Nations Governance Institute, 2004), http://www.fngovernance.org/pdf/MontureNationReBuilding.pdf.

35   Natalie Oman, "Paths to Intercultural Understanding: Feasting, Shared Horizons, and Unforced Consensus," in Bell and Kahane, *Intercultural Dispute Resolution*, 70-71.

36   Ibid., 80, 82 (emphasis in original).

37   Ibid., 82.

38   Kahane, "What Is Culture?" 38 (emphasis in original).

39   Qwul'sih'yah'maht (Robina Anne Thomas), "Honouring the Oral Traditions of My Ancestors through Storytelling," in *Research as Resistance: Critical, Indigenous, and Anti-Oppressive Approaches*, eds. Leslie Brown and Susan Strega (Toronto: Canadian Scholars Press/Women's Press, 2005), 241.

40   Ibid., 243-44.

41   Ibid., 253.

42   Jo-ann Archibald (Q'um Q'um Xiiem), *Indigenous Storywork: Educating the Heart, Mind, Body, and Spirit* (Vancouver: UBC Press, 2008), ix.

43   Ibid., 76.

44   Roger Simon, "The Pedagogical Insistence of Public Memory," in *Theorizing Historical Consciousness*, ed. Peter Seixas (Toronto: University of Toronto Press, 2004), 193.

45   Ibid., 194-95.

46   Michelle LeBaron, *Bridging Troubled Waters: Conflict Resolution from the Heart* (San Francisco: Jossey-Bass, 2002), 236-37.

Chapter 7: An Apology Feast in Hazelton

1   Hla Gwxhs Bekg'um means "welcome home." See "Apology to Gitxsan for IRS Internment," 4 March 2004, http://www.gitxsan.com/archived-news/82-apology-to-

gitxsan-for-irs-internment.html. The simgigyat are hereditary chiefs of the Gitxsan Nation. Parts of this chapter have been published previously. See Paulette Regan, "An Apology Feast in Hazelton: Indian Residential Schools, Reconciliation, and Making Space for Indigenous Legal Traditions," in *Indigenous Legal Traditions*, ed. Law Commission of Canada, Legal Dimensions Series (Vancouver: UBC Press, 2007), 40-76.

2 I dedicate this chapter to the IRS survivors of the Edmonton Indian Residential School who participated in the Hazelton ADR pilot project and to the people of the Gitxsan Nation. I was deeply honoured to work in partnership with the survivors, their advisory group, elders, hereditary chiefs, and the feast coordinator Matilda Daniels, as well as Deanna Sitter, resolution manager for IRSRC, and Brian Thorpe, senior advisor, Residential Schools Steering Committee, United Church of Canada.

3 I want to acknowledge the contribution of Matilda Daniels, who provided valuable feedback on this chapter and who, with me, co-presented a paper on the Hazelton apology feast at the Canadian Association of Law Teachers (CALT) annual conference "Law's Paradoxes," University of British Columbia, Vancouver, BC, 22-24 June 2005. I also want to thank Dr. Maggie Hodgson for her feedback regarding the Hazelton feast.

4 Gary G. Patsey, "Media Briefing: Apology Feast to the Gitxsan," media briefing kit, 19 March 2004 (author's copy).

5 Ibid.

6 Ibid.

7 See, for example, Antonia Mills, *Eagle Down Is Our Law: Witsuwit'en Law, Feasts, and Land Claims* (Vancouver: UBC Press, 1994); and Neil Sterritt et al., *Tribal Boundaries in the Nass Watershed* (Vancouver: UBC Press, 1998).

8 John Borrows, *Recovering Canada: The Resurgence of Indigenous Law* (Toronto: University of Toronto Press, 2002), 79-80.

9 Natalie Oman, "Paths to Intercultural Understanding: Feasting, Shared Horizons, and Unforced Consensus," in *Intercultural Dispute Resolution in Aboriginal Contexts*, eds. Catherine Bell and David Kahane (Vancouver: UBC Press, 2004), 83.

10 Lorna June McCue, "Treaty-Making from an Indigenous Perspective: A Ned'u'ten-Canadian Treaty Model" (LLM thesis, University of British Columbia, Vancouver, BC, 1998), 238. See also Jo-anne Fiske and Betty Patrick, *Cis Dideen Kat (When the Plumes Rise): The Way of the Lake Babine Nation* (Vancouver: UBC Press, 2000).

11 Richard Daly, *Our Box Was Full: An Ethnography for the Delgamuukw Plaintiffs* (Vancouver: UBC Press, 2005), 269-70. Note the different spelling of Gitxsan as Gitksan here.

12 Ibid., 95.

13 Fiske and Patrick, *Cis Dideen Kat*, 70. See also Daly, *Our Box Was Full*, 94.

14 Taiaiake Alfred, *Wasáse: Indigenous Pathways of Action and Freedom* (Peterborough, ON: Broadview Press, 2005), 249.

15 Val Napoleon, "Who Gets to Say What Happened? Reconciliation Issues for the Gitxsan," in Bell and Kahane, *Intercultural Dispute Resolution*, 188-89.

16 For an explanation of the tets, see Daly, *Our Box Was Full,* 74-77.

17 John Paul Lederach, "Five Qualities of Practice in Support of Reconciliation Processes," in *Forgiveness and Reconciliation: Religion, Public Policy and Conflict Transformation,* eds. Raymond G. Helmick and Rodney L. Petersen (Philadelphia: Templeton Foundation Press, 2001), 184.

18 Dominick LaCapra, *History in Transit: Experience, Identity, Critical Theory* (Ithaca: Cornell University Press, 2004), 121-22.

19 Shawn Tupper, "Apology to Hazelton ADR Participants" (author's copy). Copies of both apologies were distributed in press kits and may be held in the institutional records of government and church, but they are not widely available. For example, I could find no electronic version of either document on the Indian and Northern Affairs Canada or United Church websites.

20 Marion Best, "United Church Apology to Gitxsan" (author's copy).

21 See, for example, "Aboriginal Peoples: Justice and Right Relationships," United Church of Canada, http://www.united-church.ca/aboriginal/relationships.

22 Keith Howard, "Residential School Survivors Come Home," *United Church Observer,* June 2004, n.p., http://www.ucobserver.org/justice/2004/06/residential_school_surviviors_come_home/.

23 As Peter Seixas puts it, historical consciousness can be understood as "the area in which collective memory, the writing of history, and other modes of shaping images of the past in the public mind merge." Peter Seixas, "Introduction," in *Theorizing Historical Consciousness,* ed. Peter Seixas (Toronto: University of Toronto Press, 2004), 10. Seixas adopted this definition from the journal *History and Memory.*

24 Roger Simon, "The Pedagogical Insistence of Public Memory," in Seixas, *Theorizing Historical Consciousness,* 199.

Chapter 8: Peace Warriors and Settler Allies

1 This dialogue is part of a national initiative "1000 Conversations Across Canada on Reconciliation," http://1000conversations.ca/. It was developed by the Legacy of Hope Foundation, http://www.legacyofhope.ca/Home.aspx, and the National Day of Healing and Reconciliation, http://ndhr.ca/wordpress/?cat=4.

2 Cable Public Affairs Channel (CPAC), "Day of Hope: Roundtable on Reconciliation," video recording, 11 June 2009, http://www.cpac.ca/forms/index.asp?dsp=template&act=view3&pagetype=vod&lang=e&clipID=2913. For a summary of the dialogue, see 1000 Conversations Across Canada on Reconciliation, "#9 – A Conversation on Reconciliation, hosted by Her Excellency, the Right Honourable Michaëlle Jean, Governor General of Canada," 11 June 2009, http://1000conversations.ca/?paged=3.

3 Conversations, "#9 – A Conversation."

4 Jonathan Schell, *The Unconquerable World: Power, Non-Violence, and the Will of the People* (New York: Henry Holt, 2003), 352.

5   Ibid., 196. Schell cites Václav Havel, "Living in Truth," 57, for the quotations in this passage. Václav Havel, writer-activist and former president of Czechoslovakia and later the Czech Republic, was one of the political leaders of Czechoslovakia's non-violent Velvet Revolution, which brought down an authoritarian government.

6   David Jefferess, *Postcolonial Resistance: Culture, Liberation, and Transformation* (Toronto: University of Toronto Press, 2008), 20.

7   Ibid., 144, 145.

8   Henry A. Giroux, "When Hope Is Subversive," *Tikkun* 19,6 (n.d.): 38, 39 (emphasis in original), http://www.henryagiroux.com/online_articles/Tikkun%20piece.pdf.

9   Aboriginal Healing Foundation, *Reconciliation: A Work in Progress* (Ottawa: Aboriginal Healing Foundation, 2010), 4.

10 Ibid., 26, 27.

11 Taiaiake Alfred, *Wasáse: Indigenous Pathways of Action and Freedom* (Peterborough, ON: Broadview Press, 2005), 25.

12 John Paul Lederach, *The Moral Imagination: The Art and Soul of Building Peace* (New York: Oxford University Press, 2005), 53.

13 James C. Juhnke and Carol M. Hunter, *The Missing Peace: The Search for Nonviolent Alternatives in United States History* (Kitchener, ON: Pandora Press, 2004), 17-18.

14 Taiaiake Alfred and Lana Lowe, "Warrior Societies in Contemporary Indigenous Communities" (report prepared for the Ipperwash Inquiry), 5, http://www.attorneygeneral.jus.gov.on.ca/inquiries/ipperwash/policy_part/research/pdf/Alfred_and_Lowe.pdf. Alfred and Lowe's report is perhaps the most comprehensive empirical study of the historical and contemporary warrior societies that exist across North America.

15 Gail Guthrie Valaskakis, "Rights and Warriors: Media Memories and Oka," in Gail Guthrie Valaskakis, *Indian Country: Essays on Contemporary Native Culture* (Waterloo: Wilfrid Laurier University Press, 2005), 59.

16 Ibid., 46, 60-61.

17 Alfred and Lowe, "Warrior Societies," 19.

18 Ontario, Ipperwash Inquiry, *Report of the Ipperwash Inquiry* (Toronto: Ministry of the Attorney General, 2007), 1:97-99, http://www.attorneygeneral.jus.gov.on.ca/inquiries/ipperwash/report/vol_1/pdf/E_Vol_1_Full.pdf.

19 Thomas E. DeGloma Jr., "'Safe Space' and Contested Memories: Survivor Movements and the Foundation of Alternative Mnemonic Traditions," 2003, 3, http://www.newschool.edu/nssr/historymatters/papers/ThomasDeGloma.pdf.

20 See, for example, Healing Our Spirit Worldwide, an international initiative on healing, addiction recovery, and cultural revitalization that attracts residential and boarding school survivors from all over the world. For more information on Healing Our Spirit Worldwide, see its website: http://www.hosw.com/. Healing Our Spirit Worldwide was spearheaded by Dr. Maggie Hodgson in Edmonton in 1992. See National Day

of Healing and Reconciliation, "Maggie Hodgson," National Day of Healing and Reconciliation, http://ndhr.ca/old/about_maggie.php.

21 These bodies include, for example, National Residential School Survivors' Society, http://www.nrsss.ca/; Indian Residential School Survivors Society, http://www.irsss.ca/; and Assembly of First Nations, Indian Residential Schools Unit, http://www.afn.ca/residentialschools/index.html.

22 DeGloma, "'Safe Space,'" 5-7.

23 Ibid., 10, 11.

24 Ibid., 22-23.

25 John Torpey, *Making Whole What Has Been Smashed: On Reparations Politics* (Cambridge, MA: Harvard University Press, 2006), 56.

26 Ibid., 61.

27 Andrew Woolford, *Between Justice and Certainty: Treaty Making in British Columbia,* edited by W. Wesley Pue, Law and Society Series (Vancouver: UBC Press, 2005), 53.

28 Grand Chief Edward John, First Nations Summit, "Backgrounder: The First Nations Perspective on Clearing the Path to Justice" (presented at "Clearing the Path to Justice: A Public Forum Hosted by the Law Society of British Columbia," Wosk Centre for Dialogue, Vancouver, BC, 28 January 2009), 6-7, http://www.fns.bc.ca/pdf/Backgrounder-_ClearingPathJustice280109.pdf.

29 Jeff Corntassel, Chaw-win-is, and T'lakwadzi, "Indigenous Storytelling, Truth-Telling and Community Approaches to Reconciliation," *English Studies in Canada* 35,1 (March 2009): 137.

30 Ibid., 146.

31 Kay Schaffer and Sidonie Smith, *Human Rights and Narrated Lives: The Ethics of Recognition* (New York: Palgrave Macmillan, 2004), 116-17.

32 Jessica Senehi, "Constructive Storytelling in Intercommunal Conflicts: Building Community, Building Peace," in *Reconcilable Differences: Turning Points in Ethnopolitical Conflict,* eds. Sean Byrne and Cynthia L. Irvin (West Hartford, CT: Kumarian Press, 2000), 110.

33 For a full account of his work, see George Manuel and Michael Posluns, *The Fourth World: An Indian Reality* (Don Mills: Collier-Macmillan Canada, 1974); and Peter McFarlane, *Brotherhood to Nationhood: George Manuel and the Making of the Modern Indian Movement* (Toronto: Between the Lines, 1993).

34 Paul Tennant, *Aboriginal Peoples and Politics: The Indian Land Question in British Columbia, 1849-1989* (Vancouver: UBC Press, 1990), 81.

35 Manuel and Posluns, *The Fourth World,* 216-17.

36 George Manuel, *Speeches by George Manuel, President of the National Indian Brotherhood 1970-1976* (Vancouver: National Indian Brotherhood, 1976), 1:n.p.

37 See, for example, Robert A. Williams Jr., *Linking Arms Together: American Indian Treaty Visions of Law and Peace, 1600-1800* (Oxford: Oxford University Press, 1997);

John Borrows, *Recovering Canada: The Resurgence of Indigenous Law* (Toronto: University of Toronto Press, 2002); Matthew Dennis, *Cultivating a Landscape of Peace: Iroquois-European Encounters in Seventeenth Century America* (Ithaca: Cornell University Press, 1993); Colin G. Calloway, *New Worlds for All: Indians, Europeans, and the Remaking of Early America* (Baltimore: Johns Hopkins University Press, 1997); and Richard White, *The Middle Ground: Indians, Empires and Republics in the Great Lakes Region, 1650-1815* (New York: Cambridge University Press, 1991).

38 Rupert Ross, "When Survivors Become Warriors" (unpublished paper, n.d.), 1.

39 See, for example, United Church of Canada, "'Voicing the Past' in Kamloops," *Residential Schools Update,* October 2009, http://www.united-church.ca/files/communications/newsletters/residential-schools-update_091001.pdf; "2nd Annual TRC Info. Workshop – St. Paul, Alberta," National Day of Healing and Reconciliation, http://ndhr.ca/wordpress/?p=399.

40 The conversations are posted online at 1000 Conversations, http://1000conversations.ca/. On conferences, see, for example, "Breaking the Silence: International Conference on the Indian Residential Schools Commission of Canada," held at the University of Montreal, 26-27 September 2008, http://www.creum.umontreal.ca/spip.php?article900. For two exhibits, see "Where Are the Children? Healing the Legacy of Residential Schools," http://www.wherearethechildren.ca/; "We Were So Far Away: The Inuit Experience of Residential Schools," http://www.legacyofhope.ca/WeWereSoFarAway.aspx. Both exhibits were produced by Legacy of Hope in partnership with the Aboriginal Healing Foundation and Library and Archives Canada, with funding from Indian and Northern Affairs Canada. For more information on Legacy of Hope, see its website: http://www.legacyofhope.ca/Home.aspx.

41 See, for example, "Red Lake Hosts Residential School Exhibit," *Sagatay,* April-May 2006, http://www.wawataynews.ca/sagatay/node/89.

42 David A. Nock and Celia Haig-Brown, "Introduction," in *With Good Intentions: Euro-Canadian and Aboriginal Relations in Colonial Canada,* eds. Celia Haig-Brown and David A. Nock (Vancouver: UBC Press, 2006), 7.

43 Natalie A. Chambers, "Truth and Reconciliation: A 'Dangerous Opportunity' to Unsettle Ourselves," in *Response, Responsibility and Renewal: Canada's Truth and Reconciliation Journey,* eds. Gregory Younging, Jonathan Dewar, and Mike DeGagné (Ottawa: Aboriginal Healing Foundation, 2009), 298-99.

44 Alfred, *Wasáse,* 102.

45 Lederach, *The Moral Imagination,* ix-x.

46 John Paul Lederach, "Five Qualities of Practice in Support of Reconciliation Processes," in *Forgiveness and Reconciliation: Religion, Public Policy and Conflict Transformation,* eds. Raymond G. Helmick and Rodney L. Petersen (Philadelphia: Templeton Foundation Press, 2001), 193.

47 Anne Goodman, "Transformative Learning and Cultures of Peace," in *Expanding the Boundaries of Transformative Learning: Essays on Theory and Praxis,* eds. Edmund

V. O'Sullivan, Amish Morrell, and Mary Ann O'Connor (New York: Palgrave, 2002), 192.

48 Anne Bishop, *Becoming an Ally: Breaking the Cycle of Oppression* (Halifax: Fernwood, 1994), 124.

Selected Bibliography

Alexander, Jeffrey C., Ron Eyerman, Bernard Giesen, Neil J. Smelser, and Piotr Sztompka. *Cultural Trauma and Collective Identity.* Berkeley: University of California Press, 2004.

Alfred, Taiaiake. *Peace, Power, Righteousness: An Indigenous Manifesto.* Don Mills: Oxford University Press, 1999.

–. *Wasáse: Indigenous Pathways of Action and Freedom.* Peterborough, ON: Broadview Press, 2005.

Alfred, Taiaiake, and Jeff Corntassel. "Being Indigenous: Resurgences against Contemporary Colonialism." *Government and Opposition* 40,4 (2005): 597-614. http://www.corntassel.net/being_indigenous.pdf.

Archibald, Jo-ann (Q'um Q'um Xiiem). *Indigenous Storywork: Educating the Heart, Mind, Body, and Spirit.* Vancouver: UBC Press, 2008.

Attwood, Bain. *Telling the Truth about Aboriginal History.* Crows Nest, NSW: Allen and Unwin, 2005.

Barkan, Elazar. *The Guilt of Nations: Restitution and Negotiating Historical Injustice.* Baltimore: Johns Hopkins University Press, 2000.

Bastien, Betty. *Blackfoot Ways of Knowing: The Worldview of the Siksikaitsitapi.* Calgary: University of Calgary Press, 2004.

Battiste, Marie, and James (Sa'ke'j) Youngblood Henderson. *Protecting Indigenous Knowledge and Heritage: A Global Challenge.* Saskatoon: Purich, 2000.

Bell, Catherine, and David Kahane, eds. *Intercultural Dispute Resolution in Aboriginal Contexts.* Vancouver: UBC Press, 2004.

Bishop, Anne. *Becoming an Ally: Breaking the Cycle of Oppression.* Halifax: Fernwood, 1994.

Bodnar, John. *Remaking America: Public Memory, Commemoration, and Patriotism in the Twentieth Century.* Princeton: Princeton University Press, 1992.

Boler, Megan. *Feeling Power: Emotions and Education.* New York: Routledge, 1999.

Boler, Megan, and Michalinos Zembylas. "Discomforting Truths: The Emotional Terrain of Understanding Difference." In *Pedagogies of Difference: Rethinking*

Education for Social Change, ed. Peter Pericles Trifonas, 110-36. New York: Rout-ledgeFalmer, 2003.

Borrows, John. *Recovering Canada: The Resurgence of Indigenous Law.* Toronto: University of Toronto Press, 2002.

Bradford, William. "'With a Very Great Blame on Our Hearts': Reparations, Recon-ciliation, and an American Indian Plea for Peace with Justice." *American Indian Law Review* 27,1 (2002-03): 1-175.

Brown, Leslie, and Susan Strega, eds. *Research as Resistance: Critical, Indigenous, and Anti-Oppressive Approaches.* Toronto: Canadian Scholars Press/Women's Press, 2005.

Byrne, Sean, and Cynthia L. Irvin, eds. *Reconcilable Differences: Turning Points in Ethnopolitical Conflict.* West Hartford, CT: Kumarian Press, 2000.

Campbell, Sue. "Challenges to Memory in Political Contexts: Recognizing Disre-spectful Challenge." Paper prepared for the Indian Residential Schools Truth and Reconciliation Commission, 2008.

–. "Remembering for the Future: Memory as a Lens on the Indian Residential Schools Truth and Reconciliation Commission." Paper prepared for the Truth and Recon-ciliation Commission, 2008.

Castellano, Marlene Brant, Linda Archibald, and Mike DeGagné, eds. *From Truth to Reconciliation: Transforming the Legacy of Residential Schools.* Ottawa: Aboriginal Healing Foundation, 2008.

Cohen, Stanley. *States of Denial: Knowing about Atrocities and Suffering.* Cambridge: Polity Press, 2001.

Connerton, Paul. *How Societies Remember,* 10th ed. Cambridge: Cambridge Uni-versity Press, 2003.

Corntassel, Jeff, Chaw-win-is, and T'lakwadzi. "Indigenous Storytelling, Truth-Telling and Community Approaches to Reconciliation." *English Studies in Canada* 35, 1 (March 2009): 137-59.

Corntassel, Jeff, and Cindy Holder. "Who's Sorry Now? Government Apologies, Truth Commissions, and Indigenous Self-Determination in Australia, Canada, Guatemala, and Peru." *Human Rights Review* 9,4 (December 2008): 465-89.

Cruikshank, Julie. *The Social Life of Stories: Narrative and Knowledge in the Yukon Territory.* Vancouver: UBC Press, 1998.

Culhane, Dara. *The Pleasure of the Crown: Anthropology, Law and First Nations.* Burnaby: Talon Books, 1998.

Daly, Richard. *Our Box Was Full: An Ethnography for the Delgamuukw Plaintiffs.* Vancouver: UBC Press, 2005.

Deloria, Vine, Jr., and Daniel R. Wildcat. *Power and Place: Indian Education in America.* Golden, CO: Fulcrum Resources, 2001.

Dennis, Matthew. *Cultivating a Landscape of Peace: Iroquois-European Encounters in Seventeenth Century America.* Ithaca: Cornell University Press, 1993.

Denzin, Norman K., Yvonna S. Lincoln, and Linda Tuhiwai Smith, eds. *Handbook of Critical and Indigenous Methodologies*. Thousand Oaks: Sage, 2008.

Fiske, Jo-anne, and Betty Patrick. *Cis Dideen Kat (When the Plumes Rise): The Way of the Lake Babine Nation*. Vancouver: UBC Press, 2000.

Foner, Eric. *Who Owns History? Rethinking the Past in a Changing World*. New York: Hill and Wang, 2002.

Forester, John. *The Deliberative Practitioner: Encouraging Participatory Planning Processes*. Cambridge, MA: MIT Press, 1999.

Foster, Hamar, Benjamin L. Berger, and A.R. Buck, eds. *The Grand Experiment: Law and Legal Culture in British Settler Societies*. Law and Society Series. Vancouver: UBC Press, 2008.

Fournier, Suzanne, and Ernie Crey. *Stolen from Our Embrace: The Abduction of First Nations Children and Restoration of Aboriginal Communities*. Vancouver: Douglas and McIntyre, 1997.

Francis, Daniel. *The Imaginary Indian: The Image of the Indian in Canadian Culture*, 7th ed. Vancouver: Arsenal Pulp Press, 1992.

Freire, Paulo. *Pedagogy of Hope: Reliving Pedagogy of the Oppressed*. New York: Continuum, 1995.

Furniss, Elizabeth. *The Burden of History: Colonialism and the Frontier Myth in a Rural Canadian Community*. Vancouver: UBC Press, 1999.

–. *Victims of Benevolence: The Dark Legacy of the Williams Lake Residential School*. Vancouver: Arsenal Pulp Press, 1992.

Granatstein, J.L. *Who Killed Canadian History?* rev. ed. Toronto: Harper Collins, 2007.

Grande, Sandy. *Red Pedagogy: Native American Social and Political Thought*. Lanham, MD: Rowman and Littlefield, 2004.

Green, Joyce, ed. *Making Space for Indigenous Feminism*. Black Point, NS: Fernwood, 2007.

Haig-Brown, Celia. *Resistance and Renewal: Surviving the Indian Residential School*, 6th ed. Vancouver: Tillacum Library, Arsenal Pulp Press, 1993.

Haig-Brown, Celia, and David A. Nock, eds. *With Good Intentions: Euro-Canadian and Aboriginal Relations in Colonial Canada*. Vancouver: UBC Press, 2006.

Harris, Cole. *Making Native Space*. Vancouver: UBC Press, 2002.

Hayner, Priscilla B. *Unspeakable Truths: Confronting State Terror and Atrocity*. New York: Routledge, 2001.

Higham, C.L. *Noble, Wretched, and Redeemable: Protestant Missionaries to the Indians in Canada and the United States, 1820-1900*. Albuquerque: University of New Mexico, 2000.

hooks, bell. *Teaching Community: A Pedagogy of Hope*. New York: Routledge, 2003.

–. *Teaching to Transgress: Education as the Practice of Freedom*. New York: Routledge, 1994.

James, Matt. "Wrestling with the Past: Apologies, Quasi-Apologies, and Non-Apologies in Canada." In *The Age of Apology: Facing Up to the Past,* eds. Mark Gibney, Rhoda E. Howard-Hassman, Jean-Marc Coicaud, and Niklaus Steiner, 137-53. Philadelphia: University of Pennsylvania Press, 2008.

Jefferess, David. *Postcolonial Resistance: Culture, Liberation, and Transformation.* Toronto: University of Toronto Press, 2008.

Juhnke, James C., and Carol M. Hunter. *The Missing Peace: The Search for Nonviolent Alternatives in United States History.* Kitchener, ON: Pandora Press, 2004.

Kertzer, David I. *Ritual, Politics, and Power.* New Haven: Yale University Press, 1988.

Knafla, Louis A., and Jonathan Swainger, eds. *Laws and Societies in the Canadian Prairie West, 1670-1940.* Law and Society Series. Vancouver: UBC Press, 2005.

LaCapra, Dominick. *History in Transit: Experience, Identity, Critical Theory.* Ithaca: Cornell University Press, 2004.

Law Commission of Canada, ed. *Restoring Dignity: Responding to Child Abuse in Canadian Institutions.* Ottawa: Minister of Public Works and Government Services, 2000.

LeBaron, Michelle. *Bridging Cultural Conflicts: A New Approach for a Changing World.* San Francisco: Jossey-Bass, 2003.

–. *Bridging Troubled Waters: Conflict Resolution from the Heart.* San Francisco: Jossey-Bass, 2002.

Lederach, John Paul. "Five Qualities of Practice in Support of Reconciliation Processes." In *Forgiveness and Reconciliation: Religion, Public Policy and Conflict Transformation,* eds. Raymond G. Helmick and Rodney L. Petersen, 183-93. Philadelphia: Templeton Foundation Press, 2001.

–. *The Moral Imagination: The Art and Soul of Building Peace.* New York: Oxford University Press, 2005.

Llewellyn, Jennifer J. "Bridging the Gap between Truth and Reconciliation: Restorative Justice and the Indian Residential Schools Truth and Reconciliation Commission." In *From Truth to Reconciliation: Transforming the Legacy of Residential Schools,* eds. Marlene Brandt Castellano, Linda Archibald, and Mike DeGagné, 185-201. Ottawa: Aboriginal Healing Foundation, 2008.

–. "Dealing with the Legacy of Native Residential School Abuse in Canada: Litigation, ADR, and Restorative Justice." *University of Toronto Law Journal* 52 (2002): 253-300.

Lutz, John Sutton, ed. *Myth and Memory: Stories of Indigenous-European Contact.* Vancouver: UBC Press, 2007.

Mackey, Eva. *The House of Difference: Cultural Politics and National Identity in Canada.* Toronto: University of Toronto Press, 2002.

Manuel, George, and Michael Posluns. *The Fourth World: An Indian Reality.* Don Mills: Collier-Macmillan Canada, 1974.

Maynes, Mary Jo, Jennifer L. Pierce, and Barbara Laslett. *Telling Stories: The Use of Personal Narratives in the Social Sciences and History.* Ithaca: Cornell University Press, 2008.

McLeod, Neal. *Cree Narrative Memory: From Treaties to Contemporary Times*. Saskatoon: Purich, 2007.

Miller, J.R. *Lethal Legacy: Current Native Controversies in Canada*. Toronto: McClelland and Stewart, 2004.

–. *Reflections on Native-Newcomer Relations: Selected Essays*. Toronto: University of Toronto Press, 2004.

–. *Shingwauk's Vision: A History of Native Residential Schools*. Toronto: University of Toronto Press, 1996.

Million, Dian Lynn. "Telling Secrets: Sex, Power and Narrative in the Rearticulation of Canadian Residential School Histories." PhD diss., University of California, Berkeley, 2004.

Milloy, John S. *A National Crime: The Canadian Government and the Residential School System, 1879 to 1986*, 3rd ed. Winnipeg: University of Manitoba Press, 2001.

Mills, Antonia. *Eagle Down Is Our Law: Witsuwit'en Law, Feasts, and Land Claims*. Vancouver: UBC Press, 1994.

Minow, Martha. *Between Vengeance and Forgiveness: Facing History after Genocide and Mass Violence*. Boston: Beacon Press, 1998.

Monet, Don, and Skanu'u (Ardythe Wilson). *Colonialism on Trial: Indigenous Land Rights and the Gitksan and Wet'suwet'en Sovereignty Case*. Gabriola Island, BC: New Society, 1992.

Napoleon, Val. "Who Gets to Say What Happened? Reconciliation Issues for the Gitxsan." In *Intercultural Dispute Resolution in Aboriginal Contexts*, eds. Catherine Bell and David Kahane, 176-95. Vancouver: UBC Press, 2004.

Nelson, Jennifer J. *Razing Africville: A Geography of Racism*. Toronto: University of Toronto Press, 2008.

Neu, Dean, and Richard Therrien. *Accounting for Genocide: Canada's Bureaucratic Assault on Aboriginal People*. Black Point, NS: Fernwood, 2003.

Nobles, Melissa. *The Politics of Official Apologies*. Cambridge: Cambridge University Press, 2008.

O'Sullivan, Edmund V., Amish Morrell, and Mary Ann O'Connor, eds. *Expanding the Boundaries of Transformative Learning: Essays on Theory and Praxis*. New York: Palgrave, 2002.

Pearce, W. Barnett, and Stephen W. Littlejohn. *Moral Conflict: When Social Worlds Collide*. Thousand Oaks: Sage, 1997.

Penikett, Tony. *Reconciliation: First Nations Treatymaking in British Columbia*. Vancouver: Douglas and McIntyre, 2006.

Prager, Carol A.L., and Trudy Govier, eds. *Dilemmas of Reconciliation: Cases and Concepts*. Waterloo: Wilfrid Laurier University Press, 2003.

Pranis, Kay, Barry Stuart, and Mark Wedge. *Peacemaking Circles: From Crime to Community*. St. Paul: Living Justice Press, 2003.

Qwul'sih'yah'maht (Robina Anne Thomas). "Honouring the Oral Traditions of My Ancestors through Storytelling." In *Research as Resistance: Critical, Indigenous, and*

Anti-Oppressive Approaches, eds. Leslie Brown and Susan Strega, 237-54. Toronto: Canadian Scholars Press/Women's Press, 2005.

Ray, Arthur J. *I Have Lived Here since the World Began: An Illustrated History of Canada's Native People.* Toronto: Lester, 1996.

Ray, Arthur J., Jim Miller, and Frank Tough. *Bounty and Benevolence: A History of Saskatchewan Treaties.* Montreal and Kingston: McGill-Queen's University Press, 2000.

Razack, Sherene H., ed. *Race, Space, and the Law: Unmapping a White Settler Society,* 2nd ed. Toronto: Between the Lines, 2005.

Redekop, Vern Neufeld. *From Violence to Blessing: How an Understanding of Deep-Rooted Conflict Can Open Paths to Reconciliation.* Toronto: Novalis, 2002.

Regan, Paulette. "An Apology Feast in Hazelton: Indian Residential Schools, Reconciliation, and Making Space for Indigenous Legal Traditions." In *Indigenous Legal Traditions,* ed. Law Commission of Canada, 40-76. Legal Dimensions Series. Vancouver: UBC Press, 2007.

Rotberg, Robert I., and Dennis Thompson, eds. *Truth v. Justice: The Morality of Truth Commissions.* Princeton: Princeton University Press, 2000.

Said, Edward W. *Culture and Imperialism.* New York: Vintage Books, 1994.

Saul, John Ralston. *A Fair Country: Telling Truths about Canada.* Toronto: Viking Canada, 2008.

Schaffer, Kay, and Sidonie Smith. *Human Rights and Narrated Lives: The Ethics of Recognition.* New York: Palgrave Macmillan, 2004.

Schell, Jonathan. *The Unconquerable World: Power, Non-Violence, and the Will of the People.* New York: Henry Holt, 2003.

Schirch, Lisa. *Ritual and Symbol in Peacebuilding.* Bloomfield: Kumarian Press, 2005.

Simon, Roger. "The Pedagogical Insistence of Public Memory." In *Theorizing Historical Consciousness,* ed. Peter Seixas, 181-201. Toronto: University of Toronto Press, 2004.

–. *The Touch of the Past: Remembrance, Learning and Ethics.* New York: Palgrave Macmillan, 2005.

Slotkin, Richard. *Regeneration through Violence: The Mythology of the American Frontier, 1600-1860.* Middletown: Wesleyan University Press, 1973.

Smith, Keith D. *Liberalism, Surveillance, and Resistance: Indigenous Communities in Western Canada, 1887-1927.* Edmonton: Athabasca University Press, 2009.

Smith, Linda Tuhiwai. *Decolonizing Methodologies: Research and Indigenous Peoples.* London: Zed Books, 1999.

Tavuchis, Nicholas. *Mea Culpa: A Sociology of Apology and Reconciliation.* Stanford: Stanford University Press, 1991.

Thompson, Janna. *Taking Responsibility for the Past: Reparation and Historical Injustice.* Cambridge: Polity Press, 2002.

Timpson, Annis May, ed. *First Nations, First Thoughts: The Impact of Indigenous Thought in Canada.* Vancouver: UBC Press, 2009.

Titley, Brian E. *A Narrow Vision: Duncan Campbell Scott and the Administration of Indian Affairs in Canada.* Vancouver: UBC Press, 1986.

Torpey, John. *Making Whole What Has Been Smashed: On Reparations Politics.* Cambridge, MA: Harvard University Press, 2006.

—. *Politics and the Past: On Repairing Historical Injustices.* Lanham, MD: Rowman and Littlefield, 2003.

Treaty 7 Tribal Council, Walter Hildebrandt, Sarah Carter, and Dorothy First Rider. *The True Spirit and Intent of Treaty 7.* Montreal and Kingston: McGill-Queen's University Press, 1996.

Trouillot, Michel-Rolph. *Silencing the Past: Power and the Production of History.* Boston: Beacon Press, 1995.

Tully, James. "The Struggles of Indigenous Peoples for and of Freedom." In *Political Theory and the Rights of Indigenous Peoples,* eds. Duncan Ivison, Paul Patton, and Will Sanders, 36-59. Cambridge: Cambridge University Press, 2000.

Valaskakis, Gail Guthrie. *Indian Country: Essays on Contemporary Native Culture.* Waterloo: Wilfrid Laurier University Press, 2005.

Warry, Wayne. *Ending Denial: Understanding Aboriginal Issues.* Toronto: University of Toronto Press, 2008.

—. *Unfinished Dreams: Community Healing and the Reality of Aboriginal Self-Government.* Toronto: University of Toronto Press, 1998.

Waziyatawin. *What Does Justice Look Like? The Struggle for Liberation in Dakota Homeland.* St. Paul: Living Justice Press, 2008.

White, Richard. *The Middle Ground: Indians, Empires and Republics in the Great Lakes Region, 1650-1815.* New York: Cambridge University Press, 1991.

Williams, Robert A., Jr. *Linking Arms Together: American Indian Treaty Visions of Law and Peace, 1600-1800.* Oxford: Oxford University Press, 1997.

Wilson, Waziyatawin Angela, ed. *In the Footsteps of Our Ancestors: The Dakota Commemorative Marches of the 21st Century.* St. Paul: Living Justice Press, 2006.

Woolford, Andrew. *Between Justice and Certainty: Treaty Making in British Columbia,* edited by W. Wesley Pue. Law and Society Series. Vancouver: UBC Press, 2005.

Yamamoto, Eric K. *Interracial Justice: Conflict and Reconciliation in Post-Civil Rights America,* ed. Richard Delgado and Jean Stefancic. Critical America Series. New York: New York University Press, 1999.

Younging, Gregory, Jonathan Dewar, and Mike DeGagné, eds. *Response, Responsibility and Renewal: Canada's Truth and Reconciliation Journey.* Ottawa: Aboriginal Healing Foundation, 2009.

Index

Printed and bound in Canada by Friesens

Set in Rotis and Minion by Artegraphica Design Co. Ltd.

Copy editor: Deborah Kerr

Proofreader and indexer: Dianne Tiefensee